THE CONCEPT OF A
LEGAL SYSTEM

11. 95
Net

THE
CONCEPT OF A
LEGAL SYSTEM

An Introduction to the
Theory of Legal System

SECOND EDITION

JOSEPH RAZ

CLARENDON PRESS · OXFORD

1980

Oxford University Press, Walton Street, Oxford OX2 6DP

OXFORD   LONDON   GLASGOW

NEW YORK   TORONTO   MELBOURNE   WELLINGTON

KUALA LUMPUR   SINGAPORE   HONG KONG   TOKYO

DELHI   BOMBAY   CALCUTTA   MADRAS   KARACHI

NAIROBI   DAR ES SALAAM   CAPE TOWN

© *Oxford University Press, 1970, 1980*

First published 1970
Second edition 1980

Published in the United States by
Oxford University Press, New York

British Library Cataloguing in Publication Data

Raz, Joseph
    The concept of a legal system. – 2nd ed.
    1. Jurisprudence
    I. Title
    340.1   K230   80-40190

ISBN   0 19 825363-X
        0 19 825362-1 Pbk

Printed and bound by Weatherby Woolnough
Wellingborough, Northants

PREFACE

THIS book is based on a doctoral thesis submitted at the University of Oxford. I wish to acknowledge my great indebtedness to Prof. H. L. A. Hart. I learnt much from his published works, from his lectures, and most of all from his very patient and detailed criticism of previous drafts of this study. I am also most grateful to him for his constant encouragement and guidance.

I am greatly indebted to Dr. P. M. Hacker, with whom I had many illuminating conversations on the topics discussed, and to Dr. A. Kenny, who read and commented on two papers I wrote on Bentham and Kelsen; these served as a basis for some of the material in Chapters 3–5.

My stay at Oxford was made possible by the Hebrew University, Jerusalem, which secured the necessary funds, and especially by the kind attention and interest of Mr. E. Posnansky.

Both Professor Hart and Dr. Hacker read previous drafts of the book, and if it were not for their pains there would be many more mistakes and stylistic infelicities in the English than in fact remain.

CONTENTS

CONTENTS

ABBREVIATIONS

Some books are often referred to by the first main word in their name: e.g. *The Limits of Jurisprudence Defined* is referred to as *Limits*.

CL   Hart's *The Concept of Law*.

GT   Kelsen's *General Theory of Law and State*.

NA   von Wright's *Norm and Action*.

PTL   Kelsen's *The Pure Theory of Law*.

TP   Kelsen's *Théorie Pure du Droit*.

WJ   Kelsen's *What is Justice?*

OLG   Bentham's *Of Laws in General*. This is in substance a new edition of the *Limits*.

INTRODUCTION

THIS work is an introduction to a general study of legal systems, that is to the study of the systematic nature of law, and the examination of the presuppositions and implications underlying the fact that every law necessarily belongs to a legal system (the English, or German, or Roman, or Canon Law, or some other legal system). A comprehensive investigation may result in what could be called a theory of legal system. Such a theory is general in that it claims to be true of all legal systems. If it is successful it elucidates the concept of a legal system, and forms a part of general analytic jurisprudence.

The approach to the subject adopted here is in part historical, and starts from a critical examination of previous theories. The constructive part of the work is analytical in character, and the authors examined in the historical part all belong to the analytic school of jurisprudence.[1] From an analytic standpoint a complete theory of legal system consists of the solutions to the following four problems:

(1) The problem of existence: What are the criteria for the existence of a legal system? We distinguish between existing legal systems and those which have either ceased to exist (e.g. the Roman legal system) or never existed at all (e.g. Plato's proposed law for an ideal state). Furthermore, we say that the French legal system exists in France but not in Belgium, and that in Palestine there is now a different legal system from the one which was in force 30 years ago. One of the objects of the theory of legal system is to furnish criteria to determine the truth or falsity of such statements; these we shall call the 'existence criteria' of a legal system.

(2) The problem of identity (and the related problem of membership): What are the criteria which determine the system to which a given law belongs? These are the criteria of membership, and from them can be derived the criteria of identity, answering the question: which laws form a given system?

---

[1] Cf. Bentham, *Principles*, pp. 423 ff.; Austin, 'The Uses of the Study of Jurisprudence'; Kelsen, 'The Pure Theory of Law and Analytical Jurisprudence'; Hart, 'Positivism and the Separation of Law and Morals'.

(3) The problem of structure: Is there a structure common to all legal systems, or to certain types of legal system? Are there any patterns of relations among laws belonging to the same system which recur in all legal systems, or which mark the difference between important types of system?

(4) The problem of content: Are there any laws which in one form or another recur in all legal systems or in types of system? Is there any content common to all legal systems or determining important types of system?

Whereas every theory of legal system must provide a solution of the first two problems, since existence and identity criteria are a necessary part of any adequate definition of 'legal system', it may give a negative answer to the last two questions. It may claim that there is no structure or shared content common to all legal systems. The examination of structure and content is fundamental also to the theory of types of legal system (which is how we may name the analytic part of comparative jurisprudence).

This essay is concerned with the first three problems only, and only in so far as they belong to the general theory of legal system. Analytical jurists, apart from Hart, have paid little attention to the problem of content, and as we have chosen to develop our systematic conclusions largely through the critical examination of previous theories it will be convenient to disregard it almost completely. A few remarks on the interrelation between the problem of content and the other three problems will be made in Chapter VI and elsewhere.

All four problems of the theory of legal system have for the most part been neglected by almost all analytical jurists. It seems to have been traditionally accepted that the crucial step in understanding the law is to define 'a law', and assumed without discussion that the definition of 'a legal system' involves no further problems of any consequence. Kelsen was the first to insist that 'it is impossible to grasp the nature of law if we limit our attention to the single isolated rule'.[1] Here it is proposed to go even further: It is a major thesis of the present essay that a theory of legal system is a prerequisite of any adequate definition of 'a law', and that all the existing theories of legal system are unsuccessful in part because they fail to realize this fact.

[1] *GT*, p. 3.

In arguing for this thesis certain aspects of the general theory of norms will be considered (in Chs. III and VI). The discussion will, however, be confined to the bare minimum necessary to prove the validity of the general position.

The three most general and important features of the law are that it is normative, institutionalized, and coercive. It is normative in that it serves, and is meant to serve, as a guide for human behaviour. It is institutionalized in that its application and modification are to a large extent performed or regulated by institutions. And it is coercive in that obedience to it, and its application, are internally guaranteed, ultimately, by the use of force.

Naturally, every theory of legal system must be compatible with an explanation of these features. Because of their importance we shall, moreover, expect that every theory of legal system will take account of these features, and will, at least partly, explain their importance for the law.

The emphasis on these three features of the law is the most important factor which we share with two contemporary analytic theories of legal system—those of Kelsen and Hart. The differences between our various positions may be reduced to a difference in the interpretation of the three features, their interrelations, and their relative importance. This common denominator makes it useful to present this attempt to solve the problems in the context of a critical examination of other similar attempts.

There is, however, a great difference in the use made here of the two contemporary theories. Kelsen's theory is explained and criticized in three successive chapters (III, IV, and V) before any positive contribution to the theory of legal system is advanced. The purpose of this is to gain a more detailed understanding of the problems of the theory of legal system, and to explore some of the difficulties involved in tackling them, and at the same time to learn both from Kelsen's achievements and from his mistakes. Hart's theory, which resembles much more closely, the approach used here, is discussed in conjunction with the formulation of a positive contribution to a theory of legal system (Chs. VI to IX). Other legal philosophers who did not produce a complete theory of legal system, nevertheless held views relevant to the construction of such a theory, and some of their views are taken up and examined whenever the occasion arises.

Though Kelsen was the first to deal explicitly and fully with the concept of a legal system, there is already implicit in Austin's work a complete theory of legal system. His theory, though differing in important respects from that of Kelsen, can be profitably regarded as a variant of the same kind of theory. I propose to regard their theories as two variations of what I shall call the imperative approach. Austin's variant being the simpler, we shall begin our discussion with it and use it to describe the nature of the imperative approach (Ch. I). Austin's theory is, however, very defective, and many of its defects can be remedied within the framework of the imperative approach. Therefore the criticism of his views (Ch. II) cannot be regarded as proof of the inadequacy of the imperative approach as such, but rather as an introduction to Kelsen's theory, which is much less vulnerable.

I

AUSTIN'S THEORY OF LEGAL SYSTEM

AUSTIN in effect defines 'a law' as 'a general command of a sovereign addressed to his subjects'. His theory of legal system is implicit in this definition. To make this clear we shall divide the definition into three parts, each providing an answer to one of our three main problems: A law is (1) a general command (2) issued by some person (Austin's usual expression is 'set' or 'given')[1] (3) who is a sovereign (that is, is habitually obeyed by a certain community and does not render habitual obedience to anyone).

From the second part of the definition a criterion of identity and a criterion of membership may be derived:

Austin's criterion of identity: A legal system contains all and only the laws issued by one person (or body of persons).

Austin's criterion of membership: A given law belongs to the legal system containing laws issued by the legislator of that law.[2] That is Austin's answer to the problem of identity.

The third part of the definition contains most of the material from which an existence criterion can be extracted:

Austin's criterion of existence: (1) A legal system exists if the common legislator of its laws is a sovereign. Therefore: (2) A legal system exists if it is generally efficacious. The transition from (1) to (2) is guaranteed by the fact that a person is sovereign only if he is habitually obeyed, and he is habitually obeyed if, and only if, his commands are generally obeyed. In Chapter II (sect. 2) we shall modify the criterion to make it more exact.

The first element of the definition of law is our only clue to Austin's opinion concerning the structure of a law. He never tackled the problem directly, but he says enough about the meaning of the term 'general command' to enable us to reconstruct a rudimentary doctrine of the structure of laws. It will be one of our main contentions in this chapter that this doctrine

---

[1] Austin regards the issuing of a general command by the sovereign as legislation.

[2] Cf. Hart's summary of Austin's position, *CL*, p. 66.

excludes the possibility of any internal relation between laws constituting a necessary element in a legal system. By internal relation between laws we mean relation between laws one or more of which refer to or presuppose the existence of the others. Thereby Austin excludes *a fortiori* any specific internal structure (i.e. pattern of internal relations) which a legal system must necessarily have.

This brief summary demonstrates how Austin's theory of legal system is virtually a by-product of his definition of 'a law'. Both the theory and the definition revolve around and presuppose the applicability of one concept—the concept of sovereignty. For this reason we shall begin our detailed examination of Austin's theory by considering his concept of sovereignty, and then proceed to discuss his criterion of existence (I.2), his criterion of identity (I.3), and his theory of the structure of a law, which prepares the ground for his theory of the structure of a legal system (I.4).

I.I: SOVEREIGNTY

'Sovereignty' belonged to the philosophical and political terminology long before Austin. It had, however, been recently transformed by Bentham: 'When a number of persons', he wrote, '(whom we may style subjects) are supposed to be in the habit of paying obedience to a person or an assemblage of persons, of a known and certain description (whom we may call governor and governors) such persons altogether (subjects and governors) are said to be in a state of political society.'[1] One need only compare this passage with the following from *The Province* to realize how great is Austin's debt to his master: 'If a determinate human superior, not in a habit of obedience to a like superior, receive habitual obedience from the bulk of a given society, that determinate superior is sovereign in that society, and the society (including the superior) is a society political and independent.'[2]

Two major innovations were introduced by Bentham and adopted by Austin:

(1) Sovereignty is neither derived from nor explained by

---

[1] *Fragment*, p. 38. [2] *Province*, p. 194.

reference to morality or moral principles. It is based exclusively on the social fact of the habit of obedience.

(2) The concepts of a habit and of personal obedience, namely obedience to a specific person or group, become the key concepts in the analysis of sovereignty.

These points form the basis of Austin's theory of sovereignty, and the basis was provided by Bentham. There are, however, two differences between the passages from Bentham and Austin which should not be overlooked.

Bentham defined 'being in a state of political society'; Austin 'an independent political society'. That explains why Austin's definition consists of two conditions, one positive (the bulk of the population habitually obeys the sovereign) and one negative (the sovereign is not in the habit of obeying anyone), whereas Bentham's definition mentions only the positive condition. The negative condition is relevant only to the independence of a political society with which Bentham was not in this passage concerned. Austin comments on this omission and says that 'Mr. Bentham has forgotten to notice' the necessity of a negative condition.[1] This is not true of the *Fragment* to which Austin referred, yet it is true of Bentham's definitions of sovereign in *Of Laws in General*, his most important jurisprudential work, and elsewhere.[2] But it is no more than a technical fault. There can be no doubt that Bentham would have approved of Austin's amendment. In the *Fragment* he writes:

But suppose an incontestable political society, and that a large one, formed; and from that a smaller body to break off: by this breach the smaller body ceases to be in a state of political union with respect to that larger: and has thereby placed itself, with respect to that larger body, in a state of nature . . . [and suppose] the subordinate governors, from whom alone the people at large were in use to receive their commands under the old government, are the same from whom they receive them under the new one. *The habit of obedience which these subordinate governors were in with respect to that single person, we will say, who was the supreme governor of the whole is broken off insensibly and by degrees.* The old names by which these

[1] *Province*, p. 212.

[2] Austin's contention (ibid.) that because every political society is either an independent political society or part of it, the definition of a political society presupposes the definition of an independent society, is clearly fallacious.

subordinate governors were characterized . . . are continued *now they are supreme.*[1]

The implied definition of a supreme governor includes Austin's negative condition.

The second difference between Austin's and Bentham's concept of sovereignty, though it was never noticed by Austin himself, is of much greater importance. Austin's sovereign has four attributes, all of them of vital importance to his theory of legal system. His sovereignty is:

(1) *not subordinate*, that is (a) sovereign legislative power cannot be conferred by a law; and (b) this legislative power cannot be revoked by law;

(2) *illimitable*, that is (a) the sovereign legislative power is legally illimitable, it is the power to legislate any law whatsoever; and (b) the sovereign cannot be made subject to legal duties in the exercise of his legislative power;

(3) *unique*; for every legal system there is (a) one and (b) only one non-subordinate and illimitable legislative power;

(4) *united*: this legislative power is in the hands of one person or one body of persons.[2]

Bentham's sovereignty is certainly non-subordinate and unique, but he never said that sovereignty is illimitable or united. It is interesting to examine the development of his views on the subject: In the *Fragment* he avoids using the term altogether, and uses the term 'supreme governor' instead. He is silent on the problem of unity, and on the limitability of the supreme governors he says: 'The field . . . of the supreme governor's authority, though not infinite, must unavoidably, I think, unless where limited by express convention, be allowed to be indefinite.'[3] There is no telling whether this convention is

---

[1] *Fragment*, p. 44. My italics.

[2] It is here assumed that sovereignty can be divided and yet unique. If, for example, according to one legal system one person has non-subordinate legislative power on religious matters while another has non-subordinate legislative power on all other matters, their powers are regarded as parts of one sovereign power, which is divided between them. On the other hand, if according to one system two persons have each non-subordinate and unlimited legislative power, then sovereignty is not unique, for there are two sovereign powers in that legal system, but sovereignty is united, every sovereign power being in the hands of one person.

[3] *Fragment*, p. 94.

law or not. In his second published work on jurisprudence, the *Principles*, he tends to admit the concept of sovereignty:

To the total assemblage of the persons by whom the several political operations above mentioned come to be performed, we set out with applying the collective appellation of the government. Among these persons there commonly is some one person, or body of persons whose office it is to assign and distribute to the rest their several departments, to determine the conduct to be pursued by each in the performance of the particular set of operations that belongs to him, and even upon occasion to exercise his function in his stead. Where there is any such person, or body of persons, he or it may . . . be termed the sovereign, or the sovereignty.[1]

According to this watered-down definition of sovereignty it seems that the sovereign can be limited. On the other hand, he is both unique and united, but there is a footnote attached to this passage which says:

I should have been afraid to have said necessarily [i.e. that there is necessarily a sovereign in every country]. In the United Provinces, in the Helvetic, or even in the Germanic body, where is that *one* assembly in which an absolute power over the whole resides? where was there in the Roman Commonwealth? I would not undertake for certain to find an answer to all these questions.[2]

If the sovereign power is united, then it seems that not every state has a sovereign. We may deduce that if every state has a sovereign, then it cannot be united.

In *Of Laws in General* Bentham maintains that every state has a sovereign, but he did not abandon his view that sovereignty need not be united or unlimited:

The efficient cause . . . of the power of the sovereign is neither more nor less than the disposition to obedience on the part of the people. Now this disposition it is obvious may admit of innumerable modifications—and that even while it is constant. . . . *The people may be disposed to obey the commands of one man against the world in relation to one sort of act, those of another man in relation to another sort of act,* else what are we to think of the constitutional laws of the germanic body. . . . *They may be disposed to obey a man if he commands a given sort of act: they may not be disposed to obey him if he forbids it and vice versa.*[3]

---

[1] *Principles*, p. 325.   [2] *Principles*, p. 325, my italics.
[3] *Limits*, p. 101 n; *OLG*, pp. 18–19 n; cf. also *Limits*, p. 153; *OLG*, p. 69.

The passage is far from clear. It seems that Bentham never made up his mind on the question of the distinction between legal limitations and *de facto* limitations of sovereignty. The passage shows how he tries to explain legal phenomena by direct reference to social facts in a way which we cannot but judge to be confused. But it is clear that in the first sentence italicized above Bentham allows for a divided sovereignty and that in the sentence which follows he admits the possibility of a limited sovereignty.

Of course we should be careful not to attribute to Bentham more than he actually wrote. He did not have an explanation of divided sovereignty. He suggested no way of deciding whether a certain legal power is part of a sovereign power, and, if so, of which. Nor did he explain what are the relations, if any, between the various powers constituting one sovereign power. Similarly, he did not explain satisfactorily how sovereignty can be legally limited.[1] He was aware of certain legal phenomena which he could not reconcile with the doctrine that in every legal system there is one undivided and unlimited sovereign, and consequently he declined to subscribe to that theory.

We have elaborated this point, not only because it is usually overlooked that Bentham thought sovereignty to be divisible, but mainly because the fact that he thought it divisible and limitable prevents one from imputing to him the same views on the identity and existence problems which we have attributed to Austin. As Bentham held no other views relevant to these issues, it is Austin, and not Bentham, who is the first analytical jurist to supply us, even though without applying himself directly to the subject, an answer to these two problems, and so with a theory of legal system. For if sovereignty is divisible (or if, contrary to Bentham's and Austin's theories, it is not necessarily unique), then by tracing the origin of the laws of one system we may find several distinct legislators. And if there is no legislator common to all the laws of the system there is no bond common to them all, unless it is to be found somewhere else. Likewise, if the sovereign is legally limitable (or if he may be subordinate), the limiting law must be made by someone

---

[1] He did attempt two explanations: (1) convention, (2) limited disposition to obey; but they are not satisfactory. For his most extensive discussion of the problem see *Limits*, pp. 150–4; *OLG*, pp. 67–71.

other than the sovereign,[1] and again there may be no legislator common to all the laws of a system. Moreover, if not all the laws of the system are made by the sovereign, then obedience to the sovereign and obedience to the laws of the system are not one and the same thing, and hence Austin's existence criterion, which presupposes this identity, has to be modified.

I.2: EXISTENCE CRITERIA

A law is a general command of a sovereign to his subjects. In contrast to Bentham (and Kelsen) Austin thinks that only general commands, i.e. those obliging 'to acts or forbearances of a class', are laws. His only reason for that stipulation is conformity to 'established forms of speech'.[2] We should certainly be very reluctant to call particular commands rules, but if they are in all other respects similar to laws (e.g. laid down by competent legal authority in the exercise of its legal powers), we may disregard Austin's stipulation and admit them as (particular) laws.

For Austin a command is defined in terms of the following six conditions: c is A's command if and only if: (1) A desires some other persons to behave in a certain way; (2) he has expressed this desire; (3) he intends to cause harm or pain to these persons if his desire is not fulfilled; (4) he has some power to do so; (5) he has expressed his intention to do so; and, finally (6), c expresses the content of his desire (1) and of his intention (3) and nothing else. In Austin's own words:

A command is distinguished from other significations of desire . . . by the power and purpose of the party commanding to inflict an evil or pain in case the desire be disregarded. . . . A command then, is a signification of desire. But a command is distinguished from other significations of desire by this peculiarity: that the party to whom it is directed is liable to evil from the other, in case he comply not with the desire.[3]

The fifth condition is not mentioned here or anywhere else in the book. On the other hand, Austin regards imperfect laws, i.e.

---

[1] This point is argued in full in Ch. II, sect. 1, below.
[2] Cf. *Province*, p. 19.
[3] *Province*, p. 14 and cf. ibid., p. 17.

laws without sanctions, as deficient, laws which are not commands, and while discussing them he writes: 'Though the
author of an imperfect law signifies a desire, he manifests no
purpose of enforcing compliance with the desire.'[1] On the
strength of this passage I have introduced the fifth condition.
The last condition is a consequence of the fact that a command
is an abstract entity, i.e. is not identical either with the act of
issuing a command or with the words used in that act, just as a
proposition is not identical either with its assertion or the words
used in asserting it.

Austin does not say whether the desire (1), the intention (3),
and the power to execute that intention (4), have to exist only
at the time of issuing the command, or whether they have to
persist as long as it is valid. Both answers would be implausible.
We do not regard a law as invalid simply because its legislator has
lost interest in it. But at the same time there seems little point in
insisting on the existence of a power to punish at the time of
legislation rather than at the time when violation is possible or
likely. The most reasonable solution is that the desire (1) is a
necessary condition of c's being a law only at the time of legislation, and that at the same time it must be likely that the power
and the intention to use it (3) will exist during the law's period
of validity.[2]

The six components of the definition of a command can be
divided into three groups. The sixth concerns the content and
structure of a command and will be discussed later in this
chapter (sect. 4). Conditions (1), (2), (3), and (5) concern the
act of issuing the command, the act of legislation, and will be
re-examined in the next section. Condition (4), the power to
inflict pain on anyone who disobeys the command, which is
also called[3] the superiority of the commander, or legislator,
relative to the subject of his command-law, concerns the circumstances in which the command is made. To extract an
existence criterion from the definition of a law we have to concentrate primarily on those parts of the definition which refer
to external circumstances. We can conveniently treat the
remaining conditions as comprised in the meaning of 'a

---

[1] *Province*, p. 28.
[2] A different solution is probably appropriate to non-legal commands.
[3] *Province*, p. 24.

command', and Austin's definition of a law can be rephrased as follows: A law is (1) a command (2) of a superior to his inferior(s) and at the same time (3) of a sovereign to his subject(s). It will be seen that it is necessary to distinguish more carefully than Austin does between conditions (2) and (3).

Let us examine more closely the element of superiority. It certainly includes the power to cause harm or pain through the hands of one's agents. What degree of superiority is required? In one place Austin says that superiority is 'the power of affecting others with evil or pain and of enforcing them, through fear of that evil, to fashion their conduct to one's wishes'.[1] Obviously we should not take these words at their face value, otherwise we should be able to use against Austin the two arguments which he applied to refute Paley:

The greater the evil to be incurred in case the wish be disregarded and the greater the chance of incurring it on that same event, the greater, no doubt, is the chance that the wish will not be disregarded. But no conceivable motive will certainly determine to compliance, or no conceivable motive will render obedience inevitable. If Paley's proposition be true . . . commands . . . are simply impossible. Or reducing his proposition to absurdity by a consequence as manifestly false, commands . . . are possible but are never disobeyed or broken.[2]

Nor can superiority be equated with the power necessary to compel the disobedient to behave as required after they have already failed to do so in the first instance. This is not always logically or physically possible, and often, though possible, there is no point in insisting on it. We must therefore conclude that the superiority need only suffice to create some likelihood that the sanction specified in the law will be enforced.

As to the severity of the sanction, no minimum or maximum limits are set to it. Austin explains:

The truth is, that the magnitude of the eventual evil and the magnitude of the chance of incurring it, are foreign to the matter in question. . . . Where there is the smallest chance of incurring the smallest evil, the expression of a wish amounts to a command and, therefore, imposes a duty. The sanction if you will, is feeble or insufficient;

---

[1] *Province*, p. 24.   [2] *Province*, p. 15.

but still there is a sanction and, therefore, a duty and a command.[1]

As different laws are addressed to different people, and stipulate different sanctions, the facts establishing the superiority which is a prerequisite to the validity of every one of them are different in each case.

In this, as in other respects, Austin's sovereignty differs from superiority. The existence of the facts constituting the sovereignty of the legislator are a prerequisite to the validity of every law in the system, but they are the same facts in the case of every law. Moreover, contrary to Austin's tacit assumption, it does not follow from the sovereignty of the legislator that he is superior to the subjects of any particular purported law relative to the sanction of that law. A man can be a sovereign and yet not be superior to some of his subjects relative to certain purported laws. Austin knows, of course, that the negative condition of sovereignty—the fact that the sovereign does not habitually obey anyone—does not entail that he is superior to the subjects of his laws. But neither does the positive condition of sovereignty entail that fact. The bulk of the population can habitually obey the sovereign without being inferior relative to every law.

Austin's failure to realize the difference between being the object of habitual obedience and being superior to those who obey accounts for his view that laws are necessarily addressed to members of the same political society as that to which the sovereign belongs.

The person or persons . . . [he writes] to whom the law is set or directed, are necessarily members of the independent political society wherein the author of the law is sovereign. . . . For unless the party burthened with the duty were subject to the author of the law, the party would not be obnoxious, to the legal or political sanction by which the duty and the right are respectively enforced and protected.[2]

Of course Austin knows that 'in many cases the positive law of a given independent community imposes a duty on a stranger'.[3] He explains the difficulty by introducing the concept of partial

---

[1] *Province*, p. 16.   [2] *Province*, p. 283; see also pp. 15, 350.
[3] Ibid., p. 351.

or limited membership in a society.[1] A stranger is a partial member in so far as he is susceptible to the sovereign's power. Instead of saying that only commands addressed to subjects are law, it would be more precise to say that a command is law only if it is addressed to people who are likely to suffer the prescribed sanction, in case this should become necessary. But this is exactly what the condition of superiority amounts to. It is, therefore, possible to eliminate from the definition of law the clause 'addressed to his subjects', as redundant.

We have seen that the validity of every law presupposes that its supreme legislator (1) is superior to the subjects of that law; (2) is habitually obeyed by the bulk of the population; (3) does not habitually obey anyone. The first presupposition involves a relation between the legislator and the subjects of the particular law in question. The second involves a relation between him and the society at large. It is to this condition that we now turn.

Obeying a command involves knowing it, and to obey the commander one must know who he is. In certain contexts obeying the command implies also acting because of it. Austin certainly does not wish to imply this last condition. But how would he regard conformity to the law without knowing of its existence? We certainly regard such conformity as tending, on the whole, to support the existence of the authority rather than to weaken it. Some may even doubt whether conformity coupled with knowledge is not too thin a basis for a sovereign and a legal system. Undoubtedly much depends on the exact extent of the necessary knowledge. Austin is silent on the question, and I find it impossible to attribute to him any definite position.

Obeying the sovereign means obeying his commands. The existence of a law presupposes that the sovereign is habitually obeyed, and also, therefore, that he has issued other commands,[2] that there are other laws belonging to the same system. Hence, according to Austin, laws exist necessarily in systems, as parts

---

[1] Ibid., pp. 351 ff.

[2] It seems that Austin did not think that obedience to one law can amount to a habit of obedience. Thus he finds no difficulty in the concept of a command issued by one sovereign and directed to another (cf. *Province*, p. 139). Hence, presumably, even obedience to such a command does not deprive the sovereign of his sovereignty.

of groups of laws. It is, however, possible that at some moment during the lifetime of the system no law exists at all. It is theoretically possible, though practically absurd, for a sovereign to repeal all the existing laws and to enact new laws after an interval of, say, only a couple of days. Nor is there any logical necessity, according to his theory, for the system to include laws which are general, in the sense of applying to classes of persons rather than to individuals. This is merely convenient, and perhaps practically unavoidable: 'To frame a system of duties for every individual of the community, were simply impossible: and if it were possible, it were utterly useless. Most of the laws established by political superiors are, therefore, general.'[1]

Habitual obedience to the sovereign presupposes not only that laws have been made but also that they are habitually obeyed. A law exists only if it (1) belongs to a legal system (2) which is on the whole efficacious. Any particular law may be disregarded and constantly violated, and still exist, so long as the legal system of which it is a part is on the whole obeyed.

A system exists if its laws exist. One can, therefore, derive from what has hitherto been said on the existence of a law the following *criteria for the existence of a legal system:* A legal system exists if and only if (1) its supreme legislator is habitually obeyed, that is to say the laws of the system are by and large efficacious; (2) its supreme legislator does not habitually obey anyone; (3) its supreme legislator is superior to the subjects of every one of his laws relative to the sanction of that law.

To these we should add a fourth condition, (4) that all the laws of the system were actually legislated and were legislated ultimately, by one person, or group. This condition differs from the other conditions in that it refers to the exercise of powers, not to the fulfilment of duties. The existence of a legal system entails not only that duties are fulfilled but also that legislative powers are exercised. The fourth condition is in effect the condition of the creation of laws. A law is created, according to Austin, if it is issued ultimately by the sovereign. The fourth condition merely states the obvious, namely that if a purported legal system is to be regarded as an existing legal system its laws must satisfy the conditions of the creation of laws.

---

[1] *Province*, p. 23.

This fourth condition apart, we may say that a criterion of existence manifests the principle of efficacy if its only condition for the existence of a system is its efficacy. Austin's criterion of existence is not based solely on the principle of efficacy, though it contains it as a major component. It insists on the superiority and independence of the supreme legislator as well. Moreover, the efficacy of the system is relevant only in so far as it contributes to the personal obedience of the population to the supreme legislator.

Before leaving the subject a few words must be said on a key concept used in the analysis—society. All that Austin says about its meaning is: 'A society in a state of nature . . . is composed of persons who are connected by mutual intercourse, but are not members . . . of any society political.'[1] Elsewhere he asks: ' . . . who are the members of a given society? By what characters, or by what distinguishing marks, are its members severed from persons who are not of its members?'[2] And he answers, 'A person may be a member of a given society . . . by any of numerous modes or by any of numerous causes',[2] and these differ in 'different communities'.[3] He proceeds to explain: 'These modes are fixed differently in different particular societies, by their different particular systems of positive law or morality.'[3] The passage suggests a definition of society as all the subjects of all the laws of one supreme legislator (together with the supreme legislator himself). The subjects of a law are the persons to whom it applies. The definition is open to two objections: It would follow from it (a) that the world population as a whole may in many cases constitute a given society. Thus according to the English legal system any person commits an offence if he, for example, murders in Great Britain. (b) Suppose A is a person claiming sovereignty over two peoples, the Reds and the Greens, and he makes them all subject to his laws. In fact only the Reds obey him, whereas the Greens are effectively governed by B and disobey A's laws. We would like to say that A is the sovereign of the Reds who are an independent society. But according to the suggested definition, the Greens and the Reds are one society—both being subjects of A's laws. Therefore either their bulk habitually obeys A (which is the case if the

---

[1] *Province*, p. 200; cf. Bentham, *Fragment*, p. 38.   [2] Ibid., p. 356.
[3] *Province*, p. 358.

Reds are much more numerous than the Greens), and then *A* is the sovereign of both Reds and Greens; or their bulk does not habitually obey him, in which case he is the sovereign of neither people. Both results are unacceptable.

I propose to do without the concept of society altogether. We will define an auxiliary concept—the core of an independent society—as any number of persons who are all those who habitually obey one sovereign in preference to all other persons.[1] An independent society consists of a core and all other persons standing to them in some socially significant relation (e.g. living in the same country, sharing the same language), provided their number is large enough[2] and that the bulk of this population habitually obeys the same sovereign as the core.

This definition allows for a person to be a member of more than one independent society.

1.3: AN IDENTITY CRITERION

When in explaining Austin we say that a legal system contains all the laws made by one person or group, we do not mean that that person or group was personally responsible for their issue. The sovereign, according to Austin, is the direct or indirect legislator of all the laws in a system. The important fact is that when we trace the source of the laws of a system we end with one person (or group) who is the ultimate source of every one of them.

Austin's criteria of identity and membership are a variant of what may be called the principle of origin. The principle says that the membership of laws in a system, and the identity of the system, are completely determined by the origin of the laws; the origin of a law being the set of facts which brings it into existence. Austin's variant of the principle has three characteristic features:

(1) The origin of every law includes an act of legislation; that is, according to Austin, deliberate behaviour expressing a wish that some other persons will behave in a certain way.

(2) The ultimate origin of every law is a legislative act of one person, or body of persons. All the laws have one ultimate source (or legislator).

---

[1] Cf. Bentham, *Limits*, p. 101; *OLG*, p. 18.   [2] See *Province*, pp. 198, 207–8.

(3) The continued existence of the ultimate source is a necessary condition for the existence of the laws of the system.

Austin's criterion of identity, we may say, is based on the principle of legislative origin and assumes that all the laws of the system have one persistent ultimate source.

A person is the ultimate source (or legislator) of a law if, and only if, he is capable of being an ultimate source of this law and did issue it directly or indirectly. A person is capable of being an ultimate source of a law if he is a sovereign and is superior to the subjects of that law. A person is the non-ultimate legislator of a law if, and only if, he is competent to make and did make it, directly or indirectly. A person is competent to make a law as a subordinate legislator if, and only if, there is a law conferring upon him power to make it by certain acts. A person is an indirect legislator of a law only if it was made by the exercise of powers directly or indirectly conferred by a law whose direct legislator he was.

Direct legislation by the sovereign consists (as we have seen in section 2) in (1) entertaining a desire that some persons shall behave in a certain way and an intention to cause them some harm or pain if they do not behave in that way; (2) expressing the desire and the intention. Austin never explains how exactly delegated legislation takes place. It is plausible to suppose that the delegated authority expresses the desire and the intention. In so far as the matter lies in its discretion it clearly entertains also the desire that the subjects of its laws will behave as prescribed, and that if they do not they will be made to suffer at the hands of some of the sovereign's agents. The main difference between direct legislation by the sovereign and legislation by his delegates is that the latter must express their desires in the way prescribed by the enabling laws, i.e. the laws conferring this legislative power upon them.

Is the sovereign or any other indirect legislator supposed to entertain a wish that the subjects of laws legislated by his subordinates will behave in the prescribed way? The answer lies in the nature of the laws conferring legislative powers. Delegated legislation is made on the basis of rights conferred upon the subordinate legislator. These are sometimes accompanied by duties which dictate how they ought to be used, but this is not always the case. Sometimes the decision in what way to use the right is entrusted to the absolute discretion of the right-holder. Thus Austin distinguishes between two kinds of representatives: those who are 'subject to a trust' and those who are not.[1] He then says: 'Where such a trust is imposed by a sovereign ... the trust is enforced by legal, or by merely moral sanction. The representative body is bound by a positive law or laws: or it is merely bound by a fear that it may offend the bulk of the community.'[2] From which we can infer (a) that a legal trust is a legal duty, and (b) that not every power of a representative is coupled with such a duty, and hence that they are not identical. Nor is the power to legislate simply another duty, or even a liberty. Austin explicitly says: 'Numerous positive laws proceed directly from subjects through rights conferred upon their authors by supreme political superior.'[3] The same view is the underlying assumption of the following two passages:

If a member [of the sovereign body] ... be wholly or partially free from legal or political obligation, that legally irresponsible ... individual is restrained or debarred in two ways from an unconstitutional exercise of its legally unlimited power: 1. [moral obligation] ... 2. If it affected to issue a command which it is not empowered to issue ... its unconstitutional command would not be legally binding, and disobedience to that command would therefore not be illegal.[4]

The passage makes it amply clear that:

(1) Austin distinguishes between the absence of a right to legislate and the duty not to purport to legislate beyond one's powers.

(2) Legislative rights are not necessarily coupled with duties as to their exercise.

(3) Sometimes Austin uses the phrase 'legally unlimited' to mean 'not subject to duties', though on other occasions it must be construed as referring also to the absence of rights.[5]

The second passage proves essentially the same points and needs no further comment: The king of England is not a sovereign because

[1] *Province*, p. 229.   [2] *Province*, p. 230.   [3] Ibid., p. 159.
[4] *Province*, p. 265.   [5] e.g. ibid., p. 254.

though he is absolved completely from legal or political duty . . . if
he affected to transgress the limits which the constitution has set
to his authority, disobedience on the part of the governed to his
unconstitutional commands would not be illegal; . . . But commands
issued by sovereigns cannot be disobeyed by their subjects without
an infringement of positive law.[1]

In general, rights are conferred on a class of persons by a law
which imposes a duty on another class. It follows that power of
legislation is conferred by laws imposing duties on persons other
than the delegated legislators. Austin does not specify the nature
of the duty and the people on whom it is imposed. The only
reasonable interpretation is that the duty is imposed on the intended subjects of the subordinate legislation and that it is their
duty to obey the subordinate legislator in matters in which he is
authorized to legislate. Power to legislate is conferred by what
I propose to call 'obedience laws', that is laws imposing a duty
to obey a certain person, if he commands.

Explaining delegated legislation in terms of obedience laws
has a double advantage from Austin's point of view. It makes it
clear that by obeying a delegated authority you necessarily
obey the sovereign who ordered you to obey that authority. It
also answers our previous question about the wishes of the
sovereign in delegated legislation: Suppose the town council of
A, exercising powers given to it by the sovereign, orders every
householder to install a lamp above the front door of his house.
Does the sovereign wish the householders to fix a lamp, etc.?
In our example the same acts can be described both as fixing
lamps and as obeying the town council. The sovereign wants
the householders to do the act described by the second description. The town council wants them to do the acts described
by the first description. Their wishes are not identical, though
practically they amount to the same thing.

It is of interest to notice that Bentham, who also used the
concept of obedience laws to explain delegated legislation,[2]
gave another explanation as well. He defines a law as 'an
assemblage of signs declarative of a will conceived or adopted by the sovereign . . .'.[3] And he explains that: 'Where
the sovereign holds himself . . . in readiness to adopt the man-

[1] Ibid., pp. 266–7.   [2] e.g. *Limits*, p. 110; *OLG*, pp. 27–8.   [3] *Limits*, p. 88; *OLG*, p. 1

of another person when so ever they shall happen to have been issued, he may thereby be said to invest that person with a certain species of power, which may be termed a power of imperation.'[1] The sovereign is conceived as adopting every law of his subordinate separately by repeated acts of tacit legislation every time the subordinate issues another command. The sovereign makes the will of the subordinate his own.[2] That is why Bentham treats delegated legislation as similar in nature to legislation by reference (e.g. What *A* wrote a month ago in *x* is law as from today). Traces of the same approach are to be found in Austin. For example he writes: 'When customs are turned into legal rules by decisions of subject judges, the legal rules which emerge from the customs are tacit commands of the sovereign legislature.'[3] It seems that Austin is considering the sovereign as separately legislating every custom when a judge declares it for the first time to be legally binding. Austin apparently is not aware that he is supporting two competing theories of delegated legislation. As there is no doubt in my mind that the explanation of it in terms of obedience rules is by far the better of the two, I shall henceforward discuss only that theory.

In one passage Austin writes: 'Laws are sometimes sanctioned by nullities.'[4] If nullities are always sanctions, then this doctrine contradicts the passage from *Province*, 266–7, quoted on page 21. The doctrine that nullities are sanctions has been proved to be unacceptable by Hart.[5] Moreover Austin does not need it at all. It is introduced to explain private powers which can be completely accounted for by his doctrine of capacity.[6] One may therefore disregard the doctrine altogether.

1.4: THE STRUCTURE OF A LEGAL SYSTEM

Austin has very little to say about the structure of a legal system. The views expounded in this section are mostly inferences from the very little relevant material in the book. The scanty material reveals the trend of Austin's views on these topics, it does not suffice to establish any details. We shall

---

[1] Ibid., p. 104; *OLG*, p. 21. [2] Ibid., pp. 103–4; *OLG*, p. 21.
[3] *Province*, p. 32. [4] *Jurisprudence*, p. 505.
[5] *CL*, pp. 33–5. [6] *Jurisprudence*, p. 710.

inevitably be confined to describing somewhat hazy general positions.

Every law is a command, that is, an expression of a wish for someone's behaviour and an intention to inflict on him pain if he does not conform with the wish. In so far as it expresses a wish every law specifies some persons, the law's subjects, an act which they have to perform, and the occasion on which it has to be performed. The subject-, act-, and occasion-descriptions are combined by an imperative operator ordering the subjects to do the acts on the specified occasions. This may be presented in formal terms as follows: If x is a variable for persons, '!' the imperative operator, and A and C variables for acts and occasions respectively, then the part of a law which we are discussing, and which we will call the imperative part, can be schematically represented by the formula: $x!A$ in C.

An obedience law conferring unlimited legislative powers on a person, say P, has the same structure with respect to its imperative part, but a more complex occasion specification: $X!A$ in C_1, that is if P ordered x to A in C_2 and if C_2 is the case. If P's legislative powers are limited the formula is more complicated, but the basic structure is preserved throughout.

It seems reasonable to attribute to Austin the view that the intention to cause harm can be expressed either directly, by what may be called declaration of a punitive policy, or indirectly, by ordering some subordinate to apply sanctions to the subjects of the law if they violate it.

In cases where the intention to cause pain is expressed directly the law contains a second part—a declaration of policy. This may be the case when the legislator intends to apply the sanction himself or to deal with violations as they occur by ordering his agents on each occasion to act against each of the violators. Cases where the intention to cause harm is expressed by ordering some subordinate to apply the sanctions do not affect the content of the original law at all. This intention is expressed by a second law, which we shall call a punitive law. The punitive law, is, of course, itself backed either by some punitive law or by a policy of sanctions. A policy of sanctions, though part of a law, is not an independent law; it does not impose a duty and therefore need not be backed by a punitive law. For this reason, if for no other, Austin's theory does not involve an infinite series of laws, each providing a sanction for the violation of the other.[1]

Every law has an imperative part and some have a punitive-policy part as well. Those which have only an imperative part are laws only if they have a corresponding punitive law, that is another law which makes the violation of the first an occasion for causing harm to the violators. The relation between a law and its corresponding punitive law we shall call a punitive relation; it is an example of an internal relation.

There are innumerable possible relations among laws, many of them of interest. In searching for the structure of legal systems we shall be concerned only with one kind of relation which we call an internal relation. An internal relation exists between two laws if, and only if, one of them is (part of) a condition for the existence of the other or affects its meaning or application. Other relations will be called external relations. The internal structure of a legal system is its pattern of internal relations. Interpretation laws have an internal relation to laws which they help to interpret, because they affect their meaning. The relations between laws according to their social consequences are a very important kind of external relations. A local by-law, demanding certain sanitary conditions in pubs, complements, in different ways, both the by-law of the same local authority demanding similar conditions in restaurants, and the by-law of the neighbouring authority which demands the same conditions in pubs. A law imposing a tax on unbuilt property in towns enhances the effects of a law granting certain tax exemptions to building societies, etc.

Punitive relations are perhaps the most important internal relations implicitly recognized by Austin. A law containing an imperative part only is not an independent law at all, unless there is a corresponding punitive law. At best it is an imperfect law to be interpreted, perhaps, as part of another law, and having the effect not of imposing a duty but of permitting an act.

Our previous discussion of subordinate legislation uncovered another kind of internal relation implicitly recognized by Austin: The relation between a subordinate law and the obedience law which authorized its legislation. Such a relation

---

[1] See on this problem: Kelsen, *GT*, pp. 28–9; Hart, 'Self-Referring Laws'.

we shall call a genetic relation, that is a relation between a law and another law which is part of its origin, i.e. one of the facts which contributed to its creation.

Genetic relations present Austin with a problem. Every law imposes a duty. A duty exists only if its violation is the occasion for a sanction according to a declared policy or to a punitive law. There is only one sanction attached to violating both the law of the subordinate authority and the obedience law authorizing it. One might argue that this means there is only one duty, and consequently only one law referring to such an act. It certainly means that obedience laws differ in an important respect from other duty-imposing laws.

These are not the only internal relations which can exist between Austinian laws. To give a simple example—obeying a law may be the occasion, according to a different law, for giving the obedient subject some benefit. Our aim is, however, to find necessary internal relations, and there are no such relations according to Austin. Punitive laws can be avoided in favour of punitive policies. Obedience laws can be avoided if the sovereign chooses to remain the only legislator. Certainly punitive and genetic relations will exist in most legal systems, but they are not logically necessary. Nor are there any other necessary relations between laws. In 'The Uses of Jurisprudence' Austin enumerates five distinctions which he claims to be universally present in all mature legal systems. These are the distinction between (1) written and unwritten law; (2) rights against the world in general and rights against persons specifically determined; (3) rights against the world at large are divided into property or dominion and the variously restricted rights which are carved out of them; (4) obligations which arise of contract and of injuries and quasi contract; (5) injuries are distinguished into civil and criminal.[1] The first distinction establishes an external relation, a relation between laws according to types of origin. The rest are classifications of rights and duties which may be the basis of external relations, but do not indicate the existence of any kind of internal relations.

A theory of legal system is based on the principle of independence if according to it there is no logical necessity for a legal system to have an internal structure.

---

[1] 'The Uses of Jurisprudence', pp. 367–8.

Austin's theory may be said to be an example of a theory based on the principle of independence. The fact that every law is a command entails that every law can be an independent unit, the existence, meaning or application of which is not logically affected by other laws. Thus Austin's views on the nature of a law determine his negative solution to the problem of structure.

II

AUSTIN'S THEORY: CRITICISM

In the first chapter Austin's theory of legal system has been shown to be based on the origin and independence principles, and up to a point also on the principle of efficacy. The present chapter is an attempt to point out some of the difficulties which this theory raises. As Austin says very little about the structure of a legal system, his version of the principle of independence will not be examined until a later chapter.

The greater part of the chapter is concerned with the most important feature of Austin's theory—the role allotted to the sovereign. His theory of sovereignty has been widely and thoroughly criticized. No attempt will be made here to exhaust all the objections raised against it. My purpose is to relate some of the most important objections to the problems of the theory of legal system, thus trying to throw some new light on the significance of the problems. More attention than is usual is paid to difficulties which are revealed by a careful elaboration of Austin's theory itself, though of course the ultimate arbiter of its value is its degree of applicability to the law, as we know it.

The first section explains how and why the illimitability thesis means that Austin's theory fails to explain an important part of constitutional law. The way in which making personal obedience to the sovereign a condition for the existence of a legal system leads to a distorted picture of the duration of legal systems is examined in section 2. Another shortcoming of his existence criterion is discussed in the last section (II.5), while the remaining two sections are concerned with the failure of the identity criterion.

II.1: THE ILLIMITABILITY OF SOVEREIGNTY

In a well-known passage Austin says: 'Supreme power limited by positive law, is a flat contradiction in terms.'[1] By this he meant both that the sovereign cannot be the subject of rights

[1] *Province*, p. 254.

and duties and that his legislative power cannot be legally curtailed. The last contention is usually interpreted as a direct result of Austin's thesis that the sovereign cannot be subjected to duties. Austin did not use Hohfeld's concept of power, so the argument goes, and thought that we can limit a power only by imposing a duty not to use it. Consequently he confused lack of power with the existence of a duty. His doctrine that the sovereign cannot be put under a duty meant for him also that the sovereign's legislative powers are illimitable.

Thus we find Hart saying: 'Austin's argument against the possibility of a legal limitation on the power of the sovereign rests on the assumption that to be subject to such a limitation is to be subject to a duty.'[1] Similarly Salmond wrote:

It is considered that to limit by law the exercise of the state's legislative function is . . . impossible. . . . This principle is not commonly distinguished from the very different doctrine that the state cannot be subject to legal duties; the two are treated together and supported by the same arguments. And indeed there is no room for any such distinction in a system which defines law as the command of the state, and regards every rule as creating and corresponding to a legal duty. On this view of the nature of law, to be subject to a rule of law is the same thing as to be subject to a legal duty, and the distinction between the liability of the state to legal sanctions, and the legal limitation of its legislative powers disappears.[2]

It is true that Austin, while discussing the illimitability of the sovereign, creates the impression that he regards curtailment of legislative powers as done by imposing duties on the legislator. But, as we have seen (I.3), at least some legislators can be limited in two ways: by withholding certain legislative powers, that is certain rights, or by imposing upon them duties directing them in the exercise of those powers they possess. Austin apparently thought the second way more important,[3] but this, and the confusion which sometimes crept in, should not prevent us from realizing that the illimitability of the sovereign's legislative powers is and can be proved only by two steps:

(1) Limitation of the sovereign's legislative power construed as the absence of certain rights is impossible, because, to put it crudely, he can have no rights.

---

[1] Hart, *CL*, p. 242.   [2] *Principles*, p. 137.
[3] Cf. his argument in *Province*, p. 254.

(2) He is completely free in the exercise of his powers because he cannot be subject to legal duties.

It is easy to see the reason for the second half of the proof.
Austin explains: ' . . . if we would speak with propriety, we
cannot speak of a law set by a man to himself: though a man
may adopt a principle as a guide to his own conduct, and may
observe it as he would observe it if he were bound to observe it
by a sanction.'[1] We may add Markby's explanation: 'No man,
except by a strong figure of speech, can be said to issue commands to himself.'[2] Indeed, if we are to allow laws set by the
sovereign to himself, we must reject the command theory in
favour of some other explanation of laws, with all the consequences which may follow for the solution to the problem of
structure, which was based on the command theory.

Let us turn now to the first half of the argument. If the
sovereign cannot have rights, then the absence of rights is not a
limitation of his powers. He is simply not a person to whom
power can be given by conferring upon him rights, nor can he
be deprived of power by depriving him of rights. This method
of regulating powers does not apply to him. It does not follow
that the sovereign's power of legislation is not a legal power. By
legal power we mean the ability to change the legal situation
by an act, and the sovereign can change the laws by legislation.
But his legal power is not a legal right because it is not conferred
by law. To find out what legislative powers a subordinate has
one looks for laws conferring rights upon him. To establish the
existence or otherwise of a sovereign power one looks for social
facts, for a habit of obedience of the population, etc. And Austin
has so framed his concepts that sovereign legislative power
cannot be limited. For general disobedience to a particular law
does not mean that the sovereign had no power to make it. If
the disobedience spreads and becomes disobedience to laws in
general, the sovereign will lose not only his power to legislate
on certain matters but his sovereign power as a whole.

In brief the argument is: There are two ways of acquiring
legislative power: (a) by facts, (b) by law. The first leads only
to unlimited power. The second does not apply to the sovereign.
As the first way applies only to the sovereign this means that the

[1] *Province*, p. 255.   [2] Markby, *Elements*, p. 93.

two are incompatible. A person cannot at one time have powers acquired in both ways. Why should they be incompatible? Why cannot the sovereign have rights? Austin's argument as it stands is very unconvincing:

A man is no more able to confer a right on himself, than he is able to impose on himself a law or duty. Every party bearing a right . . . has necessarily acquired the right through the might or power of another; . . . consequently if a sovereign government had legal rights against its own subjects, those rights were the creatures of positive laws set to its own subjects by a third person or body.[1]

Austin obviously thought that his logic was so clear as not to need fuller explanation.

Willoughby suggests a more promising line of thought in support of the same thesis: 'Even as to rights, the ascription of them to the state is meaningless, since their continuance as well as their creation, their character and their content are wholly subject to the state's will.'[2] There are signs that Austin was thinking along similar lines.[3] The force of this argument is best explained by Markby:

. . . between the so-called rights of the sovereign to a tax, or a fine, and the right of a citizen to receive a debt from a fellow citizen, there are, as it seems to me, essential differences. The citizen holds his right to recover his debt, but can only exercise and enjoy that right at the will and pleasure of another, namely, the sovereign who conferred it upon him. The sovereign power, on the other hand, which imposed the tax or fine, is also the power which enforces it. Moreover, the right to payment of a debt, which is possessed by the citizen, is not only dependent on the will of another for its exercise and enjoyment, but it is limited by that will; and nothing but the external sovereign power can change the nature of the legal relation between debtor and creditor. Whereas in the case of a tax or fine, although the sovereign has expressed in specific terms, and therefore for the moment limited, the duty to be performed towards itself, it follows from the nature of sovereignty that by the sovereign will the duty may be at any moment changed. . . . It is impossible to conceive a right of so fluctuating a character . . . because we cannot conceive a right as changing at the will of its holder.[4]

[1] *Province*, p. 284.
[2] Willoughby, *The Fundamental Concepts of Public Law*, 76; see also Hobbes, *Leviathan*, p. 173.
[3] Cf. *Province*, pp. 291, 254-5.   [4] Markby, *Elements*, pp. 93-4.

To put it in my own words: *A person cannot have a right over which he has both exclusive and complete control*. One's control is exclusive if nobody else can affect by law the existence or scope of the right. One's control is complete if one can create or abolish or change the right at will.

There is no point in ascribing rights to persons if they have complete and exclusive control over them. Rights serve to distinguish behaviour which is legally permissible or effective from behaviour which is not. There is no point in drawing such a distinction unless it serves as a relatively constant standard by which to assess the behaviour of the person in question. Hence there is no point to the distinction if this person can, whenever he likes, shift the boundary of what is legally permissible or effective and no one can interfere.

Markby's argument includes the following deduction: If the sovereign can change his rights at will he can have no rights. He can change his rights at will. Therefore he can have no rights. The second premiss follows from the definition of a law. Every command of the sovereign is law, hence also every command of his to disregard a previous command is law.

The principle behind Markby's argument is sound. A man is a potential right-holder (of rights of a certain kind) only if his rights (of this kind), if he has any, are *relatively immune* from his own interference. Otherwise rights can neither limit nor guide him, by determining which of the possible courses of action open to him is permissible or effective. Markby, however, thinks that to satisfy the condition of relative immunity the potential right-holder must be able to have rights (of the kind in question) without having complete and exclusive legal control over them. This is an unnecessarily severe condition. It makes sense and it conforms to the general purposes and presuppositions of the institution of rights to consider a man as a potential right-holder (of rights of a certain kind), even if Markby's condition is not satisfied, provided another condition is fulfilled. Namely, provided it is, as a matter of fact, not often likely that when a limitation of his right is relied upon, the person will change his rights in order to avoid this limitation. In other words a *de facto* immunity of a person's rights from himself is all that is necessary to achieve the necessary relative immunity of his rights. Such a *de facto* immunity may exist either because the cost of changing the right whenever necessary is prohibitive (e.g. absorbing parliamentary time and machinery at great cost and causing other business to be delayed), or because of some pressure which prevents the right-holder from making frequent use of his legal power (e.g. public opinion).

These considerations show that Austin's thesis that the sovereign cannot have rights may be rejected, and explain the character of the rights which could consistently with the rest of his theory be ascribed to the sovereign. But even though the sovereign can have rights in general he cannot have legislative rights, and cannot, therefore, have limited legislative rights. To confer upon himself legislative rights the sovereign has to command his subjects to obey him on certain matters. Suppose that he goes even further and commands (1) his citizens to disobey him on matters p. Suppose further that later he issues a command (2) with regard to these matters. The second command partly contradicts, and therefore repeals, the first. A law (and a command) telling x to A in C partly contradicts a law (or command) telling x to not-A in C, in the sense that on no occasion can one obey the first without violating the second. If the first was legislated after the second it repeals it to the extent that it is incompatible with it. Because (2) repeals (1) it is itself a law. Thus the sovereign cannot limit his own legislative power. The law purporting to limit them is not a law at all, because there can never be an occasion to obey it. The conditions creating this occasion repeal the law itself, in so far as it applies to that occasion. If there is no occasion to rely on the limitations of the sovereign's rights there is no point in ascribing to him legislative rights; in other words, the sovereign cannot have legislative rights. Having legislative power acquired by facts excludes having legislative rights.

It also follows that (1) is unacceptable and is not a law, and therefore its contradictory, (3) a law by the sovereign ordering the population to obey him in future, is either necessary (i.e. must exist in every system), or also unacceptable. If it is necessary, then it is law regardless of whether the sovereign legislates it. Anyone who does not wish to admit the possibility of unlegislated laws must consider it as unacceptable. It should be emphasized that this argument depends on Austin's theses that laws are commands and that the sovereign cannot be subordinate.

These considerations explain the reasons for the illimitability doctrine. The consequences of the doctrine were known to Austin himself.[1] It means that certain constitutional laws, namely purported laws which either ascribe legislative rights and duties to the sovereign or determine his capacity to have legislative rights and duties, are not laws according to the theory. Or one may say that the theory fails to explain why we do regard them as laws on the same footing as other laws.

II.2: ON PERSONAL OBEDIENCE

One way in which Austin deviates from the principle of efficacy[2] is that for him the efficacy of the laws is relevant to the existence of a system only so far as it constitutes the general habit of obedience to the supreme legislator. The obedience relevant to the existence of a system is personal obedience. Laws can be obeyed even when their legislator is dead or if a body otherwise ceases to exist, but in that case by obeying the laws one does not obey their legislator. This is surely acknowledged by Austin, even though he would most probably insist that obeying a law while its legislator lives necessarily entails obeying its legislator. On the whole it is true that a person (or body of persons) cannot be obeyed after he is dead (or otherwise ceases to exist).[3]

Consequently, when a sovereign ceases to exist the legal system legislated, directly or indirectly, by him ceases to exist. This is certainly the case from the moment a new sovereign takes, as it were, the place vacated by the previous sovereign. From that moment a new legal system is created, consisting only of laws made, directly or indirectly, by the new sovereign. But even if no new sovereign establishes himself in the vacant place, and even if the population continues to obey the old laws, these are now rules of positive morality and not legal rules. For in this situation no person or body of persons is being obeyed, the obedience is not personal obedience, and a legal system exists only where there is such personal obedience.

Thus the demand for personal obedience means that the span

---

[1] *Province*, pp. 257–60.

[2] According to the principle of efficacy the existence of a legal system depends only on its efficacy. See Ch. I, sect. 2, above.

[3] There are some exceptions which do not affect our case.

of life of the supreme legislator of a legal system determines
the period of existence of the laws of the system and hence also
of the system itself. Austin knew that often old laws continue
their existence even after a new sovereign established himself,
and explains that in such cases the new sovereign tacitly legislates
them anew so that now they are his laws. In section 5, below,
this use of the concept of tacit command will be examined. But
even if this device is accepted the problem is not solved. For
lawyers distinguish—and for good reasons—between what may
be called, to use Austinian terms, a change of sovereignty
which amounts to a new start, when they say that the old legal
system has ceased to exist, and a constitutional change of
sovereignty. When a new system is created it often includes
many laws identical in content with laws of the old system and
these are usually enacted in mass, by reference to the old laws.
On the other hand, when an ordinary constitutional change of
sovereignty takes place, the same legal system continues to
exist. The laws in force under the new sovereign are not merely
identical in content with the laws legislated by the previous
sovereign, they are actually the same laws.

Austin's references[1] to the difference between a constitutional
and an un-constitutional succession of sovereigns do not affect
the crucial consequence, namely that every change of sovereignty involves a change of legal systems. This consequence is
inevitable once personal obedience has become a major component of the existence criterion. The theory of legal system
which was derived in the previous chapter from Austin's
doctrines fails in this respect to explain our existing concept of
a legal system. At the same time it provides no strong reason
why our concept should be modified.

At this point it might be useful to introduce an important
distinction, that between a legal system and a momentary
legal system. A momentary legal system contains all the laws
of a system valid at a certain moment. These are usually not
all the laws of the system. An English law enacted in 1906 and
repealed in 1927 and an English law enacted in 1948 belong to
the same legal system. Yet there is no momentary legal system
to which both belong, because they were never valid at one and
the same moment.

[1] *Province*, pp. 152 ff.

The phrase 'The English legal system at the beginning of the reign of Elizabeth II' is ambiguous. It may refer to the momentary system of that particular time or to the legal system to which this momentary system belongs. Often such phrases are used to refer to neither, but to the system of the period: that is to the laws valid at one moment or another during some span of time longer than a moment and shorter than the total duration of the legal system.

A momentary legal system is a subclass of a legal system: For every momentary legal system there is a legal system that contains all the laws of the momentary system. Two different momentary systems which are subclasses of one legal system may overlap or even be identical in their laws, or they may have no law in common.

The argument propounded in this section shows that Austin's theory of legal system contains at best an adequate explanation of a momentary legal system; its explanation of a legal system is fundamentally defective. According to his theory two different momentary legal systems which in fact belong to one system may turn out to belong to different systems only.

While we are discussing the concept of a momentary legal system one more defect of Austin's theory may be mentioned. Every theory of legal system has to satisfy the following prerequisite: It is logically impossible for a legal system to contain any empty momentary system. In other words, there is no moment at which a legal system exists but has no laws valid at that moment. The necessity for this prerequisite is intuitively clear. Austin's theory, however, does not satisfy it, as was mentioned in Chapter I, section 2, above.

11.3: THE UNITY OF SOVEREIGNTY

When Austin says that 'in every society political and independent the sovereign is *one* individual or *one* body of individuals'[1] he means that the sovereign power is both unique and united. The following argument is designed to show that his theory fails to guarantee the unity of sovereignty, and that consequently his identity criterion must at least be modified.

Sovereignty is united if all the sovereign's powers are in the

[1] *Province*, p. 246.

hands of one person or body of persons. It is divided if several persons or groups have each separately a part of the sovereign power. Hence the definition of a body of persons is of crucial importance. Austin explains:

If a body of persons be determinate, all the persons who compose it are determined and assignable, or every person who belongs to it is determined and may be indicated. But determinate bodies are of two kinds. A determinate body of one of those kinds is distinguished by the following marks: 1. The body is composed of persons determined specifically or individually, or determined by characters or descriptions respectively appropriate to themselves. 2. . . . Every individual member is a member of the determinate body, not by reason of his answering to any generic description but by reason of his bearing his specific or appropriate character. A determinate body of the other of those kinds is distinguished by the following marks: 1. It comprises all persons who belong to a given class, or who belong respectively to two or more of such classes. In other words, every person who answers to a given generic description, or to any of two or more given generic descriptions is also a member of the determinate body. 2. . . . Every individual member is a member of the determinate body, not by reason of his bearing his specific or appropriate character, but by reason of his answering to the given description.[1]

To be determined specifically, or individually, means determined by a definite description. To be determined by a generic description is to be determined by an indefinite description. According to this interpretation the first type of determinate bodies includes those bodies defined by the use of definite descriptions only. Bodies the membership of which is determined only by indefinite descriptions are of the second kind. There is no doubt that, according to Austin, a determinate body may also be a mixed body, consisting of some persons belonging to it because of a generic property they share, and some belonging to it because they satisfy a definite description. Therefore if this long quotation is to be taken as a definition of a body, any number of persons can be regarded as a body of persons, and the stipulation that sovereignty must be united is never genuinely fulfilled.

This is certainly not the ordinary concept of a body of persons.

[1] *Province*, p. 145.

Usually several persons are regarded as constituting a body only if they participate in a series of co-ordinated actions during a prolonged period, or stand in some other special relationship to one another. The discussion that follows shows that Austin did not envisage any such restriction on the use of the term.

The only other way to make sense of the idea of the unity of sovereignty is to say that sovereignty is united only if all the present members of the sovereign body generally participate in every legislative act. They need not all participate in every stage of the process of legislation, but they must generally take part at some stage or other of the process. If regularly some of the members of the sovereign body participate in legislating one kind of laws (say, laws applying to a certain area), and others take part only in the legislation of another kind of laws, then the sovereignty is divided.

According to this definition Austin actually rejects the unity thesis. When he says that in Bavaria the sovereign body is both the local government and the Imperial appellate court[1] as one body, he must be aware that they always act separately and never combine in the legislation of even one law. Similarly, when he says that the sovereign in a federal state is 'the several united governments as forming one aggregate body'[2] he knows that as a rule they do not co-operate in the legislation of the same laws. If this is the case, Austin can know that several supreme legislators are parts of one sovereign only because he has previously established on some other grounds that their laws are part of one legal system.

The unity of sovereignty being abandoned, finding out the supreme legislator of a law is not enough to establish to which legal system it belongs. True enough, all the laws of one supreme legislator belong to the same legal system, but they may not be the whole of it. There may be some other laws of a different supreme legislator which belong to the same system, the two supreme legislators being together but one sovereign. But how can one tell? Austin would presumably reply that if, and only if, a supreme legislator is legally illimitable is he a sovereign, otherwise he is only part of a sovereign. But then, how is one to know whether the rules purporting to limit a supreme legislator are legal rules or merely part of positive morality?

[1] *Province*, pp. 240-1.   [2] Ibid., p. 249.

The only criterion given by Austin is that it depends on whether he is a sovereign. Thus the argument is circular.[1]

There is no escape from the conclusion that Austin did not establish the unity of the sovereignty, and consequently his identity criterion based on the origin principle cannot be accepted. The origin principle presupposes a unity of ultimate origin.

II.4: On Legislation

The Austinian version of the origin principle suffers from even more fundamental defects than those revealed in the last section. Austin's explanation of the concept of legislation itself is of rather dubious validity. For one thing, it is usually the case, even in states where sovereignty is in the hands of a single person, that laws are created only when the sovereign follows a certain accepted procedure of legislation. But according to Austin every expression of the sovereign's desire which is a command is law, so he does not allow for the fact that the sovereign can command in ways which differ from the accepted procedure, in which case his command is not a law. When the sovereign is a body of persons, following the accepted procedure might be a defining characteristic of the sovereign body. When this happens the members of the sovereign body constitute a sovereign body and act as sovereign only when following the accepted procedure. This solution cannot, however, be applied to a single person who is a sovereign, for Austin does not distinguish between a single person's acting as a sovereign and his acting as a private citizen. And indeed there is no satisfactory way to draw the distinction within the framework of his theory.

The law is characterized by a rigid and relatively clear definition of what constitutes authoritative legal materials,[2] just as much as it is characterized by a certain vagueness about the meaning and import of the authoritative legal material. Austin's explanation of legislation introduces great uncertainties in the identification of the legal material itself.

---

[1] This argument is independent of the argument put forward in Ch. I, sect. 1, p. 10 above, though both prove the same point, namely the dependence of Austin's criterion of identity on the unity of sovereignty.

[2] This expression includes legislated enactment. It is more fully explained in Ch. IV, sect. 1, below.

Austin's explanation of legislation is even more seriously undermined by his handling of the notion of tacit command. Not that the concept in itself is objectionable, but Austin was not clear about the exact purpose it was meant to serve, and in any case misused the concept.[1]

He refers to it in order to explain how the sovereign, acting through his agents, the courts, adopts customs and laws legislated by previous sovereigns. The difficulty is to explain the existence of laws which apparently were not made by the sovereign. The solution consists in showing that though he did not make them directly he made them indirectly, and explaining how such indirect legislation takes place. It happens when a person issues an order and the sovereign who can abrogate it does not do so. Here the concept of tacit command plays the role of explaining the phenomenon of indirect legislation. This concept of tacit command has been rightly criticized as unacceptable and fictitious, and it was shown in Chapter I, section 3, above to be unnecessary. A person cannot command tacitly unless he knows of the command and can be expected to abolish it; the first element is often absent in the case of the sovereign, and to bodies of persons it is sometimes inapplicable. Moreover Austin has an alternative explanation of indirect legislation, in his doctrine about laws conferring subordinate legislative powers.

But customs and laws of previous sovereigns present a further problem, since their apparent direct legislator cannot be regarded as the sovereign's agent. Custom is not made by legislation at all, not being command in Austin's sense or in any recognized sense, and previous sovereigns cannot be subordinates of the present sovereign. It may be attempted to modify Austin's explanation of the creation of these laws, in order to by-pass the objections just mentioned, as follows: customs are not law until they are legislated by the courts, and laws of previous sovereigns are legislated for a second time by the courts of the present sovereign, thus becoming his laws. The courts, however, do not legislate them in the ordinary way, i.e. by expressing their wish that some persons should behave according to custom, etc. So they are said to legislate them tacitly, that is by (1) enforcing them while (2) being at liberty not to enforce them.

[1] See on the subject *Province*, pp. 30–2; Hart, *CL*, pp. 45–7, 63.

Here the concept of tacit command has a second and more plausible role to play.

The first role was an explanation of indirect legislation—how we can attribute to the sovereign acts done by the courts. The second role is to explain a certain irregular mode of direct legislation—how the courts legislate certain categories of laws. In the first role tacit command consists in not abolishing a law while being at liberty to do so. In the second role it consists in enforcing a law while being at liberty not to do so.

It may be thought that if the courts are not under a duty to enforce a law, then nobody else is under a duty to obey it, if only because it lacks sanctions—not being backed, as it were, by orders to the courts to punish violators (nor, presumably, by a punitive policy). But this is not quite the case. The courts' liberty not to enforce a law means only that they can repeal it by making it unenforceable, not that they are its legislators. Nor does it mean that it lacks sanction. It can be backed by sanction just like any other law, though its sanctions can be made inoperative by the courts.

This argument is merely negative. It purports to show that Austin's argument does not compel us to regard the courts as legislators of the laws under consideration. It cannot, therefore, be used to prove that the courts never legislate, that they always apply previously existing laws, which they sometimes are at liberty to repeal. Further arguments are necessary to settle for each category of laws whether they are legislated by the courts or merely enforced by them. The fate of the two types of laws considered by Austin should be settled by the following criterion: If the courts enforce a purported law (1) which was made with the intention to create a law or which is generally regarded as law; and (2) the reason for its enforcement is that it satisfies condition (1), then the courts are enforcing a law already in existence, and not a law legislated by themselves.[1]

According to this criterion, laws of previous legislators are not legislated by the courts of the present sovereign, and the case of custom is more complicated than Austin imagined. But if this be true, and as previous sovereigns cannot be regarded as agents of the present sovereign, Austin's definition of law cannot be retained. The considerations of the present section

---

[1] See on this subject Ch. VIII below.

may tempt one to replace it with a definition of law as a command enforced by the sovereign. The identity criterion will become: A system consists of all the laws enforced by one sovereign. Something like this move is made by Holland when he says that a law is 'a general rule of external action enforced by a sovereign'.[1]

II.5: ON INDEPENDENCE

Most of Austin's critics agree that his stipulation that the sovereign should be independent is inadequate to account for the independence of the legal system. Some, assuming the transitivity[2] of habitual obedience, expressed their objections by saying that the supreme legislator is not necessarily the one who is ultimately obeyed by the bulk of the population. Discarding the dubious assumption that habitual obedience is in general transitive, one is still forced to accept substantially the same conclusion: A man (or group) may still be the supreme legislator of a system although he habitually obeys some other person (or group) who regularly dictates the laws that the supreme legislator issues, but whose dictates are not laws, even when they are commands.

Almost all the critics made this point by distinguishing between two concepts of sovereignty. Bryce, for instance, wrote: 'The sovereign authority is . . . the person (or body) to whose directions the law attributes legal force, the person in whom resides as of right the ultimate power either of laying down general rules or of issuing isolated rules or commands whose authority is that of the law itself.'[3] And elsewhere: ' . . . the Practical Sovereign . . . [is] the person (or body of persons) who can make his (or their) will prevail whether with the law or against the law. He (or they) is the *de facto* ruler, the person to whom obedience is actually paid.'[4]

Dicey followed Bryce when he wrote: 'It should, however, be carefully noted that the term "sovereignty", as long as it is accurately employed in the sense in which Austin sometimes

---

[1] Holland, *The Elements of Jurisprudence*, p. 40.

[2] That is, if A habitually obeys B and B habitually obeys C, then A habitually obeys C.

[3] Bryce, *Studies in History and Jurisprudence*, vol. ii, 51.

[4] Ibid., ii. 59-60.

uses it is a merely legal conception, and means simply the power of law-making unrestricted by any legal limit. . . . But the word sovereignty is sometimes employed in a political rather than in a strictly legal sense. That body is "politically" sovereign or supreme in a state the will of which is ultimately obeyed by the citizens of the state . . . in some part of his work Austin apparently confused the one sense with the other.'[1]

Austin was aware that the sovereign is not politically omnipotent, but the distinction that he draws between legal and merely political power is unsatisfactory:

> In every monarchy, the monarch renders habitual deference to the opinions and sentiments held and felt by his subjects. But in almost every monarchy, he defers especially to the opinions and sentiments, or he consults especially the interests and prejudices, of some especially influential though narrow portion of the community. . . . Hence it has been concluded that there are no monarchies properly so called: that every supreme government is a government of a number. . . . This though plausible is an error. If he habitually obeyed the commands of a determinate portion of the community the sovereignty would reside in the miscalled monarch, with that determinate body of his miscalled subjects; or the sovereignty would reside exclusively in that determinate body. . . . But habitual deference to opinions of the community or habitual and especial deference to opinions of a portion of the community, is consistent with that independence which is one of the essentials of sovereignty.[2]

The assumption that influence exerted by means of commands must be legal influence is completely groundless. A powerful trade union, an influential archbishop, a great financial or industrial concern, or another sovereign, each of them can impose its will on the sovereign by habitually commanding him how to behave, backing their commands by threats of some harmful consequences which will follow disobedience: yet they would not thereby become the supreme legislator.

Austin's critics are therefore justified in insisting that independence, in the sense of absence of habitual obedience, is

---

[1] Dicey, *Introduction to the Study of the Law of the Constitution*, pp. 72–4; for other theorists who adopted similar positions see: Brown, *The Austinian Theory of Law*, p. 276; Buckland, *Some Reflections on Jurisprudence*, p. 82; Gray's real rulers are a variation of the political sovereign theme (see Gray, *The Nature and Sources of the Law*, p. 79); Salmond, *The First Principles of Jurisprudence*, pp. 131 ff.

[2] *Province*, pp. 218–20 n.

not a necessary characteristic of the supreme legislator. But they probably did not realize the full implication of the distinction between political and legal sovereignty. It means discarding one of the most important contributions to jurisprudence that Bentham and Austin made. For it was not out of confusion, as Dicey thought, but as a crucial step in the explanation of the nature of law, that Austin attempted to define the supreme legislator by direct reference to the social facts of habits of obedience. Austin's attempt failed, and this failure wrecked his solution of the problems of the identity and of the existence of a legal system. But the problems remained to be answered, and not one of Austin's critics mentioned in this section (with the possible exception of Salmond) made even a serious attempt to solve them. It was not until Kelsen that a new comprehensive attempt to solve the problems of the theory of legal system was made.

III

ELEMENTS OF A THEORY OF NORMS

IDEALLY the theory of legal system should be treated as part of a general theory of norms. In the present confused state of the general theory, however, there is much to recommend an attack on the problems of the theory of legal system in isolation. But such isolation can never be complete; and it is a fact that the greatest legal philosophers, including those discussed here, have developed their own theories of norms as the foundation of their jurisprudential theories.

In this chapter and the next certain parts of the general theory of norms which can be extracted from Bentham's and Kelsen's work, and which have a direct bearing on their theories of legal system, will be critically examined. This will involve consideration of four principal topics. In the present chapter we shall examine (1) Kelsen's doctrine concerning a certain class of statements, here called normative statements; (2) Bentham's account of the structure of laws in terms of acts and 'aspects of the will'; (3) Kelsen's account of the existence of legal norms. In the next chapter we shall examine (4) the theory of the individuation of laws explicit or implicit in these two writers.

It is hoped that the relevance of these four topics to the theory of legal system will be apparent from what has been said in Chapters I and II, and from the discussion which follows; but as these topics are complex and their investigation necessarily involves detailed treatment of matters apparently remote from the main subject, the following short discussion of the relation of these four topics to the theory of legal system is offered.

Legal systems being systems of laws, something must be said here on the nature of laws. The meaning of 'a law' is too controversial a subject to be taken as generally agreed upon, and of too great importance to the theory of systems of laws to be avoided altogether. Explanations of the existence, elements, and individuation of laws are parts of the analysis of the concept of a law. Normative statements are statements about laws, and some indication of their relation to laws is necessary to avoid confusion. Moreover, the existence of a system of laws entails the existence of the laws belonging to it, hence the particular relevance of the existence conditions of laws to the understanding of the existence of legal systems. It will be further argued that the problems of the structure of legal systems and of the individuation of laws are intimately interrelated; that the structure of a legal system is determined by (1) the theoretical choice of principles of the individuation of laws, and (2) by the factual incident of the richness and complexity of the legal system under consideration. Hence the relevance of the problem of individuation to the theory of legal system.

In the discussion of these topics certain aspects of Kelsen's and Bentham's theories are criticized. On occasion parts of their theories are reconstructed and combined to serve as background to the examination of the problems of a theory of legal system in the following chapters.

III.1 : NORMATIVE STATEMENTS

Kelsen's Pure Theory explores the foundations of the sciences of social norms, that is, what he terms ethics and legal science. In part this exploration is concerned with the language in which these sciences formulate their conclusions. The particular characteristic of this language is that it is a normative language, for it includes sentences used to make statements of a certain kind, here called normative statements.

'The legal norms enacted by the law-creating authorities are prescriptive.'[1] In their enactment language is used performatively.[2] Legal science, on the other hand, is descriptive: ' . . . the jurist, as the theoretical exponent of the law presents norms in propositions that have a purely descriptive sense.'[3] These rather cryptic remarks are explained in greater detail in the new edition of *The Pure Theory of Law*: 'Legal *norms* are not judgments, that is, they are not statements about an object of

[1] *GT*, p. 45.
[2] I prefer 'performatively' to 'prescriptively' as a characterization of the use of language in creating norms. Both terms are the subject of much controversy which cannot be discussed here.
[3] *WJ*, p. 268.

cognition. According to their meaning they are commands; they may be also permissions and authorizations.'[1] Because norms do not convey information, but are orders, permissions, or authorizations, they cannot be described as true or false: '. . . the norms enacted by the legal authority, imposing obligations and conferring rights upon the legal subjects are neither true nor false, but only valid or invalid.'[2] That a norm is binding and that it is valid is one and the same thing, and both mean that it exists: 'By "validity" we mean the specific existence of norms. To say that a norm is valid, is to say that we assume its existence or—what amounts to the same thing— we assume that it has "binding force" for those whose behaviour it regulates.'[3] Norms, therefore, are entities, though of course they are abstract entities rather than physical things: 'The law, as norm, is an ideal and not a natural reality.'[4] Kelsen's remarks on the relation between norms and the language used in their creation are, on the whole, confused, and need not concern us here. The remainder of this section is concerned with the relation between norms and normative statements.

Normative statements convey information and consequently can be true or false: 'The statements formulated by the science of law . . . do not impose obligations nor confer rights upon anybody; they may be true or false.'[5] The basic structure and import of normative statements are briefly explained in the following passage:

One can also say: a certain something—specifically a certain behaviour—can have the quality of 'is' or of 'ought'. For example: In the two statements, 'the door is being closed' and 'the door ought to be closed', the closing of the door in the former statement is pronounced as something that is, in the latter as something that ought to be.[6]

This remark has affinities with various ideas which were suggested by other philosophers.[7] But as Kelsen does not pursue the subject any further and is content with this very vague

[1] *PTL*, p. 71.   [2] *PTL*, p. 73.   [3] *GT*, p. 30.
[4] 'The Pure Theory of Law', 50 *L.Q.R.* 481.   [5] *PTL*, p. 73.
[6] *PTL*, p. 6.
[7] See for example Hare's distinction between phrastic and neustic in *The Language of Morals*; Stenius's semantic moods, e.g. in *Wittgenstein's 'Tractatus'*, pp. 167 ff.; and von Wright's logic of normative statements in *Norm and Action*.

passage, and as no attempt will be made here to develop a logic of normative statements, we may leave the topic at that.

In the following passage Kelsen states what amounts to an explanation of the truth grounds of normative statements: 'Rules of law in a descriptive sense . . . are hypothetical judgments stating that *according to a national or international legal order*, under the conditions determined by this order, certain consequences determined by the order ought to take place.'[1] And analogously: 'L'éthique décrit les normes d'une morale déterminée, elle nous enseigne comment nous devons nous conduire *selon cette morale*.'[2] One may say that a normative statement has the general form that p ought to be the case, and that it is true if, and only if, there is, in a certain normative system, a norm to the effect that p ought to be the case.

In discussing this doctrine the following points must be borne in mind:

(1) The term 'ought', as well as other similar terms, may be used, according to Kelsen, both performatively—to create a norm—and descriptively—to state the existence of a norm. In legal science it is used only in the latter sense: ' . . . the "ought" of the legal rule does not have a prescriptive character, like the "ought" of the legal norm—its meaning is descriptive. This ambiguity of the word "ought" is overlooked when "ought"-statements are identified with imperative statements.'[3]

(2) Furthermore, Kelsen uses the term 'ought' in a technical sense much wider than that of ordinary usage: 'The word "ought" is used here in a broader sense than the usual sense. According to customary usage, "ought" corresponds only to a command, while "may" corresponds to a permission, and "can" to an authorization. But in the present work the word "ought" . . . includes "may" and "can".'[4] In fact Kelsen uses 'ought' as a kind of variable for normative modalities. The general form of a normative statement can therefore be represented as Mp, where M stands for any normative modality.

(3) The sentences italicized in the quotations above make it

---

[1] *PTL*, p. 71.   [2] *TP*, p. 99 n. My italics.
[3] *PTL*, p. 75. It should be remembered that 'rules of law' means the same as 'normative statements about the law', and that by 'imperative statements' Kelsen is referring to imperatives.
[4] *PTL*, p. 5.

clear that normative statements always refer to a particular normative system (of course they may refer to more than one such system). The reference may be more or less explicit, as in 'In England one ought . . .', or 'According to English law one ought . . .'. It may be an implicit reference, which is the case when the system referred to is not mentioned at all in making the statement.

The existence of the system referred to is not asserted in the referring statement. It is presupposed by it. If the system does not exist, the statement is not false, but neither is it true. It has no truth value.

The normative statements discussed by Kelsen implicitly refer also to a particular moment during the lifetime of the system. They refer to a particular momentary system. Again the reference can be made explicit, and can be to longer periods of time. But following Kelsen, the temporal reference of the statements will be disregarded, and for a while it will be assumed that every statement refers to a particular momentary system.

(4) Kelsen assumes that normative statements of the form *Mp* are identical in meaning with statements that there is a norm that *Mp*: '. . . l'assertion qu'une certaine norme juridique est en vigueur . . . signifie la même chose que l'affirmation qu'une norme juridique donnée est en vigueur, laquelle affirmation signifie a son tour—et rien de plus ni de moins—que l'on doit se conduire comme la norme juridique le prescrit.'[1]

This is Kelsen's account of his notion of normative statements. His explanation is gravely at fault in so far as it purports to apply to the 'ought' statements of non-legal discourse. It can be accepted as a basis for an explanation of a certain class of statements concerning the law, which may well be called normative statements (provided it is understood that it applies only to one class of normative statements). Kelsen regards normative statements as having the form *Mp* and as describing norms. But a statement like 'The door ought to be open' does not describe a norm, because every norm, according to Kelsen, prescribes human behaviour, and no mention of this fact is made in this statement. Furthermore, statements like 'The

---

[1] *TP*, p. 109 n.

English legal system underwent radical change in the last hundred years', or 'The Israeli law of murder has not been changed since 1936', not only do not describe the content of a norm, they do not even exhibit the structure Mp. Nevertheless, all these statements are usually held to be normative statements.

Kelsen's concept of a normative statement should, therefore, be generalized as follows: A statement is a (legal) normative statement if, and only if, the existence of a (legal) norm is a necessary condition for its truth. The existence of the norm may be among the truth conditions of the statement, or it may be a condition for its having a truth value at all.

Normative statements will be said to be direct if they include only statements with either a normative operator (like 'ought to . . . ' or 'is permitted to . . . ') or a normative predicate (e.g. 'have a duty', 'have a right to'). Otherwise they will be called indirect normative statements. Thus statements like 'In 1948 a new legal system was established in Israel' are indirect.

True normative statements are either pure, or applicative, or both. A normative statement is pure if the existence of certain norms suffices to make it true. It is an applicative statement if there is a norm and a fact which together are sufficient to make it true, while none of them separately suffice to make it true. A statement is both pure and applicative if there are two independent sets of conditions each sufficient for its truth, and if in virtue of one it is pure and in virtue of the second it is applicative. Whether a statement is pure or applicative depends upon the content of the legal system. A statement of the type 'The inhabitants of Oxford ought to do A' is pure if there is a law to the effect that the inhabitants of Oxford ought to do A. It is an applicative statement if there is a law that the inhabitants of all the towns with a population of over 100,000 ought to do A, and if Oxford has a population of over 100,000.

The set of all the pure statements referring to one legal system completely describes that system. This set will be called the 'total set' of that system. Every set of pure statements which logically implies the total set of a system is a (complete) description of that system.

A complete description of a system is its proper description if, and only if, every statement in it completely describes exactly one law of the system, and there are no two statements in the description which describe the same law.

The terminology adopted here makes it possible to formulate some problems which are relevant to the theory of legal system in a new way: The criterion of identity provides the method for establishing whether any set of direct normative statements is, if true, a complete description of a legal system. The existence criteria of a legal system and of a law are both needed to provide the method for establishing whether the description is true, that is whether the system exists. The doctrines of the structure and individuation of laws and of the structure of legal systems provide a method for determining which of the descriptions of a legal system is a proper description.

This way of formulating these tasks of a legal theory may seem strange at first. Its correctness and its advantages will be explained in Chapter IV.

III.2: THE ELEMENTS OF A NORM

A. *Bentham's Account of the Structure of a Norm*

'The essential ingredients in the idea of a single or simple law are . . . the act and the aspect', explains Bentham.[1] To begin with, something must be said on Bentham's very elaborate theory of acts.

Bentham distinguishes between acts of mind, acts of discourse, and external acts;[2] of these only external acts and their omissions will be discussed here. Acts are either complex or simple. Complex acts, explains Bentham, consist ' . . . each of a multitude of simple acts, which, though numerous and heterogeneous, derive a sort of unity from the relation they bear to some common design or end; such as the act of giving a dinner, the act of maintaining a child, the act of exhibiting a triumph, the act of bearing arms, the act of holding a court and so forth'.[3]

Complex acts are (generic) acts which can be analysed as the performance of several simple acts in certain circumstances. The categories of simple and complex acts are not mutually exclusive. Many acts which can be analysed in terms of the performance of several simple acts can also be analysed in the

[1] Bentham, *Limits*, p. 178; *OLG*, p. 94.   [2] *Principles*, p. 191.   [3] Ibid., p. 194.

ordinary way in which simple acts are analysed. It is one
of the most important underlying features of Bentham's theory
of acts that it allows for different methods of describing one
and the same act situation. Complex acts will not be dealt with
here.

Acts of all the kinds mentioned can be either individual or
generic (Bentham's expression is 'classes of acts').[1] I shall
further distinguish eminently generic acts from partly generic
acts.[2] An act is eminently generic if it can be described without
reference to any individuals. Generic acts which are not eminently generic are partly generic. Kissing is an eminently
generic act, while kissing Caesar is partly generic, and kissing
Caesar now or killing Caesar are individual acts. Individual
acts are instances of generic acts.

Positive acts, says Bentham, 'consist in motion or exertion'.[3]
'Every individual act that imparts motion must have a subject
in which it begins, subjects through which it progresses, and a
subject in which it terminates.'[4] The subject in which the motion
begins is called the agent, and is always a human being. In
every positive act the three subjects can be distinguished,
though they may be identical: e.g. when a person scratches
himself. In certain individual acts, though not in all, a fourth
subject exists—objects in which the pathological effects of the
act are created (i.e. sensations of pain or pleasure).[5] Bentham
allows only human beings into this fourth category. This method
of describing acts should be modified by adding the general
presupposition that the agent must have some minimum control
over his acts.

Bentham distinguishes between two kinds of omissions:[6]
Forbearance from an act, which consists merely in not doing
the act; and deliberate forbearance. Following Bentham, I
shall use the term in its first sense, adding the following condition: A man omits doing A at time t only if there was at t an
opportunity for doing A. Thus if the door is closed I cannot
forbear from closing it, because there is no opportunity of
closing it.[7] The negative character of omissions is the property

---

[1] *Limits*, p. 126. The relevant passage is not included in *OLG*.
[2] Cf. von Wright, *NA*, p. 24, for an analogous distinction between propositions.
[3] *Principles*, p. 190.   [4] *Limits*, p. 126.   [5] Ibid., p. 121; *OLG*, p. 35.
[6] *Principles*, p. 191 n.
[7] On the concept of opportunity see von Wright, *NA*, p. 37.

of acts, not of their descriptions. Hence omissions can be described in positive terms and external acts may be described in negative terms.[1] A person can at one and the same time do several separate acts, and he can do one act and forbear from doing another.[2]

In his book *Human Acts* E. D'Arcy writes: 'To the question, "what were you doing at two o'clock this afternoon?" any of the following could be appropriate replies: "Taking a siesta", "Relaxing in an armchair", "Sun bathing", "Sitting for a portrait", "Waiting for the Carfax traffic lights to change", "Being X-rayed", "Getting my hair cut", "Sitting in Whitehall in Civil Disobedience", "Hunger striking". Each of these replies would satisfy Bentham's definition of an omission as physical non-movement, "keeping at rest"; yet we should not call any of them an omission.'[3] I suggest that hunger striking would be better called an omission, namely not eating while having an opportunity to eat (for a purpose of a certain type). It may well be that hunger striking is rarely called an omission. But this is probably due to the rarity of the occasion to discuss it in these terms. Anyway Bentham was not interested in ordinary speech habits, but rather in useful philosophical categories and classifications.

I cite the passage from D'Arcy in order to point out a pitfall to be avoided in interpreting Bentham. Contrary to D'Arcy's assumption, not everything that can be said about a person and does not entail that he moved his body describes, according to Bentham, an omission of his. Omission is not simply physical non-movement. It 'imports the negation of . . . positive agency'.[4] Therefore of D'Arcy's examples only 'Hunger striking' is an omission according to Bentham's criterion. 'Being X-rayed' and 'Getting my hair cut' are not acts at all, they are states in which a person is, things which happen to him. The other examples describe positive acts of a special kind, namely continuous acts like leaning, keeping in one's possession,[5] etc.

Using the term 'circumstances' and 'act situation' as technical terms, one can say that by definition an act situation

[1] *Principles*, p. 191.
[2] This follows from Bentham's remarks in *Principles*, p. 191.
[3] *Human Acts*, p. 41.   [4] *Principles*, p. 191.   [5] Ibid., p. 193.

is any number of facts of which at least one is an act, and that relative to any act in an act situation the other facts of the situation are circumstances. Taking the totality of facts as one act situation one can say with Bentham: 'The field of circumstances belonging to any act, may be defined a circle, of which the circumference is nowhere but of which the act in question is the centre. Now then, as any act may, for the purpose of discourse, be considered as a centre, any other act or object whatsoever may be considered as of the number of those that are standing round it.'[1]

The relation of an act to its circumstances is analogous, according to Bentham, to the relation of a substance to its properties. This implies, *inter alia*, that an act situation can be described in various ways either as an act and circumstances or as an act alone, e.g. killing by poison, or poisoning, or pulling the trigger of a loaded rifle with the result that it is discharged, or firing a rifle. As Bentham puts it: 'Here too it is with an act and its circumstances as it is with a substance and its properties you may strip a substance of its properties one by one till you reduce it to nothing; so you may an act by stripping it of its circumstances.'[2] And further on:

It may occasion a good deal of perplexity if we are not careful to observe, that the question whether such or such an act as noticed by the law be attended with circumstances, or whether it be not a mere act free from circumstances depends, altogether upon the wording: in so much that the same act precisely in one way of expressing it shall be attended with circumstances, in another not.[3]

Bentham's theory of acts has three major features:

(1) The great flexibility of act descriptions, and the partial interchangeability of various methods of act description.

(2) Simple external acts form the basis for explaining some of the other kinds of acts, particularly omissions and complex acts.

(3) The emphasis in the explanation of simple external acts is on the motion generated by the agent, that is on his movement. For the purposes of a legal theory generic and not individual acts are of prime importance.

Bentham's theory of acts can be reconstructed by making

[1] *Principles*, p. 195 n.   [2] *Limits*, p. 129; *OLG*, p. 44.   [3] Ibid.; *OLG*, pp. 43-4.

elementary acts (instead of his external acts) the basis of a comprehensive method of act description. An elementary generic act is one which secures a certain result by some movement in some mode and with a certain intention. Every elementary generic act is a positive act, i.e. involves some movement of the agent, but the kind of movement involved is not specified in the description of an elementary act. Similarly every elementary act is done in a certain mode—swiftly or slowly, perhaps using certain tools, etc.—which is not specified in its description. The generic act is defined partly by its result, that is as bringing about some state of affairs or preventing a state of affairs from being changed. Another element in the definition is a certain definite intention, the result is secured with the intention to secure a certain state of affairs. In the ordinary act the state of affairs intended is the state of affairs secured, but this is not always the case.

Elementary acts serve as the basis for the definition of other generic acts. These can be defined as an elementary act done in a specified mode (e.g. poisoning) or by a specified movement (e.g. kicking or throwing a ball), or as an elementary act which has a certain consequence, etc. Other generic acts are types of generic acts of the kinds described (e.g. killing and driving can be analysed as types of generic acts, including both elementary—intentional killing and driving—and non-elementary generic acts), or as omissions or complexes of other acts.

The type of elementary acts which has just been described is thus a powerful tool in the explanation of most of the acts which are of concern to the law.[1] In the remainder of the present study, though all kinds of acts will serve as examples, the analysis is designed to apply directly to this type of elementary acts.

The rest of this section is virtually an interpretation of pages 93–97 in *Of Laws in General*, where Bentham expounds his views

---

[1] It seems to me that all intentional acts can be analysed in terms of elementary acts (though for certain purposes other types of analysis may be more useful). Intentional actions, however 'appear to be a subclass of conscious voluntary actions. Actions which, though conscious can be inhibited with an effort and are not done on purpose, appear to be voluntary without being intentional: examples might be wincing in pain, fidgeting, sneezing, laughing, using an irritable tone of voice, brooding over an injury' (Kenny, 'Intention and Purpose', 63 *Journal of Philosophy*, p. 644).

on the structure of a law. For Bentham a law is 'an assemblage of signs declarative of a volition'.[1] It is in effect a sentence or set of sentences, though most of the time Bentham discusses it as if it were a proposition to the effect that the sovereign wants so and so.

'There are two things essential to every law,' explains Bentham, 'an act of some sort or other, being the object of a wish or volition . . . and a wish or volition of which such act is the object.'[2] The aspect, accordingly, corresponds to the wish or volition. Just as the act description describes the act, so, presumably, the aspect description describes the volition.

Many of the objections which can be made against Bentham's theory can be avoided by adopting the following simple though far-reaching modification: instead of identifying aspects with volitions or phases of volitions of the legislator, we can treat them as those elements of normative statements, namely normative modalities, which have already been mentioned. But even though much of the philosophical basis of Bentham's doctrine of the structure of a law is thus rejected, this does not mean that the doctrine itself is valueless. On the contrary, it is the best available analysis of the structure of a law by a legal philosopher of the imperative school.

Laws will continue to be regarded as non-linguistic abstract entities. A law will be said to have a structure corresponding to the structure of a normative statement which completely describes it, and it alone. Against this background Bentham's theory of the structure of norms will be explained.

A law, according to Bentham, consists of an aspect and an act, or, as must be said in view of the modifications introduced in the theory of acts above, of an act situation (including an agent specification). Some laws have parts which also consist of an aspect and an act-situation. Such parts will be called 'provisions'. Parts of a law which are not provisions are called 'clauses'.

According to Bentham there are four aspects: (1) a positive directive, (2) a negative directive, (3) a positive non-directive, (4) a negative non-directive. The four aspects will be here represented as C, P, NC, NP respectively. Representing positive act-situations by a and act situations where the act is an omission

---

[1] *Limits*, p. 88; *OLG*, p. 1.   [2] Ibid., p. 178; *OLG*, p. 93.

by $\bar{a}$, one may distinguish between four kinds of provisions: Ca or a command, Pa or a prohibition, NCa or a non-command, and NPa or a permission (a non-prohibition). The four are interdefinable: 'A negative aspect towards a positive act is equipollent to an affirmative aspect towards the correspondent negative act.'[1] That is:

(1) NPa is logically equivalent to $NC\bar{a}$.
(2) Pa is logically equivalent to $C\bar{a}$. Furthermore:
(3) Ca is the law whenever NCa is not the law, and vice versa.

The last definition is stated by Bentham among other relations between provisions:

Among these mandates there subsists such a relation, that with respect to one another some of them are necessarily repugnant and exclusive; others as necessarily concomitant. . . . A command . . . includes a permission: it excludes both a prohibition and a non-command. A prohibition includes a non-command and it excludes both a command and a permission.[2]

This means that whenever Ca is the law so is NPa, but never Pa or NCa; and whenever Pa is the law so is NCa, but never Ca or NPa. Of the relations between provisions which can be expressed in these terms the following can be taken as fundamental:

(1) It is always the law that NCa, or that NPa, or both.
(2) It is never the case that both Ca and Pa are the law.

From these together with the definitions all the other relations between provisions can be deduced. Therefore the aspects form a square of opposition.[3] One interesting consequence of the above principles is that for any given act situation it is always the case that it is the law either that NCa and that Pa or that NPa and Ca or that NPa and NCa.

So far a and $\bar{a}$ have been regarded as representing an act situation. From now on I shall distinguish between the act and the agent specification, represented as a or $\bar{a}$, and the circumstance specification represented as c and $\bar{c}$ ($\bar{c}$ being the contradictory of c). $a\backslash c$ means the performance of some positive act by some agent in circumstances c. The part of a law which specifies the circumstances in which an act should or should not,

---

[1] *Limits*, p. 180; *OLG*, pp. 95–6.   [2] Ibid., p. 181; *OLG*, p. 97.
[3] Cf. Prior, *Formal Logic*, p. 220.

etc., be done is called a 'limitative clause'. Using T as representing any of the four aspects, Bentham's term 'exceptive clause' (represented as $/c$) can be defined as follows:[1]

$Ta\backslash c$ is logically equivalent to $Ta/\bar{c}$.

A clause which is either limitative or exceptive is called by Bentham 'qualificative'.

In 'It is forbidden to take anyone's property without his consent' the last three words describe a limitative clause—when x has not agreed, the act is forbidden. The same rule can, however, be formulated as 'It is forbidden to take anyone's property unless he agrees to it.' Here the rule is formulated with the aid of an exceptive clause: It is always forbidden to do the act except in the circumstances specified. A limitative clause specifies the circumstances to which the law as it were applies. An exceptive clause specifies the circumstances to which it does not apply, which are the exception to the rule, thus logically implying that it applies in all other circumstances.

Bentham adds four more fundamental relations between provisions: 'A permission with an exception, is equipollent to a prohibition with a limitation. . . . Non-command with an exception is equipollent to a command with a limitation . . . a command with an exception is equipollent to a non-command with a limitation . . . a prohibition with an exception is equipollent to a permission with a limitation.'[2] In other words:

$Pa\backslash c$ is logically equivalent to NPa/c;
Pa/c is logically equivalent to $NPa\backslash c$;
$Ca\backslash c$ is logically equivalent to NCa/c;
Ca/c is logically equivalent to $NCa\backslash c$.

These principles have no obvious counterpart in ordinary legal discourse, for it is not always assumed that when a certain exception is explicitly mentioned no other exception exists, or that when a condition is specified no other condition exists. Therefore usually exceptive clauses cannot in ordinary discourse replace limitative clauses in the way just described.

Qualificative clauses can be analysed into a main clause qualifying the act specification and subclauses qualifying the main clause. The subclauses themselves are either limitative or

<hr/>

[1] Cf. *Limits*, pp. 208–9; *OLG*, pp. 114–15.   [2] Ibid., pp. 209–10; *OLG*, p. 116.

exceptive.[1] In 'Parking in front of government offices is forbidden in summer during working hours, except by special
permission' the clause 'in summer' is the main (limitative)
clause. 'During working hours' is a limitative subclause
qualifying the main clause, and 'except by special permission'
is an exceptive subclause qualifying the first subclause. There
is no need to explore the matter any further here.

So far legal provisions have been analysed. Every law contains
one main provision which is either a command or a prohibition
(in which case the law is obligative), or it is a non-command or
a permission (in which case the law is de-obligative). Obligative
laws may contain permissions or non-commands as subsidiary
provisions that have the effect of exceptive provisions, e.g.
'One must not keep a library book more than a fortnight. But
one may keep it longer during the vacations.'

Accepting the possiblity of de-obligative laws raises several
theoretical as well as interpretative problems. De-obligative
laws presuppose obligative laws, which they either repeal or
qualify.[2] It is doubtful whether there is much point in regarding
a repealing law (i.e. a law the sole effect of which is to repeal
one or several other laws) as existing after the laws it repealed
ceased to exist. This, with other considerations, suggests that it
is best to regard laws as repealed by acts and not by other laws.
According to this view, statutes the sole function of which is to
repeal laws do not express laws; they are merely constituents and
products of repealing acts.

De-obligative laws which only qualify obligative laws will
be discussed in some detail in Chapter VII, section 2 below. It
must, however, be mentioned here that admitting their possibility involves serious difficulties in the interpretation of
Bentham's theory. At times it seems as if Bentham explicitly
denies the possibility of de-obligative laws. Thus he says of the
provision 'Any man may export wheat when the price is not
above 44s. a quarter': ' . . . this provision is not of the imperative stamp, and on that account can not in the nature of things
constitute an independent law.'[3] Does this mean that de-
obligative laws are not independent laws? They certainly are
identical in effect with exceptive provisions in obligative laws.

[1] *Limits*, pp. 213–14; *OLG*, p. 120.
[2] Cf. *Limits*, p. 259; *OLG*, pp. 168–9; *Principles*, p. 430.
[3] *Limits*, p. 248; *OLG*, p. 157.

The only difference is, presumably, that a subsidiary exceptive provision is enacted at the same time as the main provision, while a de-obligative law is enacted later than the provision it qualifies. But, as will become clear in the next chapter, according to Bentham's own theory this is a very poor reason for such a distinction. Furthermore, accepting the possibility of de-obligative laws is incompatible with Bentham's definition of law as the expression of 'a volition . . . concerning the conduct to be observed in a certain case by a certain person . . . '[1], which seems to indicate that every law is obligative. For these reasons I shall usually regard Bentham as admitting only obligative laws.

A law may also contain independent clauses of three kinds:

(1) Expository clauses,[2] explaining concepts which are used in the law.

(2) Satisfactive clauses, which are declarations of policy designed to repair damage that may be caused through disobedience to the law.[3]

(3) Incitative clauses, that is declarations of policy—of rewards for obedience or of sanctions for disobedience to the law.[4]

Laws with more than one provision, or with independent clauses, are called 'complex laws'.

B. Kelsen on the Structure of a Norm

Kelsen's ideas on the structure of a norm are not dissimilar to those of Bentham. 'The norm', he says, 'is the expression of the idea that something ought to occur, especially that an individual ought to behave in a certain way.'[5] Kelsen's ever-present 'ought' corresponds to Bentham's 'aspect', and the individual and his behaving in a certain way correspond to the agent and the act which were distinguished in Bentham's theory. Furthermore, norms, according to Kelsen, are characteristically conditional. Their 'condition' is none other than Bentham's 'circumstances': that is that part of the norm which determines the occasions on which the agent has to act as specified. Henceforth these four elements will be called 'norm-character' (i.e. Bentham's 'aspect' and Kelsen's 'ought'), 'norm-subject', 'norm-act', and 'performance condition'.[6]

<hr/>

[1] *Limits*, p. 88; *OLG*, p. 1.   [2] Ibid., pp. 203, 221; *OLG*, pp. 302–3, 127.
[3] Ibid., p. 242; *OLG*, p. 151.   [4] Ibid., p. 225; *OLG*, p. 134.   [5] *GT*, p. 36.
[6] Cf. von Wright, *NA*, pp. 70 ff.

A norm is unconditional if, according to its performance condition, the next opportunity after the norm is issued to perform the norm-act is the only occasion to which the norm applies. A norm is also unconditional if every opportunity to perform the norm-act is an occasion to which the norm applies.[1]

Taking advantage of the great flexibility in the methods of act descriptions, I shall adopt the convention of regarding the norm-act always as eminently generic. Any individuating characteristics will be regarded as part of the description of the subject or the performance condition.

So much may be said on the basic similarity between Bentham's and Kelsen's ideas on the structure of a legal provision and of a norm. But here the similarity ends. For one thing, Kelsen does not admit anything like Bentham's complex laws. Every norm comprises, as it were, just one legal provision. Much more important is the fact that, according to Kelsen's theory, all laws are norms granting liberties, that is permissions either to do or not to do an act. His reasons for this astonishing doctrine will be explained in Chapter IV, section 2 below.

III.3: THE EXISTENCE OF NORMS

'A norm is a valid legal norm if (a) it has been created in a way provided for by the legal order to which it belongs, and (b) if it has not been annulled either in a way provided for by that legal order or by way of *desuetudo* or by the fact that the legal order as a whole has lost its efficacy.'[2] This is Kelsen's criterion of the existence of norms, or, to be precise, of derivative norms. It can be re-phrased and incorporated in a complete criterion of existence as follows:

A norm exists either from the moment an appropriate set of derivative conditions of creation obtains until the moment an appropriate derivative condition of termination obtains, or from the moment an appropriate set of original conditions of creation obtains until the moment an appropriate original condition of termination obtains, provided that the legal system to which it belongs exists.

Legal norms are of two kinds, original and derivative,

---

[1] For Kelsen's somewhat different position see *PTL*, pp. 100-1.
[2] *GT*, p. 120.

distinguished by their mode of creation and termination.[1] The existence criterion refers to creation and termination conditions, which together form the existence conditions of a norm. These will be briefly explained. As in the rest of the present chapter, the aim is merely to make clear the principles on which the theory is based; details and particular complications will be avoided whenever possible.

A. Derivative Creation-Conditions

A derivative norm comes into being the moment at least one appropriate set of creation-conditions is fulfilled. Every set of derivative creation-conditions contains conditions of two kinds: (a) the existence of a certain norm (called 'a norm-creating norm'); and (b) the occurrence of certain events (norm-creating events).

A norm-creating norm is one stipulating that if certain events occur a norm of a certain kind will come into being. An event is a norm-creating event if there is a norm that makes it a condition for the creation of another norm.

Only events fulfilling the following fourfold conditions can become norm-creating events. They must be (1) human acts, (2) which are voluntary, (3) and are performed with a special intention, (4) which is expressed in a conventional way in the act itself. (1) is the meaning of Kelsen's fundamental doctrine that norms are the objective meaning of certain human acts. (2) is expressed by the doctrine that the norm-creating acts are acts of will. The last two, (3) and (4), are expressed by Kelsen's doctrine that norm-creating acts have the subjective significance of 'ought'. That by 'subjective significance' he refers to a manifested intention is clear, for example, from the following: 'Sans doute, l'homme qui fait l'acte, et qui agit de façon rationnelle, associe à son acte une certaine signification, qui s'exprime ou traduit d'une façon ou d'une autre, et qui est comprise par d'autres hommes: c'est ce que nous appellerons la "signification subjective" des actes.'[2] The nature of the intention which Kelsen calls the subjective significance of 'ought'

[1] Roughly speaking, original norms are norms the creation conditions of which do not include the existence of other norms. Every norm which is not an original norm is a derivative norm.
[2] *TP*, p. 3.

is explained as follows: '"Sollen" est la signification subjective de tout acte de volonté d'un homme qui, dans son esprit, tend à obtenir une conduite d'autrui.'[1] The intention is to affect the behaviour of other people.

It is important to understand that it is the manifested intention that determines the content of the norm. If the act is performed with the intention of making certain people, x, behave in a certain manner, a, then the norm is that x ought to do a.

This doctrine is strongly reminiscent of those of Bentham and Austin, and is exposed to the criticism which Kelsen himself made against Austin's doctrine in *The General Theory*.[2] One of the most important points made by Kelsen is that often legislators sign or vote for a law without knowing its content, and hence also without intending that the norm subject should behave in the prescribed way. In the *Théorie Pure du Droit* Kelsen meets this point by writing: 'Lorsqu'un membre du parlement vote pour l'adoption d'un projet de loi dont il ne connaît pas le contenu, le contenu de sa volonté est une manière d'habilitation. Ce votant veut que devienne loi quoi que ce soit que contient le projet de loi pour lequel il vote.'[3] Thus the intention to affect someone's behaviour is replaced by the intention to create a norm. Kelsen seems unaware of the implications of this change. It constitutes a major departure from the Austinian conception, for it presupposes the existence of norms and conventionalized activities, and cannot serve as their ultimate explanation.[4] Austin's doctrine of legislation was formulated to account primarily for independent legislation, that is legislation which does not presuppose the existence of norms, and is not necessarily carried out within the framework of systems of norms, whereas Kelsen's doctrine applies only to legislation within the framework of normative systems.

B. *Derivative Termination-Conditions*

Norms cease to exist if a norm is enacted with the effect that they are explicitly or implicitly repealed. Sometimes a repealing norm makes the termination of a norm conditional upon the

---

[1] *TP*, p. 10.   [2] *GT*, pp. 33–5.   [3] *TP*, p. 10 n.

[4] Kelsen's modified approach is similar to that part of the general doctrine of speech acts expounded by Strawson in 'Intention and Convention in Speech Acts', *Philosophical Review* (1964), pp. 456–7, where he refers to the intention 'to further or affect the course of the practice in question'.

occurrence of a certain event or the lapse of a certain period of time. These are the ordinary ways of terminating the existence of norms. To them Kelsen adds (apart from the total collapse of the legal system as a whole) the special way of negative custom (i.e. a custom which repeals norms).

By claiming that negative custom is always and of necessity a way in which laws are terminated Kelsen abandons the Austinian position that the efficacy of a law is relevant to its validity only in so far as it affects the efficacy of the legal system as a whole. The superiority of Austin's approach will be shown in a later chapter. The following remarks are intended merely to show that even if Kelsen's position is accepted, negative custom cannot be regarded as creating norms in the same way that·positive custom creates norms. Furthermore, negative custom is not custom in the sense in which positive custom is custom.

Kelsen introduces his doctrine as follows:

A general legal norm is regarded as valid only if the human be-haviour that is regulated by it actually conforms with it, at least to some degree. A norm that is not obeyed by anybody anywhere, in other words a norm that is not effective at least to some degree, is not regarded as a valid legal norm. A minimum of effectiveness is a condition of validity.[1]

That this is a termination-condition and not a creation-condition is made clear by Kelsen's pointing out that a norm is not necessarily efficacious at the moment of its creation. There are therefore two ways in which a norm can be terminated through inefficacy: either by never becoming efficacious, or by being efficacious at one time and ceasing to be so later. Both ways, according to Kelsen, constitute negative custom.[2]

If negative custom creates repealing norms, these norms are original or derivative. They are not original, for the basic norm is the only original norm, according to Kelsen. But neither are they derivative norms, for these presuppose a norm-creating norm. And the whole point of Kelsen's doctrine is that negative custom terminates laws, even if there is no norm in the system authorizing it as a norm-creating process.[3] In this it differs from positive custom, which creates norms only if the

[1] *PTL*, p. 11.   [2] Ibid., p. 213.   [3] Ibid., p. 213.

basic norm or some other norm makes it a norm-creating process.[1] It is not logically necessary, Kelsen implies, that positive
custom should be regarded as a norm-creating process in every
legal system. Therefore negative custom either terminates the
existence of norms without creating repealing norms, or it
creates them in a way which Kelsen has failed to explain.[2]

Is a negative custom a custom at all? In order to constitute a
custom a regularity of behaviour must be accompanied by
'normative pressure': exhortations to conform to, criticism of
deviation from, and justification of conformity to, the regularity.
Kelsen's explanation does not imply that such normative
pressure is necessary in the case of termination through inefficacy. The general impression is that in these cases the norm
simply lapses by default and no positive pressure to disobey
is necessary. Moreover, a deviation from a custom is a delict,
but is a court's decision to apply a norm which has been abro-
gated by negative custom a delict? This suggests that a negative
custom is not a custom at all.

Another way in which norms can be terminated ought to be
mentioned: A norm ceases to exist if there can no longer occur
an occasion to which it applies. Thus a norm to the effect that
John ought to visit Rex once a year is automatically terminated
upon the death of Rex. A norm that entrance into a certain area
is forbidden this summer does not exist after the summer has
passed. Offences committed while the norm existed can, of
course, be punished later. No termination of a norm legalizes
offences committed while the norm was in force.

C. Original Existence-Conditions

The basic norm is the only original norm according to Kelsen.
Much will be said on it in the next two chapters. A few clarifications are, however, in place here.

The basic norm exists, i.e. it is valid: 'The basic norm is
presupposed as a *valid* norm.'[3] It is part of the legal system

---

[1] *PTL*, pp. 225–6.
[2] There are good grounds to argue that in any case norms are repealed not by
repealing-norms but by repealing-acts. I shall not argue here for this proposition,
but, like most of the philosophers discussed in this study, I shall not include repealing norms in a systematic representation of the content of a legal system.
[3] 'Prof. Stone and the Pure Theory of Law', 17 *Stanford Law Review* (1965), 1143.

because it 'has legally relevant functions'.[1] It occupies, however, a unique position within the legal system, because it alone
'is not a norm of positive law, that is, not a norm created by a
real act of will of a legal organ'.[1]

At times Kelsen expresses himself in a way which is liable to
create the impression that the basic norm is created by being
presupposed. He says, for example, that it 'exists in the juristic
consciousness' and that 'it is not . . . valid because it is created
in a certain way by a legal act but it is valid because it is
presupposed to be valid'.[2] But this impression is mistaken.
Kelsen specifically denies that basic norms are created by being
presupposed.[3] Two points should be briefly mentioned here:
First, presupposing the basic norm of a legal system is not a
condition for the existence of that system. It is merely a condition
of recognizing and understanding it as a legal system. Theoretically, a legal system can exist without anyone's presupposing
its basic norm. But a legal system cannot exist without the
basic norm itself, for without it, it lacks both unity and validity,
i.e. existence. Secondly, even though an individual's recognition
of a norm as a norm implies, according to Kelsen, his presupposing some basic norm; this fact alone is not enough to
determine the content of the basic norm which is presupposed.
To know that, one must, according to Kelsen, know all the
other norms recognized by that individual. The basic norm
which he presupposes is the norm authorizing all of them and
none other.[4] On these two accounts the presupposition of a
basic norm not only does not create it, it does not even determine
its content. It is best to regard basic norms as necessary norms,
in the sense that in every legal system there is necessarily one
and only one basic norm. Basic norms, therefore, exist without
being created. The content of a basic norm of a specific legal
order 'is determined by the facts through which an order is

---

[1] Ibid., p. 1141.   [2] GT, p. 116.

[3] See PTL, p. 204, especially the footnote. Kelsen rejects also suggestions that the
basic norm is created either by acts creating or by acts applying and obeying
other norms of the system (TP, p. 271), or that it is created by the recognition by
the population of an obligation to obey the law (PTL, p. 218 n.).

[4] Hence it is almost always the case that the basic norm of a particular legal
system is 'presupposed' only by the science of that system which presupposes it
in a different sense. This astonishing conclusion is a result of Kelsen's doctrine of
the conflict of norms, which cannot be explained in this study. Cf. on this point
Ch. VI, sect. 2 below.

created and applied'.[1] Their content varies according to the
system. 'The basic norm of any positive legal order confers
legal authority only upon facts by which an order is created
and applied which is on the whole effective.'[1] The basic norm
'qualifies a certain event as the initial event in the creation of
the various legal norms. It is the starting point of a norm-
creating process.'[2] The basic norm is thus a norm-creating
norm. It is the only norm-creating norm the existence-condition
of which does not include the existence of another norm-
creating norm. Thus it is intended to prevent Kelsen's theory
of the creation of norms from getting entangled in a vicious
circle or an infinite regress.

That the basic norm is, 'mostly unconsciously', assumed by
jurists is merely an illustration of the real point, which is that
'this presupposition alone, which is contained in the basic norm,
allows legal cognition to supply a meaningful interpretation of
the legal material.'[3] The basic norm exists, for it is necessary to
the understanding of the law. Its exact function and content
will be discussed later.

Kelsen's ideas concerning the creation of norms constitute
a great improvement upon Bentham's and Austin's ideas. His
distinction between what I called 'original' and 'derivative'
norms, the assumption that the vast majority of norms are derivative, and that the creation of derivative norms is dependent
upon the occurrence of events 'authorized' by norm-creating
norms, must be the foundations of every adequate explanation
of the creation of norms. Where he went wrong is in his interpretation of the nature of original norms and in his explanation
of the structure of norm-creating norms. These topics will be
discussed in the next chapters. He was also wrong in limiting
the class of acts that can become norm-creating acts.

Kelsen regards legislative acts (i.e. acts done with the intention to create norms) as the only norm-creating events. He
even tries to explain custom as a process of legislation:

At first the subjective meaning of the acts that constitute the custom
is not an *ought*. But later, when these acts have existed for some time,
the idea arises in the individual member that he ought to behave in
the manner in which the other members customarily behave, and

---

[1] *GT*, p. 120.   [2] Ibid., p. 114.   [3] Ibid., p. 406.

at the same time the will arises that the other members ought to behave in that same way. If one member of the group does not behave in the manner in which the other members customarily behave, then his behaviour will be disapproved by the others, as contrary to their will. In this way the custom becomes the expression of a collective will whose subjective meaning is an *ought*.[1]

Kelsen probably thought that the acts which form the regularity of behaviour are relevant to the creation of the customary law, just as much as the acts of criticizing people for failure to conform to this regularity. Acts of the first kind, where people behave in a certain way, are not performed with the intention of creating a norm of any kind. But even the acts of criticism are not performed with the intention of creating a new norm. They rather manifest recognition that a certain norm, though not necessarily a legal norm, already exists. Even if this objection is waived and these acts are regarded as performed with the intention of creating a new norm, this norm is, surely, the norm that the person criticized ought to behave in a certain way, not the much more general norm that any person of a certain class ought to behave in that way. The fact that many people criticize many others in that way means, at best, only that many particular norms are created in this way.

Because of his views on the kind of events which can be norm-creating events Kelsen fails to explain the creation of law by custom, and he does not succeed in explaining judicial legislation either. I refer to the general norms created by precedent, not to the particular norms settling the particular disputes before the courts in every case. There is no reason to suppose that judges create norms by precedent only if they intend to do so. They can create norms even without realizing that they are doing so, even though they regard themselves merely as declaring the content of already existing norms.

Kelsen's conditions for norm-creating events having been rejected, the question arises whether they should be replaced by different conditions. It seems to me that the problem should be divided into two parts: one regarding norms which are not parts of any normative system, the other regarding norms which belong to normative systems. The problem of the creation of isolated norms differs fundamentally from the problem of the

---

[1] *PTL*, p. 9; see also *PTL*, pp. 225–6.

creation of norms belonging to existing normative systems.[1] It would even be better to avoid talking about the creation of isolated norms, and to talk instead of their existence-conditions. For, unlike laws, rules of clubs, etc., isolated norms are not created at a definite time, as a consequence of a small number of easily identifiable acts. Like legal systems they come into being as a consequence of complex patterns of behaviour pursued by many people over a rather lengthy period of time. (For obvious reasons the existence of a legal system once established is backdated to a definite moment of time. This is only rarely necessary in the case of isolated norms.) Furthermore, like the existence of legal systems, the existence of isolated norms does not presuppose the existence of any other norm. Isolated norms are original norms. Most legal norms, like most of the norms which belong to normative systems, are derivative norms.[2]

The problem of the existence of isolated norms is in a way a combination of the problems of existence of normative systems and of norms belonging to such systems, though of course it differs from both questions. Only acts of certain kinds can be part of the existence-conditions of such norms. The best explanation of such acts is Hart's theory of customary rules.[3]

There are no similar limitations on the kinds of event that can qualify as creating norms which belong to normative systems. Only acts qualify as norm-creating events, but every act can create a norm if authorized by a norm-creating norm to do so.[4] A norm-creating act must, of course, determine at least in part the content of the norm created by it. But every act can determine the content of a norm, if only by being presented as an example to be imitated, the norm being a requirement to do this act in these circumstances. The norm investing an act with the character of a norm-creating act will indicate the exact way in which to interpret which norm is created by that

[1] It is only with institutionalized normative systems that we are concerned here. The sense in which legal systems are institutionalized will be examined in Ch. VIII.

[2] It will be seen in Ch. VIII below that some legal norms can be original norms, but they are the exception rather than the rule.

[3] Cf. *The Concept of Law*, pp. 54 ff.

[4] The creation of original legal norms presents special problems.

act. 'Imitate him' is probably the most primitive form of a norm-creating norm.

These remarks are intended to show that there is no general limitation on the kind of acts which qualify as norm-creating acts of derivative norms. There is, no doubt, room for further investigation, classifying and analysing the various ways in which laws are actually made. Such an investigation is, however, outside the scope of this study.

IV

ON THE INDIVIDUATION OF LAWS

THE problem of the individuation of laws is the link between the analysis of a law and that of a legal system, and as such it is of immense importance to legal philosophy. It will be here contended that previous legal philosophers, with the exception of Bentham, did less than justice to the importance of this subject. It will be argued that all of them regarded their principles of individuation, in so far as they had any, as determined exclusively by their explanations of a norm, and overlooked their relevance to the theory of legal system. It will be further argued that an adequate explanation of the structure of legal systems depends on a proper approach to the problem of individuation. These themes must, however, await another chapter. The present chapter is merely a preliminary discussion of the problem of the individuation of laws.

IV.I: THE PROBLEM OF INDIVIDUATION

The previous section is liable to mislead the reader. It is bound to leave the impression that the creation of norms is similar to the enactment of statutes by parliament, the making of regulations by government ministers, etc. In a sense this impression is right, for by enacting statutes, making regulations, giving judgments, etc., norms are created. But the creation of norms (particularly according to Bentham's and Kelsen's account of them) differs fundamentally from the creation of statutes, by-laws, regulations, etc., in two respects:

(1) By enacting a statute, making regulations, etc., the authorities create only part of a norm, the other parts of which may have been created at other times, perhaps even hundreds of years before, and often by other bodies. According to Bentham and Kelsen, parts of the same norm may have been made by ministerial decrees, while other parts have been made by local authorities, others still by judges, and so on: e.g. a municipal

by-law imposing a fine on violators of some parking regulations and the Act of Parliament setting up the courts and procedure governing such cases are both parts of the same norm.

(2) By enacting a constitution, making a statute or a regulation, etc., the legislator creates not only a part of one norm but a part of many norms, usually of a very great number of norms. Thus, for example, Kelsen thinks that a constitutional law is part of every norm created on its basis.

This section investigates the nature and significance of these two features.

It is somewhat characteristic of Kelsen that, though he has noticed the existence of these two features, he has failed to realize their full significance and implications. Kelsen knew that 'the different elements of a norm may be contained in very different products of the law-making procedure',[1] but this knowledge did not affect his thought in the way in which the realization of the same fact affected Bentham.

The discovery that a law is not identical with a statute or a section in a statute, etc., that many statutes from all the branches of the law, including civil as well as penal law, contribute to the content of every law, was the most important turning-point in Bentham's thinking on legal philosophy.[2] This discovery and the problems it raised were crystallized in one central question: 'Wherein consists the identity and completeness of a law?'[3] And again: 'What is a law? What are the parts of a law? The subject of the questions, it is to be observed, is the *logical*, the *ideal*, the *intellectual* whole, not the *physical* one: the *law* and not the *statute*.'[4]

It is not in the least surprising that the jurisprudential division of a legal system into laws differs from the ordinary division of it into statutes, sections, sub-sections, regulations, by-laws, etc. These are distinguished according to the authority which issued them, the occasion on which they were issued, their subject matter, and various stylistic considerations. Even

---

[1] *GT*, p. 45.

[2] This is not the place to comment on the development of Bentham's thought. Suffice it to say that this discovery caused him to leave the *Principles* unfinished (cf. paragraph 32 in his Preface to that book); it moved him to write, and determined the problems and approach of, *Of Laws in General*, his major jurisprudential work.

[3] *Principles*, p. 122. [4] *Principles*, p. 429.

lawyers and the general public when wishing to learn the law on a particular point usually prefer to consult books (e.g. Halsbury's *Laws of England, Chitty on Contracts*) which adopt a different division of the law, and which bring together all the legal material on a certain subject, regardless of the authority that enacted it or of the time of its enactment. It is only to be expected that the jurisprudential division of the law will more closely resemble the lawyers' division of it than that of the legislators.

The crucial question is what exactly are the principles underlying the jurisprudential division of the law. This I will call the problem of individuation. It will be discussed in some detail in the following chapters. At present, by way of introduction, the discussion is concerned with Bentham's and Kelsen's views on the subject, and with the consequences for the theory of legal system of the mere fact of posing the problem of individuation.

In the first place it is for legal philosophers to decide on principles of individuation of laws. Only by using these principles to represent the legal material in a form which is very different from its original form can one represent it as consisting of distinct laws. Hence it is possible to know the content of a legal system without knowing the identity of any of its laws. This is presupposed by Kelsen when he says: 'It is the task of the science of law to represent the law of a community, i.e. the material produced by the legal authority in the law-making procedure, in the form of statements' of a certain structure.[1] It is possible to identify and understand this legal material without knowing how to divide it into laws.

Legal philosophy has a double task. First, it has to formulate criteria by which to determine the identity of the authoritative legal material of which Kelsen spoke. Second, it has to formulate principles of individuation of laws, in order to determine how much of the matter contained in the whole system goes to make up one law.

It is, consequently, tempting to say that in the previous section the creation conditions of legal material were explained. When these conditions are fulfilled some authoritative legal material is created, though it does not necessarily constitute

[1] *GT*, p. 45.

just one complete norm. It should, however, be remembered that legal material, in Kelsen's sense of this term, is brought into being only when the creation of laws involves linguistic behaviour, and probably only when the content of a law (or a reference to it) is expressed in writing as part of its creation. Consequently no legal material is created when a customary law comes into being. The previous section, therefore, is best regarded as explaining the creation of laws or *parts of laws*.

The previous pages provide the explanation of the odd way in which some of the tasks of the theory of legal system were formulated at the end of Chapter III, section 1 above. It was stated there that the criterion of identity provides the method for establishing whether any given set of direct normative statements is, if true, a complete description of a legal system; and that the doctrines of the structure and individuation of laws and of the structure of legal systems provide a method for determining which of the descriptions of a legal system is a proper description, i.e. a description in which every statement describes just one complete law.

This formulation presupposes that it is possible to identify a legal system without knowing whether it exists or not. The system exists only if the description is true, but it is possible to determine what the description is without knowing whether it is true or not. In 1967 one could know what was Smith's legal system for Rhodesia, and know what was the British legal system for Rhodesia, even if one had doubts which of them was the legal system existing in Rhodesia.

This formulation of the tasks of a legal theory further presupposes that it is possible to know what is a complete description of a legal system without knowing which of its descriptions is a proper description. It is possible to identify a system without identifying its laws. This is a more precise way of saying, as has been said earlier in this section, that it is possible to know the content of a legal system without knowing the identity of any of its laws.

The problem of the structure of a law can be regarded as part of the problem of individuation. It is, however, important to realize that the two are not identical. Suppose that the following statements are all true:

(1) All adult males ought to inform the Home Office of any change in their address within a fortnight of changing their address.

(2) All adult females ought to inform the Home Office of any change in their address within a fortnight of changing their address.

(3) Every corporation ought to inform the Home Office of any change in the address of its head office within a fortnight of changing the address.

(4) Every person ought to inform the Home Office of his address within a fortnight of the passing of this Act, and thereafter within a fortnight of changing his address.

The four statements have the same structure and it is the structure of statements describing complete laws. But this in itself does not mean that each of them describes one complete norm. It may be that (1) and (2), and perhaps even (3), describe parts of the content of one norm. Perhaps this norm is completely described by (4). Perhaps it is not completely described by any of the four statements. How is one to decide? Is the time or occasion of creation of the legal material on which these statements are based relevant to the decision? Is its formulation relevant? Or does everything depend on the logical relations between these statements? One thing is clear: None of these questions can be answered merely on the basis of the doctrine of the structure of laws.[1]

Bentham is probably the only legal philosopher who understood the necessity and importance of principles of individuation apart from the doctrine of the structure of laws. Consequently, after expounding his views on the structure of laws he began a systematic investigation of the other principles of individuation.[2]

---

[1] It is assumed all along that, if there is more than one proper description of a system, then all the proper descriptions have equal claim to be regarded as individuating the laws and representing their structure. This means, of course, that a law can be regarded as having several alternative structures (for, as has been pointed out before, a pure normative statement describing one and only one complete law represents its structure). If for any reason it is considered desirable to regard a law as having just one structure, then it will be necessary to use a stricter doctrine of the structure of laws, one which goes beyond the principles of individuation. Whereas these principles determine only which complete description is a proper description, the doctrine of structure will determine which of the proper descriptions represents the structure of the laws.

[2] See especially *Limits*, pp. 247–9, 256–61; *OLG*, pp. 156–8, 165–71.

Without entering into the details of Bentham's view on the subject a few remarks can be made about some of his principles.

He was almost exclusively concerned with the arrangement of authoritative legal material, and his ideas are in fact relevant only to the representation of legislative material. They do not throw much light on judicial legislation. For him 'to fix the individuality of a law . . . is to ascertain what a proportion of *legislative matter* must amount to in order on the one hand not to contain less, on the other hand not to contain more, than one whole law.'[1] Bentham regarded the creation of laws by the courts as 'a kind of legislation',[2] but he never succeeded in putting forward a reasonable theory of judicial law-making. His approach to the problem of individuation can be seen as resting on five fundamental principles:

(1) Every law is a norm prescribing certain behaviour as obligatory in certain circumstances, for every law is an expression of the legislator's will that certain acts should be done by certain persons in certain circumstances. Bentham himself says at one point: 'Whatever business the law may be conversant about, may be reduced to one sort of operation, viz. that of creating duties.'[3]

Hitherto the terms 'a legal norm' and 'a law' have been used as if they had the same meaning. From now on they will be distinguished: 'A law' will be used to designate the basic units into which a legal system is divided, and 'a legal norm' for a law directing the behaviour of human beings by imposing duties, or conferring powers.[4] It is Bentham's most important principle of individuation that every law is a norm. It is, moreover, a norm of the type here called a prescription, i.e. a duty imposing norm. This principle is manifested in his doctrine of the structure of laws by the fact that every law must contain one provision which is a command or a prohibition. It means that all the other provisions and sections in the legal system must be arranged round these main provisions and be related to them as explanations, qualifications, warnings, etc.

---

[1] *Limits*, p. 247; *OLG*, p. 156.
[2] Cf. his analysis of legislation in the *Limits*, pp. 90 f; *OLG*, pp. 3 f.
[3] *Limits*, p. 55; *OLG*, p. 249. Here, as often elsewhere, Bentham disregards the possibility of 'legislative invitations', i.e. laws backed by rewards (Cf. *Limits*, pp. 224–7; *OLG*, pp. 133–6).
[4] More on norms in Ch. VI.

(2) An expression of the legislator's will, a prescription to people to behave in a certain way, amounts to the imposition of a duty, and thus to the creation of a law, *only if* it is backed by sanction, either by way of an incitative or a satisfactive clause or by punitive laws stipulating sanctions for the violation of the prescription.[1]

(3) Subject to the second principle, every act situation which is commanded or prohibited by the legislator is the core of a separate law. The fact that a law ordering the judges to punish murderers implies a prohibition of murder does not entail that there is just one law (that directed to the judges); there are two laws, although one of them entails the other.[2]

(4) Conflicts of laws are resolved before the representation of the law in its proper form. The proper description of a legal system does not describe any conflict of laws. Nor does it provide the means for resolving such conflicts. The rules by means of which conflicts between two laws are resolved refer, among other things, to the relative importance of the legislators of the laws and to the dates at which they were made—facts which are not expressed in the proper description of the system, according to Bentham's theory.

(5) The individuation of laws partly depends on the way in which the legislator happened to formulate the legal material: e.g. if a statute has been made at one time to the effect that

(i) 'Every male' shall do A in conditions C, and if several years later another statute has been made saying that

(ii) 'Every female' shall do A in C,
then, according to Bentham, the legal system includes two separate laws, one corresponding to (i), the other corresponding to (ii). Had the second statute been formulated as follows:

(ii') 'Every person' shall do A in C,
then, according to Bentham, the legal system contains just one law corresponding both to (i) and (ii').

In the foregoing analysis de-obligative laws have been disregarded. That every law is a norm is as fundamental a

---

[1] The sanction need not always be a legal sanction. A law may impose a duty even if the only sanction for its breach is a moral or religious sanction. Cf. *Limits*, p. 151; *OLG*, pp. 68–70, 248.

[2] Cf. *Limits*, p. 234–5; *OLG*, pp. 143–4; 'A General View of a Complete Code of Laws', Bowring (ed.) *The Works of J. Bentham*, vol. 3, p. 159.

principle to Bentham as any. De-obligative laws are not norms, but Bentham seems to have been unaware of this conflict between his views. For reasons explained in Chapter III, section 2 above I preferred to continue to ascribe to him the view that all laws are norms and to disregard the possibility of de-obligative laws. It is worth noting, however, that accepting their possibility will involve some further modifications in the account given above of Bentham's principles of individuation: not all the conflicts between laws would be resolved prior to their representation in the proper form. The conflicts between de-obligative laws and the obligative laws which they qualify would remain unresolved. Obviously, not every law would be backed by a sanction, and it seems that the occasion on which an exemption to a general duty was enacted would determine whether it would be part of the obligative law imposing the duty, or an independent de-obligative law; this would increase the relevance of the actual circumstances of legislation to the problem of individuation.

IV.2: KELSEN'S APPROACH TO THE INDIVIDUATION OF LAWS

Kelsen's ideas on the nature and structure of norms are sufficiently similar to those of Bentham to confront his theory with the same problems and difficulties concerning the principles of individuation. Kelsen, unfortunately, did not have that clear understanding of the nature of the difficulties which characterizes Bentham's thought on the subject. He did not recognize the necessity of formulating principles of individuation, and consequently his theory does not provide a complete solution to the problem. It contains, however, enough material to shed considerable light on some aspects of his implicit approach to the problem.

Kelsen, like Bentham, would presumably regard differences in the occasion of creation, and in the legislative authority, as irrelevant to the individuation of laws. He finds no difficulty in regarding one law as containing parts legislated on different occasions and by different authorities. He considers, for example, constitutional law as part of every other law.[1] Furthermore, again as with Bentham, the way in which the science of

[1] *GT*, p. 143.

law is advised to represent the law does not allow for the representation of conflicts of laws. The proper description of the law, according to Kelsen, does not describe conflicting laws. This is the implication of the following passage: '. . . the principle of non-contradiction must be posited in the idea of law, since without it the notion of legality would be destroyed. This presupposition alone, which is contained in the basic norm, allows legal cognition to supply a meaningful interpretation of the legal material.'[1]

Bentham's first and most important principle of individuation, namely that every law is a norm and a prescription, is rejected by Kelsen in favour of a different principle: that every law is a norm and a permission, that is, every law grants a permission. But the discussion of another of Kelsen's principles of individuation must precede the examination of this principle.

Bentham's other principles, mentioned above, are replaced in Kelsen by another principle, which is incompatible with them: 'All the norms of a legal order are coercive norms, i.e. norms providing for sanctions.'[2] The explanation of this principle must begin with a few remarks on Kelsen's concept of a sanction.

Sanctions are implemented by acts. Acts which implement sanctions will be called 'sanction-applying acts', and sometimes simply 'sanctions'. An act is a sanction-applying act only if it causes some advantage or disadvantage to a person.[3] Kelsen does not in fact discuss laws based on rewards in any detail. A disadvantage 'consists in a deprivation of possessions—life, health, freedoms or property'.[4] Kelsen says that the disadvantage or evil is *applied* to the violator of the law, a phrase which indicates that the sanction is an act done to the violator by someone other than himself. This is by no means always the case. Deprivation of property, for example, can be achieved by ordering the violator to give up some property of his, and not only by ordering another person to take it from him.

The sanction 'has the character of a measure of coercion. This does not mean that in carrying out the sanction physical

---

[1] *GT*, p. 406. The subject is discussed in detail in *PTL*, pp. 205 ff.
[2] *GT*, p. 29.   [3] *GT*, p. 15.
[4] *GT*, p. 18. Good name should be added to the list, as well as injuring other feelings (e.g. by killing or hurting one's relatives). In this way some of Kelsen's difficulties in *GT*, p. 55 can be solved.

force must be applied. This is necessary only if resistance is encountered in applying the sanction.'[1] It should be noticed that the act-applying sanction itself, and not merely the use of force, is here called coercive. Contrary to the implication of the passage from which the quotation is taken, not every legal sanction can be enforced by force. Deprivation of property can sometimes be implemented by the annulment or withdrawal of certain rights in ways which are not open to physical obstruction.[2] Some sanctions, on the other hand, must by their very nature be applied by force, e.g. whipping and execution. It is, of course, possible to order self-whipping or suicide, but these are different sanctions.

In light of the foregoing remarks procedure will be as follows. Legal sanctions will be regarded as two acts connected in the following way: One, which is the sanction-applying act, is done by the violator of the law and is to his own disadvantage in the sense explained above.[3] The other act is done by someone else, should the violator not perform the first act, and it is intended to cause either the same or a different disadvantage to the violator. A sanction which cannot be applied by the violator of the law himself consists only of an act of the second sort.

A sanction is a coercive sanction if it allows for the use of force. Contrary to Kelsen's opinion, not all legal sanctions are coercive.

An act is not the application of a sanction, even though it is to the disadvantage of a person, unless it is stipulated by a norm as a consequence of a certain act of that person.[4] 'In all civilized states', Kelsen explains,

administrative organs are . . . authorized to evacuate forcibly inhabitants of houses that threaten to collapse, to demolish buildings in order to stop the spread of fires, to slaughter cattle striken with certain diseases, to intern individuals whose physical or mental condition is a danger to the health or life of their fellow citizens. . . . These coercive acts—to which administrative organs, especially

---

[1] *GT*, p. 18.

[2] Cf. 'The deprivation of other rights can also be stipulated as punishment.' *PTL*, p. 109.

[3] Acts of the first kind are in general to the disadvantage of persons of this class. It is not a necessary condition that the act will be to the disadvantage of the violator on every occasion.

[4] *PTL*, p. 34.

organs of the police, are authorized—differ from sanctions, . . . in that they are not conditioned by a certain human conduct against which the coercive act, as a sanction, is directed.[1]

Coercive acts of these kinds are not sanctions: this is not because they are to the benefit of all whom they affect (for Kelsen assumes that they are to the detriment of some persons),[2] but because the law which authorizes their performance does not make it dependent on any behaviour of the persons who stand to suffer from these acts.

Kelsen's concept of a sanction is based on the notions of an act to the disadvantage of a person, and of a violation of a law (which, if it is a condition for a sanction, is called delict[3]). It is also intimately connected with the concept of responsibility. A person is liable to a sanction if he is responsible for his own delict. Sometimes, as Kelsen acknowledges,[4] a person is held responsible for acts of other persons. An act to the detriment of a person is a sanction against him if its performance is conditioned, by law, upon a delict of another person for whom the first one is responsible. Kelsen, however, does not explain the nature of responsibility,[5] and this is not the place to enter into this complex subject.

This explanation of legal sanction is based primarily on the *General Theory of Law and State*. In the *The Pure Theory of Law* Kelsen repeats his explanations of disadvantage and coercion, as well as his distinction between administrative coercion and sanctions.[6] But in this book legal sanctions have lost their importance with respect to the individuation of laws. In one place Kelsen says: 'As a coercive order the law is distinguished from other social orders. The decisive criterion is the element

[1] *GT*, pp. 278-9.
[2] Kelsen does not discuss the special problems of 'legal paternalism': namely, enforcing a person to his own good. Acts of this kind are regarded by him as acts to the disadvantage of the person who is enforced. This view results from the fact that he considers an act as disadvantageous to a person if it is so on most occasions on which it can be performed to the disadvantage of some human beings. It would have been more reasonable to consider merely whether the performance of the act on the occasions specified by the law would be, in general, to the disadvantage of the law's subjects.
[3] *GT*, p. 54.   [4] *GT*, p. 55.
[5] All he says is that there is some relation between the person who committed the delict and the person who is held responsible.
[6] *PTL*, pp. 33-4, 108.

of force—that means that the act prescribed by the order as a consequence of socially detrimental facts ought to be executed even against the will of the individual and, if he resists, by physical force.'[1]

Not coercive sanctions but coercive acts as such are made here the distinctive characteristic of law (*le droit*). This produces a most significant change in the principles of individuation, for Kelsen had always tacitly assumed that the distinctive characteristic of the law in general is also the distinctive characteristic of every legal norm. Therefore the change in his views about the distinction between law and other social orders brings about a change in his principles of individuation of laws:

Si l'on conçoit le droit comme un ordre de contrainte, c'est-à-dire comme un ordre qui institue des actes de contrainte, alors les propositions de droit qui en décrivent les normes apparaissent comme des assertions aux terms desquelles, quand des conditions, determinées, c'est-à-dire fixées par l'ordre juridique, sont données, un certain acte de contrainte également défini par l'ordre juridique doit être accompli.[2]

The general form of a law, according to Kelsen, is: *A* ought to be done when conditions *C* obtain. His original principle of individuation means that *A* must be an act (or a compound of acts as explained above) applying a sanction. All those parts of the legal material of a system which do not stipulate a sanction are either part of the specification of conditions for the application of sanctions, or are not part of the law at all (which is the fate of preambles to statutes or constitutions etc., as well as of some imperfect laws).[3] Coercive acts which are not applications of sanction, i.e. administrative coercion, are always among the conditions for the application of sanctions. Sometimes they are duties imposed on the administration, and failure to carry them out makes the officials responsible liable to sanction. They are always an exception to norms forbidding the use of force.

The new doctrine propounded in *The Pure Theory of Law* means that, apart from being (as before) part of the conditions of the application of sanctions or norms prescribing sanctions, administrative coercive acts are specifically permitted by separate norms which do not stipulate sanctions.

[1] *PTL*, p. 34. [2] *TP*, p. 149. [3] Cf. *PTL*, pp. 52 ff.

The reasons for this change of doctrine have already been outlined. It is based first on Kelsen's view that the characteristic properties of law in general are present in every individual law; and second, on the belief that law is distinguished from all other social normative systems by being the only one which prescribes coercive acts.

The errors of the first step will be exposed later. As for the second belief, there is no reason to suppose that it is true. Lynching or vendetta may be prescribed by certain positive moral systems without turning them into legal orders. Similarly, non-legal social orders can prescribe corporal punishment of children by their parents, pupils by their teachers, etc. Coercion may also be authorized or even prescribed by non-legal social orders in cases of danger to the community or part of it.

More important still is the fact that Kelsen's definition of law in *The Pure Theory of Law* as a coercive order conflicts with the guiding principle for the definition of normative social orders which he himself has adopted. 'It is the function of every social order', he explains,

> . . . to bring about a certain reciprocal behaviour of human beings. . . . According to the manner in which the socially desired behaviour is brought about, various types of social orders can be distinguished. These types . . . are characterized by the specific motivation resorted to by a social order to induce individuals to behave as desired . . . [in one type] behaviour conforming to the established order is achieved by a sanction provided in the order itself.[1]

According to this principle of classification of social orders, law is distinguished by Kelsen from other social orders by the fact that it resorts to coercive sanctions as standard motives for conformity. In the *Théorie Pure du Droit* Kelsen repeats the same principle of classification of normative orders in almost the same words:

> . . . la fonction de tout ordre social est de provoquer une certaine conduite des hommes qui lui sont soumis, . . . Cette fonction de motivation est remplie par les représentations des normes qui ordonnent ou interdisent certains actes humains. Les façons différentes dont ils prescrivent ou prohibent permettent de distinguer

[1] *GT*, p. 15.

parmi les ordres sociaux plusieurs types. . . . Certains ordres sociaux prescrivent une certaine conduite humaine sans attacher aucune conséquence à l'obéissance ou à la désobéissance de leur commandement. D'autres, en même temps qu'ils ordonnent une certaine conduite, y attachent l'octroi d'un avantage, une récompense, ou bien attachent à la conduite contraire un désavantage, une peine, au sens le plus large de ce dernier terme.[1]

If this principle of classification is adopted, then law is defined as the only social order using socially organized coercive sanctions as standard motivation for conformity. The individuation principle derived from this definition is clearly that every law is a norm stipulating a sanction.

Whatever the deficiencies of this definition of law, it must be admitted that it is based on much more significant facts (assuming they are facts) than Kelsen's new definition of law, based, as it is, merely on the assumption that no other social order prescribes coercive measures, which throws no great light on the mechanics or 'social technique' of the law.

Preferring on these grounds Kelsen's earlier definition of law, I am bound by Kelsen's own logic to prefer also his earlier principle of individuation. The rest of the discussion is based on this principle, namely that every law is a norm stipulating a sanction.[2]

The preferred principle of individuation stands, however, in need of closer inspection. But as this inspection bears on Kelsen's theory of the structure of a legal system, it will be postponed till that subject is taken up in the next chapter.

Kelsen's principle of individuation, which we have been discussing, explains the kind of act that every law stipulates. The general form of a law is to the effect that an act ought to be performed by certain persons in certain conditions. It has been shown that the act is always a sanction-applying act, which entails that the conditions of its performance include some act of the person who stands to suffer from the application

[1] *TP*, p. 34.
[2] Kelsen's new principle of individuation is not supported by an analysis of norms prescribing administrative coercion, about which very little is said. The discussion is still centred on the sanction-stipulating norms. Moreover, in an article published in 1966 'On the Pure Theory of Law', Kelsen returns to his old definition of law and his old principle of individuation. These facts suggest that his new principle is only a half-digested afterthought.

of the sanction.[1] What is the force of the 'ought' in this formulation? What does it mean to say that every law *stipulates* or
provides for a sanction?

It is reasonable to assume it means the law *requires* that the
sanction should be applied when the specified conditions are
fulfilled, and that not applying the sanction in such circumstances amounts to a violation of the law. It is true that failure of a
person to apply a sanction stipulated by one law is not always
a condition for the application of another sanction stipulated
by a second law and directed against that person. This means,
according to Kelsen, that the norm-subject of the first law does
not have a duty to apply the sanction, for to be under a duty to
do an act means that not doing it is a condition for the application of a sanction.[2] But it is not impossible to make sense of the
concept of 'being required to behave in a certain way' without
reference to the concept of 'being liable to a sanction'. In such
a sense it is customary to say that judges and other officials
ought to apply the law, to execute sanctions, etc., even if they
are not made subject to sanctions when they fail to do so. These
facts did not escape Kelsen's attention. He even gives a partial
explanation of some of them. People say that a person ought,
or is required, to behave in a certain way when the legislator
has enacted a law expressing his intention that that person
should behave in that manner, even when no sanction is
provided to back this prescription. Kelsen, however, thinks that
such intention 'must be regarded as legally irrelevant',[3] thus
rejecting any attempt to distinguish between 'is legally required'
and 'is a legal duty'.

Kelsen uses 'ought' to signify 'is required to', 'has a permission to', and 'has a power to'.[4] He seems to think that the
'ought' in the proper description of norms has any one of
these meanings according to the circumstances.[5] He seems
ready to say that a person has the power to apply a sanction.
In one place he says that 'in case of a legal order providing for
coercive acts as sanctions an individual is authorized to perform
these acts under the conditions stipulated by the legal order.'[6]

[1] This is not a complete principle of individuation. The individuation of laws
depends, according to Kelsen, on the individuation of sanctions, a subject on which
he says nothing.
[2] See *GT*, p. 59; *PTL*, p. 115.   [3] *PTL*, p. 52.   [4] *PTL*, p. 5.
[5] *PTL*, pp. 118–19.   [6] *PTL*, pp. 15–16.

I shall regard every sanction-stipulating norm as granting a permission. In Chapter VI the problem of which of them also confer powers will be discussed.

Kelsen seems to think that a law prescribes a sanction if there is another law making failure to execute the sanction a condition of another sanction. But in that case the application of the sanction is prescribed by the norm making failure to apply it a delict, and not by the norm stipulating the sanction.[1] Consequently every sanction-stipulating norm, that is every law, is a permission to apply a sanction.

IV.3: KELSEN VERSUS BENTHAM—A COMPARISON

Even though what we have said in the last two sections about Bentham's and Kelsen's principles of individuation does not present their complete doctrines of individuation of laws, it provides some insight into the nature of the problems involved. It can also serve as a basis for a partial comparison of their views on the subject, which in itself helps us to understand what considerations are relevant to solving the problem of the individuation of laws. As will be seen later the comparison helps also to point out the strong connection between the problem of individuation and the theory of legal system.

'Every rule of law obligates human beings to observe a certain behaviour under certain circumstances.'[2] Being a permission, a norm can obligate only implicitly. It obligates in this sense: the fact that a norm permits one person to behave in a certain way under certain conditions entails that another person has a duty to do or abstain from doing a certain act.

A person 'is legally obligated to refrain from the delict. . . . An individual is legally obligated to the behaviour the opposite of which is the condition of a sanction directed against him.'[3] As every law is a permission to apply a sanction, every law entails a duty. It must, however, be remembered that whereas a law permits explicitly it obligates implicitly. Strictly speaking it is a simple permission: x may do A when y does B and other conditions obtain. But this permission to x to do A entails an obligation on another person mentioned in the description of the law, namely y, to avoid doing another act which is likewise mentioned in the description, namely B.

[1] On this point see the next section.　　[2] *GT*, p. 3.　　[3] *GT*, p. 59.

It can be said that a Kelsenian law amounts to two Bentha-
mite laws. Bentham's principal law, imposing an obligation on
x to behave in a certain way, say *A*, and his punitive law, imposing an obligation on another person, say *y*, to apply a sanction
against *x* by doing *B*, if *x* fails to fulfil his obligation to do *A*,
become in Kelsen's theory one law: A permission to *y* to do *B*
if *x* does not do *A*. This is the most important difference between
their respective principles of individuation. The same legal
material which, according to Kelsen, goes to make up one law,
is regarded by Bentham as establishing two laws.

The fact that Kelsen regards the application of the sanction
as permitted, whereas Bentham regards it as obligatory,[1] does
not reflect a difference in the amount of the legal material. It
testifies to a different interpretation of the same legal material.[2]
Bentham regards the fact that the legislator expressed his
intention that a sanction should be applied as making its
application a duty, provided that disobedience were punished
by some other sanction. The further sanction is merely a
necessary, and not a sufficient, condition for the existence of a
duty to apply the first sanction. Kelsen, on the other hand,
makes the sanction for a failure to apply the first sanction, or
to do any other act, both a sufficient and a necessary condition
for the act's being a duty, and regards the intention of the
legislator as irrelevant.

This at any rate seems to be the consequence of remarks like
the following: 'The statement "An individual is legally obligated to behave in a certain way" is identical with the statement "A legal norm commands a certain behaviour of an
individual". And a legal order commands a certain behaviour
by attaching a sanction to the opposite behaviour.'[3]

By saying that a legal order obligates to do an act by making

---

[1] According to Bentham, the application of sanctions is not obligatory merely
when their existence is declared in incitatory clauses, i.e. in policy-declaring
clauses.

[2] There are none the less two differences in the legal material accepted by the
two philosophers as establishing the existence of one law: (1) Kelsen regards
declarations of policy as irrelevant, whereas Bentham considers them as part of
the relevant legal material. (2) Kelsen thinks that a permission to apply a sanction
in case an act is not performed is sufficient to make the performance of that act a
duty. Bentham seems to think that the application of the sanction must be obligatory or a declared policy.

[3] *PTL*, p. 115.

failure to perform it a condition for the application of a sanction Kelsen exposes himself to the following criticism:

If we confine our attention to the contents of the law as represented in the canonical form 'if *A* then *B* ought to be' it is impossible to distinguish a criminal law punishing behaviour with a fine from a revenue law taxing certain activities. Both when the individual is taxed and when he is fined the law's provisions when cast into the Kelsenian canonical form are identical. Both cases are therefore cases of delict unless we distinguish between them by reference to something that escapes the net of the canonical form, i.e. that the fine is a punishment for an activity officially condemned and the tax is not. It may perhaps be objected that a tax, though it consists of a compulsory money payment as some sanctions also do, is not a 'sanction'. . . . But this does not really avoid the difficulty but only defers it; for we shall have to step outside the limits of juristic definition in order to determine when a compulsory money payment is a sanction and when it is not.[1]

The last remark in the quotation suggests that there is a certain ambiguity in Kelsen's position: It is not clear whether every act which is to the disadvantage of a person, and the performance of which is made by law dependent upon the behaviour of that person, is a sanction, or whether some further condition has to be satisfied. As Hart points out, if there is a further condition then Kelsen failed to disclose what it is.

In fact Kelsen writes as if there is no such further condition. This is a surprising conclusion, for it means that while Kelsen insists that the legislator must manifest an intention to prescribe the behaviour of other people in order to create any authoritative legal material at all, he considers that same intention completely irrelevant to the interpretation of the legal material thus created. Nevertheless, there is no escape from that conclusion. It is based on Kelsen's definitions of 'a sanction' and 'a duty',[2] and particularly his definition of 'a delict'.

Kelsen is most emphatic: 'C'est seulement par le fait que l'ordre juridique les érige en conditions d'actes de contrainte prévus par lui que des comportements, actions ou abstentions,

---

[1] Hart, 'Kelsen Visited', 10 *U.C.L.A. Law Review*, pp. 720–1.
[2] See for the first *PTL*, pp. 34–5, 111; and for the second the previous page.

prennent le caractère d'actes illicites ou délits.'[1] But, as Kelsen knows,

> the delict, i.e., the fact that one party has not fulfilled the contract, is not sufficiently characterized by saying that it is 'a condition of the sanction'. The making of the contract and the suit of the other party are also such conditions. What then is the distinctive characteristic of that condition which is called the 'delict'? Could no other criterion be found than the supposed fact that the legislator desires conduct contrary to that which is characterized as 'delict', then the concept of delict would be incapable of a juristic definition ... such explanations only amount to saying that the delict is against the purpose of law. But that is irrelevant to the legal concept of the delict.[2]

Instead of referring to the 'legislator's intention', 'the official intention', or 'the purpose of the law' Kelsen defines the delict simply as 'the behaviour of that individual against whom the sanction is directed as a consequent of his behaviour'.[3] This definition fails to distinguish, for example, between making a binding promise and breaking it. It makes both acts parts of the delict. Every act of a person which is a condition to the application of a sanction against him is part of a delict.

By disregarding everything apart from the fact that a delict is a condition for a sanction Kelsen vitiates his own doctrine of individuation. His principles of individuation depend on the possibility of deducing, from a statement that a person is permitted to apply a sanction, that another person is obligated to behave in a certain way. But the statement that doing an act makes a man liable, by law, to some unpleasant consequences does not entail that he has a legal duty to avoid doing it. This is only the other face of Hart's criticism quoted above. The fact that earning money makes one liable to pay income tax does not entail that one has a duty to avoid earning money.

Disregarding this criticism of Kelsen's doctrine of individuation (his doctrine can be rectified in order to accommodate the criticism), it must be asked what are the reasons for accepting it in the first place. Why should it be preferred to Bentham's doctrine, for example?

---

[1] *TP*, p. 152.   [2] *GT*, p. 53.

[3] *GT*, p. 54, see also *PTL*, p. 114. Kelsen allows for certain exceptions which are irrelevant to the discussion.

First there is Kelsen's implicit belief that the characteristic properties of legal orders, the features that distinguish them from other types of social normative orders, are the properties which distinguish every legal norm from every non-legal social norm. It seems that only this belief can explain the change in Kelsen's view on individuation in *The Pure Theory of Law*.[1] This belief demonstrates the prevalent tendency to regard the definition of a law, not the explanation of a legal system, as the main problem of jurisprudence. It shows also that Kelsen, who should have known better, is not exempt from that tendency. For the belief that every legal norm can be distinguished from every other norm by the fact that every legal norm and no other norm stipulates a coercive sanction is incompatible with Kelsen's other belief that 'it is impossible to grasp the nature of law if we limit our attention to the single isolated rule.'[2]

In a sense almost all the rest of this study is designed to convince the reader of the truth of this quotation. The law should be distinguished from positive morality, etc., by characteristics of legal systems which are not shared by each of their laws. Only if this procedure is adopted does it become possible to account for the special place that coercive sanctions occupy in the law. It is not true that only the law stipulates coercive sanctions, nor is there any reason for saying that every law stipulates a coercive sanction (if only because not all legal sanctions are coercive). But it is true that one characteristic of the law is that it makes a systematic use of coercive sanctions, and that coercive sanctions are of great importance in understanding its nature as a specific 'social technique'. This point will be taken up in another chapter.

Another reason for Kelsen's principles of individuation is implicit in the *General Theory of Law and State*. Whatever the motives for which people obey the law, the law itself, as has been explained in Chapter III, section 5, above, provides a standard motive for obedience by stipulating sanctions. Law is characterized by its special 'social technique', 'the social technique which consists in bringing about the desired social conduct of men through the threat of a measure of coercion which is to be applied in case of contrary conduct'.[3] The way in which the law 'relies' on this standard motivation, the way

[1] Cf. Ch. IV, sect. 1 above.   [2] *GT*, p. 3.   [3] *GT*, p. 19.

in which the liability to sanctions is related to acts which are required by law, so as to become a standard motive for fulfilling these duties, is made clear if laws are individuated according to Kelsen's principles.

There is no doubt that it is desirable to make clear the relation between duties and sanctions. The question is whether Kelsen has chosen the best way to do so. Why should the relation be presented as a relation between two parts of one law rather than as a relation between two laws, as it is by Bentham?[1] It will be argued later that Bentham's laws are too complex to be the basis of a reasonable division of a legal system. Such arguments apply with even greater force to Kelsen's laws. It is also possible to argue that Kelsen's principle does not represent correctly the relation between the duty and the sanction. It focuses attention on the sanction and the delict. The existence of the duty has to be inferred. But the duty and not the sanction is the law's main concern. The sanction is there to ensure the performance of the duty. Kelsen's representation creates the impression that duties are by-products of sanctions.

Furthermore, Kelsen's laws are permissions, whereas according to his own theory the most important fact about the law is that it prescribes behaviour, not that it permits it. The importance of duties, as well as their relation to sanctions, is more clearly represented by Bentham's method of describing the law than by Kelsen's.

In his latest book, *The Pure Theory of Law*, Kelsen admits the possibility of norms prescribing duties which are valid only if another norm exists stipulating sanctions against violators of the first norm.[2] But he still maintains that in the law the two are but one norm, explaining that the law 'se caractérise par le fait qu'il ordonne une certaine conduite précisément en attachant à la conduite contraire un désavantage'.[3] This remark refers to Kelsen's view that the legislator's intention and the law's purpose are irrelevant to the question which act is a duty. This doctrine has already been criticized, and even if it were true there is no reason why it should affect in any way the principles of individuation.

On the other hand, Kelsen's quoted remark may refer to the

---

[1] I am disregarding the case of satisfactive and incitative provisions.
[2] *PTL*, p. 28.   [3] *TP*, p. 35.

wording of statutes. As Bentham points out, 'were a law to say "Let the judge cause every man that commits murder to be put to death", the prohibition thereby given would be not a whit less intelligible than if it were to say, " let no man on pain of death, commit murder".'[1] Is Kelsen's remark intended to justify his principle of individuation, on the ground that the legislator usually formulates prohibitions by directing the courts to punish people for committing the forbidden act? If this is the meaning of Kelsen's remark then it is surely wrong. Bentham's conclusion from the same fact is the correct one:

The versatility of language is endless, and its variety inexhaustible. There is no trusting, therefore, to mere words. To understand any subject, but more particularly that of law, to have a clear perception of the ideas that belong to it, we must strip them of their fallacious covering and judge of them by themselves.[2]

In the *General Theory of Law and State* yet another argument is put forward in support of Kelsen's principle of individuation: 'If it is assumed that the . . . norm which forbids theft is valid only if the norm attaches a sanction to theft, then the first norm is certainly superfluous in an exact exposition of law. If at all existent, the first norm is contained in the second, which is the only genuine legal norm.'[3]

Suppose that the purported duty-imposing law is entailed by the law's providing a sanction for not fulfilling the duty it purports to impose; is that fact a sufficient reason to think that there are no duty-imposing laws, that statements purporting to describe such laws describe only the consequences of the existence of norms stipulating sanctions? Bentham for one thinks that it is not:

The law which converts an act into an offence, and the law which directs the punishment of that offence, are properly speaking, neither the same law nor parts of the same law. . . . These laws are so distinct that they refer to different actions—they are addressed to different persons. The first does not include the second, but the second implicitly includes the first. Say to the judges, 'You shall punish thieves', and a prohibition of stealing is clearly intimated. In this point of view, the penal code would be sufficient for all purposes.[4]

[1] *Limits*, p. 234; *OLG*, p. 143.   [2] *Limits*, pp. 234–5; *OLG*, pp. 143–4.
[3] *GT*, p. 61.   [4] *A General View*, p. 160.

Logical superfluity in the presentation of the law, in the proper description of the law, is a thing to be avoided, but not at all costs. Bentham suggests another, and an overriding, consideration: Every act-situation which is required by law is subject to a separate law prescribing it, unless it is an instance or a species of another act-situation which is itself the subject of another law.

V

KELSEN'S THEORY OF LEGAL SYSTEM

AUSTIN'S concept of sovereignty was the main target of the criticism of his theory of legal system in Chapter II above. The concept of sovereignty is the corner-stone of Austin's theory of legal system. Kelsen does not use any concept of sovereignty similar to Austin's and thus avoids many of the shortcomings of Austin's theory. It is, however, interesting that this did not prevent him from adopting a theory of legal system which is similar to Austin's theory: Both theories are based on the principle of efficacy as the basis of their solutions of the problem of existence, both base their respective solutions of the problem of identity on the principle of origin, and, finally, their solutions of the problem of the structure of legal system are based on the principle of independence.

In the present chapter the explanation of Kelsen's theory of legal system is designed to emphasize both its similarity to and its difference from Austin's theory. It is further argued that Kelsen's theory is inadequate and that its shortcomings are due to the fact that it is based on the principles of origin and independence. The criticism of the principle of efficacy is deferred to another chapter. It will be suggested that any theory based on the principles of efficacy, origin, and independence is open to objections similar to the objections raised in this study against Austin's and Kelsen's theories.

V.1: THE EXISTENCE OF A LEGAL SYSTEM

Kelsen's criterion of the existence of a legal system can be formulated as follows: A legal system exists if, and only if, it reaches a certain minimum degree of efficacy.

The efficacy of a system is a function of the efficacy of its laws, but Kelsen says nothing about the nature of the connection and how the degree of efficacy is to be determined. The efficacy of a norm can be manifested in two ways: (a) by the obedience of those on whom a duty is imposed by that norm;

(b) by the application of the sanction permitted by the norm.

By effectiveness of a legal norm, which attaches a sanction to a certain behaviour and thus qualifies the behaviour conditioning the sanction as illegal, that is, as 'delict', two facts may be understood: (1) that this norm is *applied* by the legal organs (particularly the law courts), which means that the sanction in a concrete case is ordered and executed; and (2) that this norm is *obeyed* by the individuals subjected to the legal order, which means that they behave in a way which avoids the sanction.[1]

Kelsen gives no indication of what the relation between the two types of manifestation of efficacy must be if the norm is to be considered efficacious. Nor is it clear how the efficacy of a norm can be measured or otherwise determined.[2]

According to Austin, it will be remembered,[3] a legal system exists if, and only if, (a) its supreme legislator is habitually obeyed; (b) its supreme legislator does not habitually obey anyone; (c) its supreme legislator is superior to the law-subjects relative to every law. The last condition is omitted by Kelsen. If its purpose is to ensure that the law's teeth can bite, then this is usually implied by the general efficacy of the legal system, which in turn usually means that sanctions are actually applied.

It has been seen that obedience to the supreme legislator entails obedience to his laws, whereas obedience to the laws does not entail obedience to their legislator. By making the existence of a system dependent upon obedience to the legislator, and by denying the existence of laws applying to the supreme legislator, Austin was forced to assume that every change of supreme legislators means a change of legal systems,[4] though, of course, Austin does not explicitly state this consequence of his theory. Kelsen does away with the sovereign, and presumably every case of obedience to the law is, according to Kelsen, relevant to the existence of the legal system. In this way a change of supreme legislator does not by itself affect the continuous

---

[1] *PTL*, p. 11.

[2] On these problems see Ch. IX below. It is worth noting that Kelsen seems to attribute equal weight to the violation of a duty and the non-application of a sanction in determining the efficacy of a norm. This suggests that the application of the sanction is required and not merely permitted by law.

[3] See Ch. I, sect. 2 above.

[4] Cf. Ch. II, sect. 2 above.

existence of the legal system. A new system is created only when the change of supreme legislators is unconstitutional.

The second of Austin's conditions—the independence of the supreme legislator—disappears with the concept of sovereignty itself, and the problems it created[1] are avoided. Thus, by replacing personal obedience to the sovereign by obedience to the laws and the application of sanctions, Kelsen is able to improve upon Austin's criterion of the existence of a legal system. But their criteria have this in common—that both make the efficacy of a legal system the criterion of its existence.

V.2: THE CRITERION OF IDENTITY

Austin thought of a legal system as the set of all the laws enacted, directly or indirectly, by one sovereign. Kelsen substitutes the basic norm for Austin's sovereign, and leaves the rest of the definition unaltered: A legal system is the set of all the laws enacted by the exercise of powers conferred, directly or indirectly, by one basic norm. In his own words: 'All norms whose validity may be traced back to one and the same basic norm form a system of norms, or an order.'[2]

Austin's criterion for membership of a law in a system is: A law belongs to a system if, and only if, it was enacted by the sovereign who enacted all the other laws of that system. Kelsen's criterion is: A law belongs to a system if, and only if, it was enacted by the exercise of powers conferred by the basic norm that conferred the powers by the exercise of which all the other laws of the system were enacted. In his own words, 'That a norm belongs to a certain system of norms . . . can be tested only by ascertaining that it derives its validity from the basic norm constituting the order.'[3]

Kelsen remains faithful to the principle of origin: The identity of a legal system, as well as the membership of a law in a system, is determined solely by the facts of its creation, by its origin. But the source of unity is no longer one legislative body, it is one power-conferring norm. The basic norm replaces the sovereign, otherwise nothing has changed.

Something must be said at this stage about the content of the basic norm. Kelsen tends to succumb to the temptation to

[1] Cf. Ch. II, sect. 5 above.   [2] *GT*, p. 111; cf. *PTL*, p. 195.   [3] *Ibid.*

make every basic norm include in its content all the conclusions of his theory of norms. The temptation is natural, considering that for him basic norms are necessary norms and conditions for the understanding of the law.[1] All the conclusions of the theory of norms are necessary, and all of them are conditions for the understanding of the law. The distinction between a statement of the content of a norm and a general truth about the law is blurred, because such general truths are based on and reflected in the content of norms. That the Israeli supreme court has legislative power is not a statement of the content of any Israeli law. But it is a conclusion drawn from one section of an Israeli statute, which adopts the doctrine that inferior courts are bound by the decisions of the supreme court. Is the general truth that there is no contradiction between valid norms of one system derived in a similar way from any particular norm of the system? Obviously not. The general truth about law is equally reflected in the relations of any number of norms, and has no special relation to any one of them.

Kelsen thinks otherwise. Thus, for example, he thinks that it is the basic norm of every legal system which guarantees the internal coherence of that system. The principle of non-contradiction, he says, 'is contained in the basic norm'.[2] For similar reasons he regards every basic norm as stipulating that every norm provides for a sanction.[3] He asserts in general that every basic norm, though not identical with, nevertheless contains the definition of, law.[4]

However, following another remark made by Kelsen, our discussion from now on is based on the assumption that 'the content of a basic norm is determined by the facts through which an order is created and applied.'[5] Accordingly, the definition of law and the principle of non-contradiction are not regarded as 'contained' in basic norms.

The basic norm, Kelsen says, is formulated as follows: 'Coercive acts ought to be performed under the conditions and in the manner which the historically first constitution, and the norms created according to it, prescribe. In short: One ought to behave as the constitution prescribes.'[6] One may doubt

[1] Cf. Ch. III, sect. 3 above.   [2] *GT*, p. 406; cf. pp. 401 ff; *PTL*, p. 207.
[3] e.g. *GT*, p. 406; *PTL*, p. 50.   [4] *PTL*, p. 50.   [5] *GT*, p. 120.
[6] *PTL*, p. 201.

whether this is the best possible formulation. Its merits will be examined below. What matters for the present discussion is the intended legal effect of a basic norm: 'The ultimate hypothesis of positivism is the norm authorizing the historically first legislator. The whole function of this basic norm is to confer law-creating power on the act of the first legislator and on all the other acts based on the first act.'[1]

The concept of a basic norm is one of two concepts on which Kelsen's criterion of identity is founded. The other is the concept of a chain of validity, which is explained by the following passage:

To the question why this individual norm is valid as part of a definite legal order, the answer is: because it has been created in conformity with a criminal statute. This statute, finally, receives its validity from the constitution, since it has been established by the competent organ in the way the constitution prescribes. If we ask why the constitution is valid, perhaps we come upon an older constitution. Ultimately we reach some constitution that is the first historically and that was laid down by an individual usurper or by some kind of assembly. . . . It is postulated that one ought to behave as the individual, or the individuals, who laid down the first constitution have ordained. This is the basic norm of the legal order under consideration.[2]

A chain of validity is a set of all those norms such that (1) each of them authorizes the creation of just one of the others of the set, except at most one which does not authorize the creation of any norm; and (2) the creation of each of them is authorized by just one norm in the set, except for one norm, the creation of which is not authorized by any norm in the chain.[3] A chain of validity can be represented graphically as shown in Fig. 1. Every line represents a norm which authorizes the creation of the norm represented by the line immediately above it. The circles represent the legislative

---

[1] *GT*, p. 116.   [2] *GT*, p. 115.

[3] It is worth noting that the concept of a chain of validity is used in Kelsen's criterion of identity of a legal system. It cannot, therefore, be part of the definition of a chain of validity that only norms belonging to one system can belong to one chain of validity. This is a consequence of the definition of a chain of validity and of its use in the criterion of identity. It is not part of the definition of a validity chain, for this would presuppose an independent criterion of identity.

An individual norm.

A general norm.

A norm of the present constitution.

A norm of the first constitution.

The basic norm.

FIG. 1.

powers.[1] One person may have legislative powers derived from several norms.

Two chains of validity may have all their norms but one in common. Two such chains can be represented in one diagram:

Individual norms.

A general norm.

The constitution.

The basic norm.

FIG. 2.

Other chains of validity may differ in more than one norm. Kelsen insists, however, that: (1) There is at least one norm common to any two chains of validity which belong to the same legal system. (2) Moreover, there is one norm which is part of all the chains of validity of one system. (3) In every legal system the norm which belongs to all the chains of validity, or 'validity chains' as they will also be called, of the system, is the basic norm, which is the last norm (that is the one represented by the bottom line) of every chain of validity.

On the basis of these points all the validity chains of one

[1] Lines and circles, norms and legislative powers, alike will be called 'links' in the chain.

system, that is the complete legal system, can be represented in one diagram:

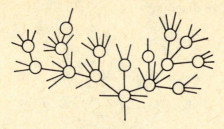

FIG. 3.

This tree diagram[1] of a legal system is, of course, much simplified. Legal systems contain a much greater number of laws and legislative authorities. The tree diagram demonstrates how two ideas—that of validity chains and that of a basic norm—are combined by Kelsen to solve the problems of identity and of membership within the bounds of the principle of origin.

The concept of validity chains, though first used systematically to this purpose by Kelsen, is not peculiar to his theory. It can be applied, for example, to Austin's theory. This was first done by Bryce in his modified Austinian theory. Bryce wrote:

A householder in a municipality is asked to pay a paving rate. He inquires why he should pay it, and is referred to the resolution of the Town Council imposing it. He then asks what authority the council has to levy the rate, and is referred to a section of the Act of Parliament whence the Council derives its powers. If he pushes curiosity further, and inquires what right Parliament has to confer these powers, the rate collector can only answer that everybody knows that in England Parliament makes the law, and that by the law no other authority can override or in any way interfere with any expression of the will of Parliament. Parliament is supreme above all other authorities, or in other words, Parliament is Sovereign.[2]

[1] Some of the commentators on Kelsen's theory use the pyramid as a model of legal systems. I prefer the tree diagram, for it makes clear the hierarchical organization of the law, which is Kelsen's main object in using the pyramid model, while avoiding some undesirable implications of the use of the pyramid model. The tree diagram is free from the implication that one norm cannot authorize the creation of both general and individual norms, or that one authority cannot legislate both constitutional and individual norms. Perhaps the most important undesirable implication of the use of the pyramid model is that there is the same number of layers in the pyramid of every legal system.

[2] *Studies in Jurisprudence*, vol. ii, p. 52.

By adapting this procedure to Austin's original theory it becomes possible to represent the Austinian picture of a legal system by a tree diagram:

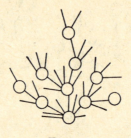

FIG. 4.

Thus represented, Austin's solution to the problem of identity is seen to rest on the combination of two concepts: validity chains and sovereignty. Kelsen accepts the first, and thereby also the principle of origin, and rejects the second, substituting his own concept of a basic norm. The focal point, the uniting link, is not one legislator but one law.

Austin's attempt to solve the problem of identity failed because of the inadequacies of the concept of a sovereign. In the next section the question is raised whether Kelsen's substitute, the concept of a basic norm, is adequate to the role assigned to it in Kelsen's criterion of identity. Later on, in section 4, the contribution of the concept of chains of validity to the solution of the identity problem is subjected to close scrutiny.

V.3: THE CRITERION OF IDENTITY—THE ROLE OF THE BASIC NORM

The basic norm is assigned a double role, it provides the answer to two separate questions: 'What is it that makes a system out of a multitude of norms? When does a norm belong to a certain system of norms . . . ? This question is in close connection with the question as to the reason of validity of a norm.'[1] The second of these roles, the basic norm as the ultimate reason for the validity of other legal norms, has been touched

[1] *GT*, p. 110. Cf. *PTL*, p. 193.

upon in Chapter III above, and will be further discussed in the next chapter. This section is concerned only with the function of the basic norm in the solution of the problems of identity and of membership.

Kelsen repeatedly asserts that the only function of a basic norm is to authorize the creation of the first constitution. It may be thought, therefore, that the first constitution, as well as the basic norm, must be part of every chain of validity of every norm in a legal system. This would mean that even if there are no basic norms there is no difficulty in establishing the identity of legal systems. A legal system, instead of being defined as a basic norm and all the norms deriving their validity from it, will be defined as a first constitution and all the norms deriving their validity from it.

The fallacy in this argument is that the first constitution is not necessarily one norm; it may be, and often is, a set of norms which came into force by the exercise of one legislative power, for example, by one act of legislation. A first constitution may include several norms, each conferring different legislative powers on different bodies. For example, one norm of the first constitution may determine the legislative power of the federal parliament, while another norm in the constitution determines the powers of the state parliaments. Furthermore, the first constitution may contain ordinary norms, namely norms which do not confer legislative powers but impose duties and provide sanctions to back them.

Kelsen's criterion of identity presupposes that there is one norm which belongs to the chain of validity of every norm in a legal system. The first constitution may contain several norms, some belonging to certain chains of validity, others belonging to other chains. The basic norm is the only norm belonging to every chain of validity, and it is therefore essential to the success of Kelsen's criterion of identity.[1]

The criteria of identity and membership are intended to provide a method by which it is possible to find out for any given norm whether or not it belongs to a given legal system, and this may be used to establish the total membership, i.e.

---

[1] It is essential, of course, only if one wishes, as Kelsen does, to base the criterion of identity on a norm which unites the system by belonging to every chain of validity of every norm in the system. Cf. the next section for other possibilities.

the identity, of the system. According to Kelsen, the question whether a certain norm, N_1, belongs to a certain system is settled by finding out whether the system contains a norm authorizing the creation of N_1. If it does—N_1 belongs to that system, if not—it does not.

Let us suppose that it has been established that no derivative norm authorizes the creation of N_1. It follows that either N_1 is authorized by the basic norm or it does not belong to that system. How is one to discover the content of the basic norm? Kelsen's answer, as has already been mentioned, is: ' . . . the content of a basic norm is determined by the facts through which an order is created and applied',[1] which means in effect that once one knows which norms belong to a legal order, and only then, one is in a position to discover by which acts they were created, and thus to discover the content of the basic norm of the system. It is not possible to reverse the process and discover which norm belongs to the system by reference to the basic norm.

The same point can be proved by another argument: If N_1 belongs to a given legal system, then either it authorizes the creation of all the other norms of the system, i.e. it is the whole of the first constitution of the system, or it has been created by the exercise of the same legislative powers by the exercise of which the first constitution has been created, in which case it is part of that first constitution. For if N_1 authorizes the creation of the rest of the system, then any basic norm authorizing it authorizes the rest of the system. Similarly, if N_1 has been created by the exercise of the powers by which the first constitution has been created, then any basic norm conferring these powers unites N_1 and the first constitution (with all the norms authorized by it) in one legal system (N_1 thereby becomes part of the first constitution). If, on the other hand, none of these conditions are fulfilled, then no one basic norm can authorize both N_1 and the rest of the system. Nothing more can be learnt about the membership of N_1 in the given system from Kelsen's theory, yet it is clear that any of these conditions can be fulfilled even if N_1 does not belong to the given system.

Example I. Suppose that a country, A, which was hitherto ruled by another country, B, has gained its independence.

[1] *GT*, p. 120.

Suppose further that independence was assumed by a declaration and a new constitution adopted by an assembly of notables, and that on the basis of that constitution elections were held and further laws were enacted. There is a general consensus of both lay and professional opinion in A that they are living under a legal system among the norms of which the norms of the new constitution were the first to be enacted. The fact that in country B a law, N_2, was passed on the basis of their first constitution, N_1, prior to A's independence, which conferred unlimited legislative powers in all matters concerning the population of A on the above-mentioned assembly of notables, is regarded as having a great political but no legal significance for A. It is widely assumed in A, although the matter has not been put before the courts, that N_1 and N_2 are not a part of the legal system of A. This opinion is completely justified, even though N_1 does authorize all the norms of the legal system of A, and thus fulfils the first of the two alternative conditions deduced above from Kelsen's theory.

Example II. Suppose, on the other hand, that there has been no peaceful transfer of powers from the government of B to the independent state in A, and that B, after a lengthy struggle against the Liberation Movement in A, has unilaterally relinquished its rule over A. A slight confusion results when, apart from the laws issued by the central committee of the Liberation Movement, the leader of a splinter group, called the Revolutionary Liberation Movement, attempts to seize absolute power and issues several purported laws, and among them N_2 is the only one which does not conflict with any laws enacted by the central committee. After two days things settle, and the leader of the Revolutionary Liberation Movement goes into voluntary exile, abandoning his attempt to seize power. The status of his purported laws has not been decided by the courts, but there is no doubt that they, and N_2 among them, are not part of the legal system of A. Nevertheless, many purported basic norms can be suggested which authorize both N_2 and all the laws enacted by the 'lawful authorities'. For example: 'Everybody ought to behave in the way prescribed by the leadership of any of the liberation movements.' Therefore N_2 fulfils the second of the alternative conditions for membership derived above from Kelsen's criterion of membership.

The two examples prove that the basic norm cannot play the role assigned to it by Kelsen's criteria of membership and identity, and, hence, that his criteria fail to fulfil their function. The concept of a basic norm should determine where every validity chain ends and what is its scope, but it fails to do so. In fact it does not contribute anything to the criteria of identity and membership.

What, then, is the meaning of Kelsen's phrase to the effect that basic norms are the foundation of the unity of legal orders? It may help to recall the first part of the quotation with which the present section began. In it Kelsen posed two questions: 'what is it that makes a system out of a multitude of norms? When does a norm belong to a certain system of norms?' The second question is the problem of membership and of identity. It is the question of the criterion for determining which are the norms that constitute this or any other legal system. The first question is completely different. It is the question of the ordering principle of legal systems. It presupposes that the problem of identity has been solved, and that the composition of the system is known; it then proceeds to ask: Given that these are the norms of the system, how can they be ordered into a systematic whole? This is, in fact, a problem very similar to the problem of the structure of the system (the only difference is that Kelsen does not confine his question to the internal structure of the system).

The above arguments show that basic norms have no bearing on the problem of identity. That Kelsen has been misled into believing that the basic norm has relevance to the problem of identity is probably due, at least partly, to his failure to distinguish between the problem of the discovery of the norms which belong to a system and the problem of their arrangement.

As a matter of fact, the basic norm has, contrary to Kelsen's most firm belief, no real importance for the arrangement of the norms of a legal system. For the arrangement and structure of a legal system, according to Kelsen, is represented by the tree diagram. The ordering principle of the tree diagram and the key to the structure of a legal system is the concept of a chain of validity. The tree diagram can exist even if the basic norm is omitted from it. It will, in that case, become an Austinian tree diagram, with a 'basic (legislative) power' instead of a basic norm. The structure and arrangement of the legal system, its unity, remain virtually unaffected by the elimination of the basic norm.

V.4: THE CRITERION OF IDENTITY—THE CHAIN OF VALIDITY

In the previous section it has been argued that the basic norm has no relevance whatsoever to the criterion of identity (and to the doctrine of structure). Of course, Kelsen claims that the basic norm is important for reasons which have nothing to do with the identity and structure of legal systems, reasons derived from his general theory of norms. His arguments will be critically examined in the next chapter. For the rest of this section, however, the basic norm will be completely disregarded, and the success of a criterion of identity, similar to Kelsen's but based solely on the concept of chains of validity, will be examined.

If we eliminate the basic norm from a Kelsenite tree diagram it is transformed into an Austin-type tree diagram; instead of resting on a basic norm the tree comes to rest on a basic (legislative) power. The basic power is the power authorizing the first constitution. The criterion of identity becomes: A legal system consists of the first constitution and all the laws created, directly or indirectly, by the exercise of powers conferred by the first constitution. A law belongs to a given system if, and only if, it is either part of the first constitution or has been enacted by the exercise of powers directly or indirectly conferred by it.

A first constitution can be defined as follows: A law belongs to a first constitution if, and only if, its creation was not authorized by any other law. Several laws belong to the same first constitution if, and only if, each of them belongs to a first constitution and all of them were created by the exercise of the same legislative power.

This solution of the problem of identity resembles Austin's solution in that it acknowledges the existence of a legislator who has legislative powers which were not conferred by law. Like Austin's sovereignty, the basic authority can be said to be unlimitable, in the sense that the validity of laws created by its exercise is determined not by reference to any norm-creating norm but by their efficacy. The basic authority is the legal power to enact every law which will become the foundation of an efficacious legal system.

The difference between Austin's criterion and this modified version of Kelsen's criterion is a result of the fundamental difference between Austin's sovereignty and the basic power. A most disturbing feature of Austin's theory is his insistence on the *continuous* existence of the sovereign. A legal system exists only so long as there is an authority which has illimitable legislative powers which were not conferred by law. Kelsen's basic power, on the other hand, need not be ever-present. A legal system continues to exist even after the holder or holders of its basic power ceased to exist (e.g. the first absolute monarch died or the constitutive assembly has been disbanded).

Kelsen expresses himself on occasions as if the first constitution is always created by one legislative act, as if it comes into being on one occasion. The considerations advanced in the previous sections have demonstrated that this is not always the case. A constitutional assembly may promulgate the first constitution in parts on several occasions, each part coming into force when promulgated. Nor need the basic power be entrusted to the hands of one body only. There may be two constitutional assemblies acting simultaneously or in succession (assuming, of course, that there are settled ways to deal with possible conflicts of laws arising from their activities). But even though the continuous presence of a legislator whose authority is not derived from any law is possible, according to the modified version of Kelsen's doctrine, it is not necessary.

Austin's tree diagrams are diagrams of momentary legal systems. The fact that all the tree diagrams of all the momentary systems belonging to one system have the same sovereign at their base means that the sovereign exists so long as the system exists. A modified Kelsenian tree diagram, though similar to the Austinian diagram in having a power (and not a norm) at its base, has a different meaning. It represents not a momentary legal system but a continuous legal system (from its foundation up to a certain specified time). The basic power represented in it must have existed, but need exist no more. The hierarchy of legislative powers in Kelsen's theory is not, like Austin's hierarchy, a vertical momentary hierarchy, it is a horizontal hierarchy stretched over a period of time.

The difference between the sovereignty and the basic power[1] is Kelsen's main improvement upon Austin's criterion of identity. But it has been achieved at a very high price. The improvement is made possible by positing obedience to the laws, instead of obedience to the sovereign, as a condition for the existence of a legal system. This change is desirable on other grounds as well, but it has one unfortunate by-product. It increases the importance of the concept of chains of validity to the criterion of identity.

In Austin's theory a common link in their chains of validity is a necessary but not a sufficient condition for two laws to belong to one system. That N_1 and N_2 have a common link is not sufficient proof that they belong to the same system. A further necessary condition is that no sovereign power is a link in their chain of validity such that it is below one of them but not below the other. In other words, two laws belong to the same system only if they were enacted, directly or indirectly, by the same sovereign.

The value of this condition is made clear by considering again the first of the two examples considered in the previous section, the example of the peaceful transfer of powers. The norm N_3 of the new legal system of A and the norm of the legal system of B conferring power on the assembly of notables (designated as N_2) have, as has been explained, links common to their chains of validity. The two chains are represented by the tree diagram in Fig. 5.

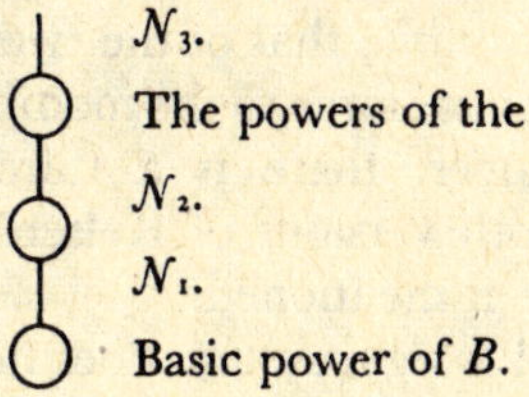

N_3.
The powers of the assembly of notables.
N_2.
N_1.
Basic power of B.

FIG. 5.

---

[1] The concept of a basic power is not my innovation. It is implied by Kelsen's theory, though he assigns, not to it, but to the concept of a basic norm, the key role in his criteria of identity and membership.

They do not belong to the same system, according to Austin, because the sovereign of A (the assembly of notables) enacted N_3 but not N_2.

According to the modified version of Kelsen's criterion of identity a basic power is recognized not by being habitually obeyed but by not being created by any law. But there is a law, namely N_2, conferring upon the assembly of notables all the legislative powers it has. Therefore, according to Kelsen, its legislative power is not a basic power, and consequently N_1, N_2, and N_3 appear by the modified version of Kelsen's criterion of identity to belong to the same system.

This conclusion can be avoided only by abandoning the principle of origin and regarding N_3 as the first constitution not because it has been enacted by the exercise of a basic power but because it is recognized as such by the courts. Considerations of this nature will be examined in another chapter. Kelsen accepts the principle of origin, and therefore, in order to avoid the shortcomings of Austin's theory, he is compelled to regard having a common link in the chains of validity both a necessary and a sufficient condition for membership of two laws in the same system, thereby exposing his theory to the above-mentioned criticism.

This criticism is practically identical with the first of the points made in the previous section against Kelsen's original criterion of identity. Basing the criterion of identity on a basic power instead of on a basic norm does not help to avoid the weaknesses of the criterion, because they are inherent in the principle of origin itself.

The second point of criticism, made in the previous section with the help of the second example, that of the two liberation movements, also applies with equal force to the modified version of Kelsen's doctrine.[1] Moreover, there is a third point of criticism, which applies to both versions of Kelsen's criterion of identity and has not yet been mentioned.

The continuous existence of a legal system does not depend, according to Kelsen, on the continued presence of the first sovereign. But it depends on the possibility of tracing back the

[1] Austin's criterion of identity would have emerged unscathed from this problem too, had it been based on an adequate concept of the individuation of sovereign power.

reason for the validity of every law to the first constitution. This view is erroneous. A legal system in which precedent does not create law can change gradually into a system in which it does create law. There is no need to suppose that the power to legislate by making precedents was conferred upon the courts by the first constitution or by any other law. Indeed, the courts themselves may acknowledge that they possess this power only many years after they have acquired it. In such a case there is no reason to suppose that one legal system ceased to exist and a new system was created. Nor is it at all clear what can count as the basic norm or the basic power of the 'new system'. Similarly, in states in which parliament is limited by a constitution it may happen that it will enact an unconstitutional law that will be accepted as law by the population and the government alike, and will be enforced by all the courts. If such a law has little constitutional importance (e.g. if it regulates the manufacture of matches), then there is no reason to think either that it is not a law at all or that by legislating it the old legal system ceased to exist and a new legal system was created. To conclude, it is impossible to explain the conditions of continuous existence of a legal system on the basis of the principle of origin alone—other considerations must be taken into account.

v.5: THE STRUCTURE OF A LEGAL SYSTEM

The account hitherto given of Kelsen's theory attributes to him two incompatible views: first, that every norm imposes a duty by permitting the application of a sanction; and second, that some norms do not impose duties but confer legislative powers. Kelsen acknowledges that there is a difficulty here:

Analytical jurisprudence, as presented by Austin, regards law as a system of rules complete and ready for application, without regard to the process of their creation. It is a static theory of the law. The Pure Theory of Law recognizes that a study of the statics of law must be supplemented by a study of its dynamics, the process of its creation. This necessity exists because the law . . . regulates its own creation.[1]

Kelsen's 'study of the statics of law' affirms that every norm imposes a duty by stipulating a sanction. He is aware, however,

[1] *WJ*, pp. 278–9.

of a necessity to supplement this view and reconcile it with
another, allowing for norms conferring legislative powers.

Kelsen attempts to effect this reconciliation in the following
passage:

The norms of the constitution which regulate the creation of the
general norms to be applied by the courts and other law-applying
organs are thus *not independent complete* norms. They are *intrinsic parts*
of all the legal norms which the courts and the other organs have to
apply. On this ground constitutional law cannot be cited as an
example of legal norms which do not stipulate any sanctions. The
norms of the material constitution *are laws only in their organic connection* with those sanction stipulating norms which are created on
their basis. What, from *a dynamic point of view*, is the creation of a
general norm determined by *a higher norm*, the constitution, *becomes
in a static presentation* of law one of the conditions to which the sanction
is attached as consequence in the general norm (which, from the
dynamic point of view, is the lower norm in relation to the constitution). *In a static presentation of law, the higher norms of the constitution
are, as it were, projected as parts into the lower norms.*[1]

This must be regarded as Kelsen's general explanation of
norms which confer legislative powers without stipulating
sanctions. It will be explained in three stages, each adding to
the previous one and modifying it:

A. *Two Alternative Principles of Individuation*

In several places Kelsen explains his concepts of dynamic
and static points of view,[2] but his explanations add little to what
is said in the passage quoted above. A legal system, Kelsen
seems to say, i.e. the totality of the legal material belonging to
it, can be examined from two points of view. These points of
view differ from each other by the way in which they arrange
and divide the legal material; that is to say, the two points of
view are two different principles of individuation. The static
principle of individuation is the one explained in Chapter IV,
section 2 above. According to it every law is a norm imposing a
duty by stipulating a sanction. The dynamic principle of
individuation is less clear; the only thing certain is that it
allows for norms which confer legislative powers as well as
norms which impose duties and stipulate sanctions.

[1] *GT*, pp. 143–4. My italics.   [2] e.g. *PTL*, p. 70.

Just as the static principle of individuation is based on the concept of a coercive sanction, so the dynamic principle of individuation is based on the concept of a legislative power. Unfortunately Kelsen's only explanation of legislative powers is given on the basis of the static principle of individuation and cannot serve as a basis for a different and independent principle. In the absence of an independent definition of legislative power, Kelsen's dynamic point of view never amounts to more than a programme for a dynamic principle of individuation. The programme itself is, however, quite clear and Kelsen himself knows that it involves a new criterion of 'a law': 'If one looks upon the legal order from the dynamic point of view . . . it seems possible to define the concept of law in a way quite different from that in which we have tried to define it in this theory. It seems especially possible to ignore the element of coercion in defining the concept of law.'[1]

B. *The Possibility of Projecting One Classification onto the Other*

As the dynamic and static principles of individuation are two ways of arranging and dividing the same legal system, it should be possible to project or map one division onto the other, because a one–many relation must exist between all the elements in any of the divisions and some of the elements of the other division. As Kelsen says: 'In a static presentation of law, the higher norms of the constitution are as it were projected as parts into the lower norms.'[2] This means that a static norm, like 'If the constitution authorizes parliament to legislate criminal laws, and if parliament stipulates a sanction for theft, then if a person commits theft he ought to be punished', is projected onto two dynamic norms: 'Parliament is authorized to legislate criminal laws', 'The officials are authorized to apply sanction to thieves.' Therefore every static law is projected in this way onto several dynamic laws. Reversing the process, and trying to project the dynamic arrangement onto the static, is, of course, also possible. One dynamic norm will be projected onto several static norms. For example, the dynamic law, 'Parliament is authorized to enact criminal laws', is projected onto the static law against theft mentioned above, as well as onto the criminal law against arson: 'If parliament is

[1] *GT*, p. 122.   [2] *GT*, p. 144.

authorized to legislate criminal laws, and if parliament stipulates the application of a sanction against people who commit arson, then if a person commits arson the sanction ought to be applied against him.

Legislative powers when represented in a static presentation of the law are competence or capacities, i.e. conditions for sanctions.[1] But Kelsen provides no criteria to distinguish competence to legislate from other types of competence that are neither delict nor claim rights. Hence he fails to provide even a 'static' definition of legislative powers.

C. *The Primacy of the Static Principle*

The explanation given above demonstrates the technique of projecting static norms onto dynamic norms, and vice versa. It does not prove that the projection can always be made. In fact it is not always possible to find parts of static norms corresponding to dynamic norms. If a norm confers legislative powers, and if no use has been made of these powers, that is if no norm has been created by the exercise of these powers, then it has no counterpart in a static representation of the law. Legislative powers become, according to the static principle of individuation, conditions for the application of sanctions stipulated by the use of these powers. If no sanction has been stipulated, then the legislative powers do not exist, so far as the static principle is concerned.

This means that the dynamic and static principles of individuation apply to different legal material. The static principle regards a statute conferring legislative powers as part of the legal material only after at least one sanction has been stipulated by the use of that power. Kelsen resolves this discrepancy between the two principles by stipulating that a purported dynamic norm is a legal norm only if it can be projected onto a static representation of the law: 'The norms of the material constitution are law only in their organic connection with those sanction-stipulating norms which are created on their basis.'[2]

This stipulation indicates the primacy of the static principle of individuation. Kelsen's general theory of norms compels

---

[1] *GT*, p. 90. In *PTL*, p. 146, Kelsen modified his definition to include the application of sanction as a competence.

[2] *GT*, p. 144.

him to an even more extreme position. It is the very foundation of his theory of the individuation of laws that every law is a norm. According to his general theory of norms, all norms are of one mould—they all direct human behaviour by imposing duties backed by sanctions. Legal norms are further distinguished by stipulating coercive sanctions. Hence not 'everything which has been created according to this procedure is law in the sense of a legal norm. It is a legal norm only if it purports to regulate human behaviour . . . by providing an act of coercion as sanction.'[1]

Dynamic norms are, therefore, not norms at all. The unavoidable conclusion is that the dynamic point of view does not, after all, provide an alternative principle of individuation of laws, not even a subordinate one. It is a study of the division of static norms into parts which are neither norms nor laws.[2]

Tree diagrams present legal systems from a dynamic point of view. Many of the lines represent purported norms which do not provide for sanctions. Hence, according to Kelsen's doctrine as here explained, they are not norms but only parts of norms. Tree diagrams are primarily diagrams of segments of norms. The relations between lines in a tree diagram are not relations between norms but between segments of norms. It follows that every chain of validity represents only one norm. The lines representing a chain of validity correspond to parts of the norm represented by the chain of validity as a whole. Tree diagrams represent two kinds of relations: genetic relations, represented by relations between lines which belong to the same chain of validity; and relations of partial identity between different chains of validity.

Kelsen's picture of the structure of a legal system is of a

---

[1] *GT*, p. 123.

[2] In *The Pure Theory of Law* Kelsen uses extensively the concept of dependent norms (cf. pp. 51, 54 ff.), which seems to designate any entity described by a normative statement that is part of some complete description of a legal system, but not of a proper description of it, i.e. which does not describe one complete norm. Dynamic norms are one kind of dependent norms. Though Kelsen does not explicitly say that they are parts of static norms, he repeats all the arguments that make this conclusion unavoidable. There is no need to introduce a new class of entities—dependent norms. Normative statements, like, for example, that *x* has legislative powers, can be true and can be part of a complete description of the legal system. But, according to Kelsen's theory, they do not describe one complete law. They describe part of the content of many laws.

network of lines related by genetic relations. But genetic relations exist only between parts of one chain of validity, i.e. between segments of one and the same law. Kelsen replaces the theory of the structure of a legal system by a theory of the structure of single norms. Relations between segments of laws occupy the place designed for relations between laws.

Every norm is a self-contained and independent entity, standing in no necessary relation to any other norm. Hence it follows for Kelsen that the principle of independence of laws is accepted and dictates the absence of any necessary internal structure to legal systems.

The basic norm, in so far as this concept is acceptable, is a dynamic norm. It does not stipulate a sanction[1] and therefore it must be regarded as a part of static norms. The basic norm 'The so and so has power to make the first constitution' becomes 'If (according to the basic norm) the so and so has power to make the first constitution . . . then a sanction ought to be applied.'

This basic segment is part of the content of all the norms of one system. Thus, if the basic norm is accepted, there is one common relation between norms—all the norms of one system are partly identical, they all have one segment in common.

v.6: ON INDEPENDENT NORMS

The discussion of the status of the dynamic point of view, as well as the comparison between Bentham's and Kelsen's principles of individuation,[2] illustrates the interdependence of the principle of individuation and the structure of legal systems. By preferring the static to the dynamic principle of individuation Kelsen excludes the possibility of an internal structure based on genetic relations. By rejecting Bentham's principle he excludes the possibility of punitive internal relations.[3]

The most decisive reason for preferring a principle of individuation which results in a rich variety of internal relations to a principle which excludes the possibility of internal relations is that only such a principle can work. Much of this section is

[1] For the possibility of a different interpretation of 'a basic norm' see the next section.
[2] See Ch. IV, sect. 3 above.
[3] i.e. the relation between a law and the corresponding punitive law. Cf. Ch. I, sect. 4 above.

concerned with proving just why Kelsen's principle of individuation and other similar principles do not and cannot work, why they cannot be the basis of a complete and correct description of the law. But Kelsen's and similar principles of individuation must be rejected on other grounds as well.

First, Kelsen's principle individuates laws which are very different from the ordinary image of laws. Every law is a permission, every law is addressed to officials, every law is a combination of constitutional and procedural as well as substantive law.[1] Such a concept of a law has very little relation to the concept of a law used by both the lay and the professional public.

It may be claimed that explaining the law and explaining the 'common-sense' concept of law are two completely different things. But I doubt whether the two can be completely separated. An adequate explanation of law is the best starting-point for the explanation of the common-sense conception of law. The common-sense conception is made clear by explaining its deviation from the theoretical concept. This approach makes it a desideratum of the theoretical concept of a law that it approximate to the common-sense concept.

Second, in deciding on a principle of individuation two conflicting aims should be borne in mind and a proper balance be struck between them. The first is to define small and manageable units of law, units which could be discovered by reference to a small and easily identifiable portion of the legal material. The other aim is to define units which are relatively self-contained and self-explanatory so that each contains a significant part of the law. Naturally, the more is 'put' into one law the more self-contained and self-explanatory it is. At the same time it gets more complicated and more difficult to discover.

Kelsen's principle of individuation pays no heed to the need of relative simplicity. It guarantees the greatest degree of self-sufficiency: everything relevant to the existence and application of a law is contained in it (the full specification of

---

[1] Moreover, every law creating an offence or a civil wrong against property contains large parts of property law, corporation law, etc. Kelsen's approach makes for much repetition: many laws contain the same constitutional arrangements, the same parts of property law and of procedural law, as their parts. This repetition is an additional reason for rejecting Kelsen's principle of individuation; cf. Ch. VI below.

the conditions under which a duty is acquired, the full specification of the procedure through which it is enforced, and the law authorizing the enactment of the rest, are all parts of one norm). This makes, of course, for complex norms. To find out the content of any one norm the whole of the legal material has to be scrutinized. Such norms have the further oddity that there is no occasion to refer to a complete norm. Whatever the purpose for which one may refer to the law, one is almost always interested in some greater or smaller part of a Kelsenite norm, and only very rarely in a norm as a whole. This is a clear indication that the complexity of Kelsenite norms serves no useful purpose, at least none of the purposes which should determine the division and individuation of laws.

These quantitative considerations are obviously not the only ones determining the principle of individuation. The principle must provide a rational classification and division of legal systems. But the quantitative considerations do a great deal to explain why Kelsenite laws differ from the common-sense view of laws and why the common-sense view has much to recommend it.

It might be thought that there is a good chance of overcoming these objections by identifying a law not with a norm, as Kelsen does, but with a part of a norm. It is difficult to assess fully the advantages of such a move, because Kelsen says relatively little about the parts of norms and their relations, and especially because there is no clear indication of what should count as 'a part' of a norm. It is clear, however, that the move must ultimately fail, for its success depends on the assumption that Kelsen's principle of individuation does allow for a complete, even though not a proper, description of legal systems. Three different considerations prove this assumption to be mistaken.

It has already been pointed out that, according to Kelsen, there are no laws conferring legislative powers before some use has been made of the powers they confer.[1] This is one phenomenon, and there are many similar; all of them prove that Kelsen does not explain properly the concept of legislative powers. For the same reasons a law conferring legislative powers ceases to exist when all the laws created up to date on its basis

[1] Ch. V, sect. 5 above.

cease to exist, even though the legislative authority still has the power to make new laws.

Another class which Kelsen is forced to disregard completely consists of laws repealing laws that confer legislative powers. These, like other repealing laws, are not represented in a systematic exposition of the content of a momentary legal system, but they have their effects by eliminating the repealed law from the list of valid laws. Not so, according to Kelsen's theory. Imagine that a special committee, exercising powers conferred upon it by the town council in a by-law, has ordered tenants of council flats to fix a list of occupants, with their names and flat numbers, in the entrance hall of their house, and has stipulated that failure to do so will make offenders liable to a fine of £5. Suppose further that the by-law authorizing the committee's order has been repealed, but that the order is still valid. According to Kelsen the by-law was one of the conditions for the fine. Has it ceased to be such a condition? Omitting the by-law from the conditions for the fine makes it necessary to omit also the act of parliament which authorized the creation of the by-law, and with it disappear the constitutional laws authorizing the act of parliament, creating the impression that these laws have also been repealed. If, on the other hand, the cancelled by-law is still regarded as a condition for the fine (as indeed it must be: Kelsen's formulation says only ' . . . if the council has decided that . . . ', and it has; the later cancellation alters nothing), then the repealing law has no visible effect. In his representation of the law Kelsen simply disregards it.

All such anomalies flow from Kelsen's failure to do justice to laws conferring legislative powers. By representing them as conditions for sanctions enacted on their basis, Kelsen assumes that their effect is merely to establish the validity of laws already in existence. He overlooks the fact that they confer legislative powers which have not yet been exhausted, that new laws can yet be created on their basis. But this forward-looking aspect of these laws is their real legal meaning: by repealing a law conferring legislative powers the laws which have already been created on its basis are unaffected; the only change is that it cannot be used for creating new laws.

Kelsen is attempting to represent each norm as regulating

its own creation. This is bound to lead to even more paradoxical consequences. 'If the parliament has decided that thieves shall be punished and if the competent court has ascertained that a certain individual has stolen, then . . . '[1]: this is Kelsen's example of the way constitutional laws are incorporated into norms. The quoted statement, however, describes only the constitutional law, or part of it. If it is the law that parliament has the power to make criminal laws, then it follows that if parliament has decided that thieves shall be punished and if the competent court has ascertained that a certain individual has stolen, then . . . ; just as it follows that if parliament has decided that people over 50 years old who have never committed theft shall be punished, then. . . . If the basic norm is added to every norm, each norm is made to begin with the clause 'If the so and so have made the first constitution to the effect that . . . '. Every such law is logically entailed by the basic norm itself, and adds nothing to it. Instead of incorporating constitutional laws into ordinary norms Kelsen has inadvertently developed a description of law which asserts the existence of part of the basic norm, or of part of the first constitution, only, and overlooks all the rest of the law. Kelsen overlooked the fact that in order to assert the existence of a criminal law against theft it is not enough to say 'If parliament has decided that thieves shall be punished . . . '; it is necessary to state that parliament has indeed decided that thieves shall be punished. . . . But when formulated in this way the Kelsenite norm is seen to be what it really is—not one norm but a group of distinct norms: The so and so have power to make the (first) constitution; they made a law that parliament has power to enact criminal laws; (parliament made a law that) thieves should be punished, etc. Kelsen's method of describing the law completely defeats its own purpose.

Finally, it should be noted that Kelsen does not give his own principle the most rigorous interpretation. His doctrine that every norm stipulates a sanction has been interpreted above as meaning that every norm permits the application of a sanction. According to this interpretation, an example for a norm would be: If parliament has decided that thieves shall be punished and if *A* has been found guilty of theft and if the court has decided that he ought to serve a period not exceeding

[1] *GT*, p. 143.

five years in prison, then the responsible policeman ought to put him in jail for that period.

Kelsen, however, adopts a looser interpretation of 'stipulates a sanction' and takes it to mean either 'permits the application of a sanction' or 'permits to permit the application of a sanction'. He, therefore, allows norms like the following: If parliament has decided that thieves shall be punished and if A has been found guilty of theft, then the court ought to decide that he ought to serve a period not exceeding five years in prison. The permission given in such a norm to the court is not to apply a sanction itself but to issue a permission to the police to apply the sanction.

One may well wonder why, if Kelsen allows norms removed one step from the application of a sanction (a permission for a permission to apply a sanction), he does not allow norms removed two or any number of steps from the application of a sanction (a permission for a permission for a permission to apply a sanction, etc.). Had he done so he could have regarded every law conferring legislative powers, and not only laws authorizing the courts to make laws permitting the application of sanctions, as independent norms. The constitutional law authorizing parliament to make criminal laws can be regarded as a permission to parliament to permit the courts to permit the police to apply sanctions.

This interpretation of constitutional laws can be applied also to basic norms. Indeed Kelsen's formulation of the basic norm, 'Coercive acts ought to be performed under the conditions and in the manner which the historically first constitution . . . prescribes',[1] supports this approach. It can be interpreted to mean that the authors of the first constitution are permitted to permit the application of sanctions and to permit to permit the application of sanctions, etc.

Kelsen's theory of constitutional law is, however, just one of many signs that he did not realize that he was following a loose interpretation of 'to provide for a sanction'. He declares that the standard form of a law is 'if such and such conditions are fulfilled, then such and such a sanction shall follow.'[2] And he regards such a norm as obeyed (or applied) only if a sanction is executed.[3] His discussion of the structure and content of

[1] *PTL*, p. 201.   [2] *GT*, p. 45.   [3] *GT*, p. 61.

laws and of the existence of legal systems is completely based on this position, which is compatible only with the strict interpretation of 'providing for a sanction'.

Needless to say, even if Kelsen's theory were to be rewritten to suit the loose interpretation, thus admitting the existence of genetic relations between laws, it would avoid only a few of the objections raised in this and the previous section. All the laws even of this improved theory would still be (1) directed only to officials; (2) granting permissions and only indirectly imposing duties; (3) too complex to identify and to handle; and (4) repetitive, in that large parts of family law, property law, company law, etc. are parts of a great many laws (of all the laws of contract and all the laws of torts, for example).

VI

LEGAL SYSTEMS AS SYSTEMS OF NORMS

Hitherto this study has been concerned almost exclusively with two objectives: the clarification and explanation of the major problems of the theory of legal system, and the critical exposition of some important attempts made by previous theorists to solve these problems. It seems that the study of the theory of legal system is still in its infancy, because the nature of the problems involved in it has not been fully understood, nor has their importance been clearly apprehended. For this reason our study up to this point has been largely directed to exposition and criticism, but from this chapter onward its principal concern will be to suggest new and more promising approaches. This is, however, a change only of emphasis, for the constructive suggestions involve reference to previous theories. They are largely presented as modifications and (it is hoped) improvements on the imperative theory of norms which is to be found in Kelsen's work. These modifications utilize some of the ideas to be found in other writers, including Bentham and Hart.

Hence, in the first section of this chapter we shall attempt to extract from Kelsen's work a coherent imperative theory of norms, and in the second section to disentangle it from elements in his theory which we consider unsatisfactory and, indeed, unnecessary; in particular from his doctrine of a non-positive basic norm. In the third section we shall state general requirements that every set of adequate principles of individuation must satisfy, as a preliminary to an account, in the fourth and fifth sections, of two important types of laws and other modifications in the imperative theory of norms needed to permit their recognition as distinct types of legal norms. In the next chapter several types of laws which are not norms will be discussed.

In our discussion it will be made clear that the nature of each type of law can be understood only by understanding the internal relations of laws of each type to other laws. The general concern of this chapter, and also of the next, is, therefore, the problem of the structure of legal systems. Chapter VIII deals with the problem of identity, and in Chapter IX some observations are made concerning the criteria for existence of a legal system.

VI.1: IMPERATIVE NORMS

In the discussion of Kelsen's concept of a norm we shall neglect his theory that legal norms are fundamentally permissions. Laws are, therefore, regarded as directly imposing duties on the law subjects to perform the law acts, i.e. the norm acts of legal norms, and not, as Kelsen regards them, as directly granting permissions and only indirectly imposing duties.

'The specific meaning of a norm is expressed by the concept of "ought". A norm implies that an individual ought to behave in a certain manner.'[1] But the 'ought', says Kelsen, cannot be fully explained,[2] which seems to mean that his concept of a norm cannot be fully explained. As a matter of fact, Kelsen does offer a full explanation of his concept of a norm. This explanation has, however, to be assembled from many different and sometimes conflicting passages.[3] The interpretation here offered is an attempt to arrive at a coherent understanding of the basic ideas underlying Kelsen's conception, and of the nature of some of the problems with which he was preoccupied.

Kelsen's ideas concerning the nature of norms can be divided into two groups: The first group explains the nature of norms as *guiding and justifying behaviour*. The second group is concerned with the nature of norms as *justified standards* of behaviour. The first group explains in what sense, to Kelsen, all norms are imperatives, and is discussed in this section. The concept of a basic norm is the central concept in the second group, which is discussed in the next section.

Four main ideas contribute to Kelsen's concept of a norm as an imperative: Norms are (1) standards of evaluation (2) guiding human behaviour, (3) supported by standard reasons for compliance, in the form of the prospect of some evil ensuing

---

[1] *WJ*, p. 210.   [2] e.g. *PTL*, p. 5.

[3] It seems to me that most of the conflicts between various statements cannot be explained as an evolution of Kelsen's views over the years, but that he oscillates from one position to another and back again.

upon disobedience, and (4) created by human acts intended to create norms; i.e. to set standards of behaviour, guiding behaviour and supported by the prospect of some evil ensuing upon disobedience, as standard motivation.

In the first place, norms are *standards of evaluation:*

What turns this event into a legal or illegal act is not its physical existence, but the objective meaning resulting from its interpretation. The specifically legal meaning of this act is derived from a 'norm' whose content refers to the act; ... The norm functions as a scheme of interpretation'.[1]

Norms make possible the normative interpretation or evaluation of behaviour:

The judgment that an actual behaviour is such as it ought to be according to an objectively valid norm is a value judgment—a positive value judgment. It means that the actual behaviour is 'good'. The judgment that an actual behaviour is the opposite of the behaviour that conforms to the norm is a negative value judgment. It means that the actual conduct is 'bad' or 'evil'.[2]

If the norm is a legal norm the behaviour is judged to be either legal or illegal, lawful or unlawful.

The phrase 'the immediate range of a norm (or a law)' can be defined as follows: An individual act will be said to be within the immediate range of a norm if, and only if, it is done by a norm-subject in circumstances which are an instance of the performance conditions of the norm, and if it is an instance of the generic act which is the norm-act or an instance of the omission of that norm-act. A norm serves as a direct standard of evaluation of acts within its immediate range only.[3] An individual act belonging to the immediate range of a norm has a positive value (i.e. is commendable, good, legal,

[1] *PTL*, pp. 3–4.
[2] *PTL*, p. 17. On Kelsen's doctrine of values see also *PTL*, pp. 17 ff., *TP*, p. 80 n., *TP*, p. 109 n., *WJ*, pp. 35 ff., *WJ*, pp. 139 ff., as well as *GT*, pp. 47 ff., where Kelsen introduces the concept of standard of valuation. Kelsen is, of course, mistaken in thinking that acts have values only in consequence of their conformity or non-conformity with norms.
[3] There are various ways of defining the total range of a norm. It can, for example, be defined as comprising all the acts the performance of which logically entails the performance of acts of the immediate range. A norm serves as an indirect standard of evaluation of all the acts belonging to its total range. The method of evaluation is, however, more complicated, and will not be discussed here.

etc.) if it is an instance of the duty-act, otherwise it has a negative value.

Evaluating behaviour according to standards set by legal norms is an essential part of the function of judges and other officials who are professionally concerned with treating people according to their behaviour evaluated according to law. It is likewise an activity in which ordinary people are expected to be on occasions engaged, if only in order to judge their past or planned behaviour according to law.

In the second place, norms are *principles guiding behaviour*, and according to Kelsen, they guide behaviour by prescribing a specific course of action: 'The laws of nature formulated by natural science *must* conform to the facts, but the facts of human action and refrainment *ought* to conform to the legal norms described by the science of law.'[1] That a norm N imposes a duty on x to do A in C means that x is required to do A in C or that doing A in C is prescribed for x.

Every guide to behaviour is also a standard for evaluation—individual acts can be evaluated according to whether or not they are the prescribed behaviour. On the other hand, not every standard of evaluation is a guide for behaviour, for example, it is possible to evaluate states of affairs which are neither actions nor consequences of acts. For a standard of evaluation to be a guide it is necessary (1) that the standard should relate to human behaviour, and (2) that the existence of the standard, or (what amounts to the same thing) the facts giving rise to its existence, will in fact be a reason for persons whose behaviour the standard evaluates to choose to perform an act having a certain value rather than another act.

This, it seems to me, is the ultimate reason for the philosophical principle that 'ought' implies both 'can' and 'can abstain', to which Kelsen subscribes: ' . . . a norm that were to prescribe that something ought to be done which everyone knows beforehand must happen necessarily according to the laws of nature always and everywhere would be as senseless as a norm which were to prescribe that something ought to be done which one knows beforehand is impossible according to the laws of nature.'[2]

Both this quotation from Kelsen and the much stricter

[1] *PTL*, p. 88.   [2] *PTL*, p. 11.

necessary condition I suggested above leave many questions unanswered. Some are general philosophical problems—what is meant by ability to act, and what by ability to choose? Need every norm-subject be able to act and to choose on every occasion to which the norm applies? Some questions have particular relevance to the law: How should retroactive laws be understood? How is strict liability to be interpreted? As the discussion of each of these questions would involve a lengthy detour none of them can be discussed here.[1]

In the third place, norms are created by acts of will with what Kelsen terms the subjective meaning of 'ought'. The meaning of this doctrine has already been fully discussed in Chapter III, section 3 above. It implies that the existence of a norm N to the effect that x ought to do A in C entails that some person expressed his wish that x should do A in C or that (provided one deals with an institutionalized context) some person expressed his wish that a norm N should be created. This description of the ways in which norms are created has been criticized above (Chapter III, section 3 above).

In the fourth place, norms are 'backed' by sanctions. It can be argued that for a standard of valuation to exist it must be substantiated, i.e. there must be some standard reason[2] for some people to apply the standard. At any rate, it is clear that guides to behaviour exist only if accompanied by a standard reason for following them. This is clearly recognized by Kelsen who stipulates that guides of behaviour are substantiated by some standard reason (not always sufficient and not always heeded) for preferring the prescribed behaviour to other alternatives.[3] That much is presupposed by Kelsen when he says that types of social order 'are characterized by the specific motivation resorted to by the social order to induce individuals to behave as desired'.[4]

---

[1] For Kelsen's views on retroactive laws see *PTL*, pp. 13 f. As will become clear in the next chapter, I do not consider that every law must be a norm. I can, therefore, admit that retroactive laws are not (or not completely) norms, and yet maintain that they are laws. The principle of individuation suggested below must, however, be modified to account for retroactive laws, etc.

[2] By a standard reason for doing an act in certain circumstances I mean a reason for doing that act which is present whenever the circumstances exist.

[3] This standard reason for compliance is a standard reason for people other than the norm-subjects to take the norm into account in evaluating the behaviour of the norm-subjects.

[4] *GT*, p. 15.

There are, according to Kelsen, three types of standard reason: (1) An advantage stipulated by the same or another norm to follow upon conforming to the norm in question; (2) A disadvantage stipulated by the same or another norm to follow upon an act violating the prescription of the norm in question; (3) The direct appeal of the act prescribed by the norm.[1]

Kelsen regards reasons of the second kind as the standard reasons resorted to by the law. He further insists (1) that a norm is a legal norm only if the disadvantage to follow upon its violation is stipulated by a legal norm, and (2) that the disadvantage is stipulated by the same norm for the obedience to which it is a standard reason.

It should be remembered that by saying that a disadvantage is a standard reason it is not meant that the author of the norm intends or wishes the norm-subjects to obey the norm for that reason, or that they usually do so, or that they are justified when they do so. All that is meant is that the disadvantage is a reason for conforming to the norm.

It should be noticed also that the standard reason for a legal norm consists in the combination of two things: (1) A sanction stipulated by a legal norm; (2) The fact that the legal system as a whole is efficacious.[2] These facts confer a certain probability that a disadvantage will be suffered by the norm-subjects if they violate the law, and this probability of disadvantage is the standard reason. To be sure, by adding other facts and calculating the probability on a wider basis it may be diminished substantially for most cases or for some particular cases. But this is beside the point. What counts is the probability based only on the stipulation of the sanction and the existence, and hence the general efficacy, of the legal system.

These are the four points which conjunctively explain the first part of Kelsen's concept of a norm in general and of a legal norm in particular. The first two in themselves do not explain much. They point to certain connections between

---

[1] Cf. *GT*, p. 15. Given a theory of values wider than Kelsen's, one may add the value of the act prescribed when done by the norm-subject in the specified circumstances. There are other kinds of standard reasons, some—like the personal authority of the author of the norm—are indirectly admitted by Kelsen elsewhere.

[2] According to Kelsen, there is also the fact that the norm stipulating the sanction is not totally inefficacious.

certain groups of what are known by the conveniently vague phrase 'normative terms'. This is useful, but the vagueness of the clarification given leaves much to be explained. The last two points should, however, be understood as a partial explanation of the first two points. This is also how Kelsen himself regards them. Thus, when confronted with accusations such as Alf Ross's suggestion that 'the idea of a true norm or demand is a logical absurdity, the fallacy implied in all ethical absolutism',[1] Kelsen says:

La tentative du positivism logique, de présenter l'éthique comme une science des faits empiriques résulte manifestement de la tendance, parfaitement légitime en elle-même, à l'exclure du domaine de la spéculation métaphisique. Mais il est satisfait à cette tendance si l'on reconnaît que les normes qui forment l'objet de l'éthique sont les significations de faits empiriques posés par des hommes dans le monde de la réalité.[2]

Here he draws in effect on the third point, that norms are created by certain acts of will, to explain the non-metaphysical sense in which they can be said to be demands and standards of valuation.

The last two points outline the factual context which, according to Kelsen's theory, justifies talking about norms, standards of valuation, and guides of behaviour. Spelling out the kind of facts which must obtain if any statement about existing norms is to be true and the relation between statements about norms and other parts of the normative language are the essence of the explanation of the concept of a norm.[3]

Kelsen's stipulation concerning the creation of norms has been criticized in detail (Chapter III, section 3 above) and will not be further discussed. The other points mentioned in this section will be examined somewhat more fully later in this chapter. Though we shall now proceed to discuss the second group of Kelsen's ideas concerning the nature of norms, including the idea of a non-positive basic norm, it seems that the latter are not required for an adequate analysis of norms.

[1] A review of Kelsen's *What is Justice*, 45 *Cal. L.R.* 564, 568.   [2] *TP*, p. 80 n.
[3] Cf. Hart's suggestion that the term 'a legal right' is explained once the truth-conditions of statements of the form 'X has a right' are given, and it is stated that statements of this form are used to draw conclusions of law in particular cases. Similar explanations, Hart claims, can be given to other problematic legal terms: *Definition and Theory in Jurisprudence*, pp. 14–17.

VI.2: THE BASIC NORM AND DYNAMIC
JUSTIFICATION

According to the concept of a norm as explained in the previous section, orders backed by threats are norms. They guide the behaviour of the persons ordered, they are standards by which behaviour can be evaluated, they are made by human beings with the intention of influencing other people's behaviour, and they are supported by a standard reason, namely the avoidance of the threatened sanction.

Orders can be distinguished from laws on other grounds, but they are normative in the same sense as laws, that is, provided the four points elaborated in the previous section constitute a satisfactory account of a norm. Two differences between laws and orders might be mentioned here: First, there are ample opportunities and reasons to refer to content of laws without referring to the circumstances of their creation. Thus, a lawyer often has a reason to refer to various laws relating to contracts and to discuss their significance and bearing on his clients' affairs, and in such discussions the circumstances in which the laws were created are often (though of course not always) completely unimportant. On the other hand, it is characteristic of orders that they are usually discussed with reference to the actual context in which they were given. Whereas knowing that every person has, under certain circumstances, to pay a certain rate of income tax is for many purposes all the information required; knowing that Smith and his family were ordered to give £20 to Brown is usually an incomplete piece of information, and one needs also to know who gave the order, when and in what circumstances it was given, if the information is to be relevant and useful for the usual purposes involved.

The fact that there are so many occasions and reasons to refer to laws in abstraction from the circumstances of their creation is the justification for regarding laws as abstract entities. There is no similar general case for regarding orders as abstract entities in the same sense.[1]

[1] At least two concepts of an order as an abstract entity should be distinguished. They differ in that, according to one, identity of content is both necessary and sufficient for the identity of the orders, whereas, according to the second concept, it is a necessary but not a sufficient condition for the identity of the orders. If *a* and

One should, on the strength of this argument, supplement the four points made in the previous section by stipulating that unnecessary entities should not be allowed. Orders, therefore, are not norms, whereas laws are norms.

There is a second distinction between orders and laws which should be mentioned here. Every law belongs to a normative system for every law belongs to a legal system. Orders sometimes do and sometimes do not belong to normative systems.[1] This means that every legal norm belongs to a group of legal norms interrelated in certain ways, while orders do not always belong to such groups. As has been explained in the previous chapter, Kelsen tries to use his concept of a basic norm to explain this systematic interrelation of legal norms. The fact that orders are not always interrelated in a similar way is one reason why Kelsen thinks the concept of a basic norm (or a basic order) is not necessary for the analysis of orders as such.[2] It is obvious, however, that Kelsen has also other reasons for employing his concept of a basic norm in the analysis of norms and not employing it in the analysis of orders.

---

b, each independently of the other, order c to do A in C, then according to the first concept both gave the same order, whereas according to the second concept they gave two different orders with the same content. The first concept can be said to represent orders as linguistic entities, for in this sense orders can be identified with the meanings of certain context-free imperative sentences. I do not wish to dispute the necessity of regarding orders as linguistic entities.

Laws, and norms in general, are entities of the second kind, i.e. identity of content is necessary but not sufficient to establish the identity of two laws. England and the United States may have two laws identical in content, which are nevertheless two distinct laws, just because they belong to two different legal systems. Likewise, the English parliament may enact a law having the same content as a law which was once valid in England, yet it does not re-enact the same law, but a different law with the same content. (This is not to say that difference in circumstances of creation always entails difference in identity: What should be said when parliament merely extends the period during which a certain law is in force, and how should one interpret a case where parliament re-enacts a law which is anyhow valid? These problems require a deeper probe into the logic of norms than is possible here.)

It is the necessity of this second, non-linguistic, concept of an order as an abstract entity which is discussed above.

[1] Orders which do belong to normative systems are regarded as norms and are treated as part of the normative system. Legal orders, for example, are discussed in legal theory. It is, perhaps, arguable that there can be no normative systems consisting only of orders.

[2] Legal orders and other orders which belong to normative systems are fully analysed only by reference to the basic norm of the system to which they belong.

According to Kelsen's theory, orders are made by appropriate acts of persons in a suitable position (e.g. a position of strength or of personal authority). Legal norms, on the other hand, come into being as a consequence of a combination of human acts and other legal norms: for Kelsen no norm can be created by human acts alone. The existence of every positive norm presupposes the existence of another norm authorizing its creation. Kelsen thinks that an infinite regress is avoided, and can only be avoided, by assuming the existence of a basic norm in each normative order which is not created at all, for it is a necessary norm. As the occurrence of another order (or the existence of another norm) is not a necessary condition for the occurrence of an order, the concept of a basic norm (or a basic order) has no place in the analysis of orders.

It might be thought that Kelsen's doctrine that the creation of every norm presupposes another norm is a mere manifestation of the systematic relations between norms. In fact, Kelsen insists on this doctrine for other reasons as well, reasons which are of the utmost importance to his theory of norms. He regards the doctrine as a necessary consequence of the fundamental principle that 'Nobody can assert that from the statement that something is, follows a statement that something ought to be, or vice versa.'[1] From this he concludes that acts cannot by themselves create norms: ' . . . the objective validity of a norm, which is the subjective meaning of an act of will that men ought to behave in a certain way, does not follow from the factual act, that is to say, from an *is*, but again from a norm authorizing this act, that is to say, from an *ought*.'[2]

The fact that Kelsen does not apply this argument to orders indicates that he regards them as normative in a sense different from that in which norms are normative. As the four points of the last section apply equally to norms and orders, this implies that the last section did not fully explain Kelsen's concept of a

---

[1] *PTL*, p. 6.

[2] *PTL*, pp. 8–9. In a footnote Kelsen identifies his principle with Prior's statement 'il est impossible de déduire une conclusion éthique de prémisses entièrement non-éthique', *TP*, 12 n. This principle is unsound. At most it can be claimed that (some) normative conclusions presuppose a normative assumption. The assumption need not be a premiss, it may be a rule of derivation. According to this interpretation of the principle, the statement that a norm exists can be derived from statements that certain acts were performed, given appropriate rules of derivation.

norm. Kelsen regards orders, as such, as 'subjective ought' and norms as 'objective ought'. What, for Kelsen, is absent in the concept of an order which prevents it from being an objective 'ought'?

To answer this question it is necessary to review a number of different considerations by which Kelsen seems to have been influenced in his distinction between subjective and objective 'ought', and a number of different and sometimes conflicting interpretations of his doctrine of the basic norm.

Thus it is easy to detect one factor which may induce us to distinguish between orders backed by threats (the only kind of orders that Kelsen considers) and norms. Both may be substantiated by the fact that a sanction is likely to follow disobedience. Consequently, both orders and norms can be appealed to in order to justify behaviour conforming to them. They provide a reason for the behaviour they prescribe, and thereby also justify it to a certain degree. It may be that because of other conflicting considerations the behaviour is unjustified, but at least it has a partial justification. That does not, of course, mean that norms and orders are themselves justified. It might be thought that one of the differences between norms and orders is that norms are necessarily justified demands, whereas orders, even though sometimes justified as well as justifying, are not necessarily so. Such a difference can explain the difference in normativity between norms and orders in Kelsen's theory which is reflected in calling orders 'subjective ought' and norms 'objective ought'. Similarly it explains why norms 'derive' their validity from other norms, whereas no analogous stipulation is necessary, according to Kelsen, in the case of orders: The norm which contributes to the creation of another norm is part of its justification.

The thesis that:

(1) Every norm is a justified demand,
should be distinguished from other related theses, all of which have some support from Kelsen's statements on the subject, namely

(2) Norms are not necessarily justified, but 'ought' statements that x ought to do A in C mean both that such a norm exists and that it is justified.

(3) Such 'ought' statements do not mean that the norm

described is justified, but that it is justified if the basic norm of the system to which the norm belongs is justified.

(4) Such 'ought' statements do not mean that the norm described is justified conditionally or unconditionally, but stating them implies that the speaker thinks the norm is regarded as justified by the bulk of the community to which the system including the described norm applies.

(5) Such 'ought' statements do not mean that the norm described is justified conditionally or unconditionally, but stating them implies that the speaker considers them to be justified.

Does Kelsen accept any of these or any of the many different but related theses which can be formulated? It is impossible to examine here all the relevant passages in Kelsen's works. I shall, however, try to suggest an answer based on some of the key passages. Only legal norms will be considered, but other norms will be referred to on occasion.

First thesis (see p. 131): Kelsen rejects this thesis explicitly: 'The legal rule says: If *A* is, *B* ought to be. And thereby it says nothing as to the value, moral or political, of the relationship. "Ought" remains a pure *a priori* category for the comprehension of the empirical legal material. . . . The category has purely formal character. . . . It is an epistemological transcendental category in the sense of Kantian philosophy . . . in this it reserves its radically anti-ideological tendency.'[1] This passage is reinforced by many others which make it clear that Kelsen does not regard the law as necessarily good or justified in any sense.

It is tempting to think that though the law is not justified in any absolute sense it exists only if it is accepted as justified by the community to which it applies. This interpretation is supported by the following passage: 'If the "ought" is also the objective meaning of the act, the behaviour at which the act is directed is regarded as something that ought to be, not only from the point of view of the individual who has performed the act, but also from the point of view of the individual at whose behaviour the act is directed, and of a third individual

---

[1] *L.Q.R.* (1934), 485.

not involved in the relation between the two.'[1] Kelsen, however, rejects this interpretation: ' . . . the doctrine of the basic norm is not a doctrine of recognition. . . . According to the doctrine of recognition positive law is valid only if it is recognized by the individuals subject to it, which means: if these individuals agree that one ought to behave according to the norms of the positive law.'[2] Thus Kelsen rejects the first thesis in both its interpretations.

Second and fourth theses (see pp. 131–2): There can be no doubt that Kelsen rejects both these theses. In fact I only mentioned them because of their interest within the context of some other theory of norms. Kelsen himself is committed to the idea that (objective) 'ought'-statements describe norms and nothing else. Hence he cannot accept the second thesis. He is also aware that there are legal systems which are not regarded as good or justified by the people they govern. Nevertheless, one may describe these systems by 'ought' statements. Therefore, the thesis that stating an 'ought'-statement implies that the speaker believes that the norm described is accepted as justified by its norm-subjects, if it is to be accepted at all, must be modified by specifying special contexts in which the implication does or does not hold. No such specification is to be found in Kelsen's work. His discussion of linguistic problems shows that he is not aware that by the act of stating the speaker may imply things that are not part of the meaning of the statement made. This consideration applies equally to the fifth thesis, which must also be rejected.

In the quotation from the *Law Quarterly Review* cited above Kelsen is clearly trying to distinguish between two ideas of 'ought'—a material 'ought', which carries the implication that the norm described is good or just; and a formal 'ought', which does not carry the implication. Because Kelsen lacks an adequate linguistic theory to help him in expressing his ideas, it is difficult to tell what exactly he does mean by that distinction. It is, nevertheless, clear that, according to Kelsen, in describing the law only the formal 'ought' is to be used: 'Right (the law),

[1] *PTL*, p. 7.
[2] *PTL*, p. 218 n. In this respect it seems that, according to Kelsen, legal norms differ from social morality. The latter is created by custom, and hence it is created only if the community considers that it ought to behave in the prescribed way.

according to the theory here developed, is a certain order (or organization) of might.'[1] Yet law is regarded 'not as a mere factual assembly of motives, but as a valid order, as Norm'.[2] This is made possible by the basic norm: ' . . . the basic norm, in a certain sense, means the transformation of power into law.'[3]

By interpreting organized force as a system of norms one need not assume that it is good or just. The only reason why there is no basic norm to a system of orders of an organized group of gangsters is that 'this order does not have the lasting effectiveness without which no basic norm is presupposed.'[4]

All these passages and many others tend to sustain the concept of a legal norm explained in the previous section, and to support the suggestion made in the beginning of this section that, according to Kelsen, the only difference between laws created by certain acts of will and orders is in the relatively prolonged existence and the systematic interconnections of laws. These ideas also justify the statement that basic norms exist if they are regarded only as common bonds determining the identity of normative systems and the validity of orders as part of such systems. The ultimate aim of these pronouncements is to make possible the assertion that ' . . . positive law . . . is justified only by a norm or a normative order with which positive law, according to its contents, may or may not conform, hence be just or unjust.'[1] From which it follows that the basic norm has nothing to do with the justification of laws.[5]

However, as often as not Kelsen deviates from this position. He constantly identifies the question 'What is the reason for the validity of the law?' with the question 'Why should the law be obeyed?'[6] To these questions he answers 'The basic norm', 'Because of the basic norm'.

Kelsen recognizes and discusses in some detail a special method of justifying norms, which can be called 'dynamic' justification. It can be defined by two characteristics:

(1) A norm is justified on the basis of another norm.

(2) The justifying norm is a norm-creating norm, and the justification consists in showing that the justified norm was

[1] *PTL*, p. 214.   [2] 51 *L.Q.R.* 518.   [3] *GT*, p. 437.   [4] *PTL*, p. 47.
[5] *PTL*, p. 217.   [6] *WJ*, p. 257.

created in the way stipulated by the justifying norm.[1] (Needless to say one may proceed and ask for the justification of the justifying norm.)

He is aware that a legal norm which is part of the creation-condition of another legal norm *can be* referred to as a (dynamic) justification of that norm. He fails, however, to distinguish between the existence-conditions of a norm and their possible use as a justification of it, and by identifying the two he is driven to the conclusion that existing norms are necessarily justified. Aware of the threatening contradiction between his views, he seeks to avoid it by edging towards the third thesis:

Third thesis (see p. 131): 'Ought'-statements mean that a norm exists and that it is justified if the basic norm of the system to which it belongs is presupposed. Kelsen says, for example, that 'legal positivism answers the question why law is valid by referring to a hypothesis that may or may not be accepted—in other words by *justifying obedience to law* only conditionally.'[2] I would prefer to say that legal positivism does not justify the law at all, but that it describes and analyses a method which *can* be used to justify laws.

Kelsen, however, thinks otherwise and concludes that 'the "ought" of positive law can only be hypothetical.'[3] By this he seems to subscribe to the third thesis. Unfortunately, this is not the end of the story, for Kelsen is trapped by his identification of validity with the existence of a norm on the one hand and with its justification on the other. The statement that legal norms are only conditionally justified is synonymous for him with the statement that legal norms are only conditionally valid, i.e. that they enjoy only conditional existence: 'As the absolute validity of its norms corresponds to the idea of natural

---

[1] For some undisclosed reasons Kelsen adopts the odd view that there are only two types of normative systems: Dynamic systems, all (or perhaps most of) the norms of which are justified by dynamic justification, and static systems, all (or perhaps most of) the norms of which are justified because statements describing them are entailed by statements describing other norms. The basic norms of dynamic systems invest some person or body of persons with legislative powers, and are presupposed. The basic norms of static systems are not norm-creating norms, and they are not presupposed, but regarded as self-evident. See on this subject: *GT*, pp. 112 f., 399 f.; *PTL*, pp. 195 ff. Kelsen further maintains that no norm is really self-evident: *PTL*, p. 196. We need not discuss this theory here.

[2] *WJ*, p. 263.   [3] *GT*, p. 394.

law, the merely hypothetical-relative validity of its norms corresponds to that of positive law.'[1] This conclusion contradicts Kelsen's own views (examined above) on the non-ideological nature of laws, and is itself untenable.

The way out of this confusion is to reject the identification of the validity of a norm with the justification of a norm, and to accept the third thesis. Or, one may, as I have suggested, go even further and regard the fact that some legal norms are usually among the existence-conditions of other legal norms, not as justifying these norms, but only as providing a possible way in which they can be justified. The third thesis can, accordingly, be rejected.

It is obvious from the discussion so far that Kelsen's views on the question of norms as justified demands revolve around the interpretation of the concept of a basic norm. Do basic norms justify legal norms? and, if so, in what sense? Kelsen regards basic norms as the source of validity and as the source of unity of legal systems. Their function in uniting legal systems has been examined in the previous chapter. It is with basic norms as the source of validity of the law that we are concerned here.

Kelsen's discussion of this subject is beset by confusion. The basic norm is said to be presupposed. Kelsen speaks of it as presupposed in two different ways. It is presupposed by legal theory, it is 'the ultimate hypothesis of positivism'. It is also said to be presupposed by any person who regards the law as a system of norms, i.e. any person who uses normative terms in referring to laws: 'That the basic norm really exists in the juristic consciousness is the result of a simple analysis of actual juristic statements.'[2] These two statements do not necessarily conflict, but Kelsen tends on occasion to equate the presupposition of a basic norm by ordinary persons with its acceptance as justified or good. In some passages he says that anarchists, for instance, do not presuppose the basic norm and regard law not as a normative system but as mere power relations.[3] Similarly: 'A communist may, indeed, not admit that there is an essential difference between an organisation of gangsters and a capitalistic legal order which he considers as the means of ruthless exploitation. For he does not presuppose—as do those who interpret the coercive order in question as an objectively

[1] *GT*, p. 394.   [2] *GT*, p. 116.   [3] *GT*, pp. 413, 425.

valid normative order—the basic norm.'[1] Legal theory does not presuppose the basic norm in the same sense. It is not the business of legal theory to justify the law, but to explain it.

If presupposing the basic norm means accepting it as justified, then there may exist legal systems which apply to populations who do not presuppose their basic norms. Neither the existence of legal systems nor the existence of their basic norms (for there is a basic norm in every legal system) depends upon the basic norm's being presupposed.[2]

It should be understood, notwithstanding certain remarks of Kelsen's suggesting the contrary view, that the anarchist, communist, or anyone who does not presuppose the basic norm can still describe the law using normative statements. Normative statements do not imply 'any approval of the described legal norm'.[3] Kelsen is right in saying: 'Even an anarchist, if he were a professor of law, could describe positive law as a system of valid norms, without having to approve of this law.'[4] This is, however, no reason for him to contradict both his former and latter statements that the anarchist does not presuppose the basic norm, as he does in that same footnote.

Why should legal theory be said to presuppose the basic norm and not merely to analyse and describe it, as it does the other norms? Kelsen considers every norm as created by legislative acts. This is, of course, not true of the basic norms. Hence he says that one presupposes their enactment. A fiction is accepted that basic norms are enacted.[5]

One can therefore, without loss, dispense with the idea that legal theory presupposes the basic norm. We have seen that norms are not always justified demands. The concept of a norm is that analysed in the previous section (subject to the substantial modifications introduced in the next sections). The difference in normativity between legal systems and orders can be explained by the fact that legal systems have a built-in possibility of dynamic justification of most of their norms.

---

[1] *Stanford L.R.* (1965), 1144.   [2] Cf. Ch. III, sect. 3 above.
[3] *PTL*, p. 79.   [4] *PTL*, p. 218 n.
[5] 'On the Pure Theory of Law', 1 *Isr.L.R.*, p. 6. Here Kelsen attributes the fiction not to legal theory but to everyone thinking about the law. The important thing is that this is a different sense of 'to presuppose'. Another possible interpretation of the view that legal theory presupposes the basic norm is that it finds the concept of a basic norm necessary or helpful in explaining the law.

What is the fate of the basic norms? They do not help to
establish the unity and identity of legal systems, nor do they
help in arranging the norms of legal systems.[1] They are said to
be the source of validity of legal norms, but in that role they do
not justify these norms. Neither are they made necessary by the
principle that any derivation of a normative statement is based
on some normative assumption. Is there any reason for accepting the existence of basic norms? There is one more argument
that should be considered.

In enacting the first constitution its authors exercise legal
powers. According to Kelsen, this means that there is a norm
which conferred upon them these powers. That norm could not
have been enacted (had it been enacted the same argument can
be applied to the powers of its legislators), yet it must exist. The
same argument can be applied to every legal system, and therefore such an un-enacted norm, i.e. the basic norm, must exist
in every legal system.

This argument is based on the mistaken assumption that a
man can have legislative powers only if they were conferred on
him by a law. Legislative power is simply the ability to create
or repeal laws.[2] The authors of the first constitution have
legislative power, which is not given to them by law, to make
the first constitution. The first constitution is law because it
belongs to an efficacious legal system (a fact which cannot be
determined until some time after the constitution is first issued).

Even if every legislative power must be conferred by law, as
Kelsen claims, his argument establishes only the possibility and
not the necessity of basic norms. For the powers of the authors
of the first constitution can be conferred upon them by an
ordinary law of the system. Kelsen's argument shows only that,
if every legislative power must be conferred by law, basic norms
must exist in systems where no ordinary law confers the
appropriate powers on the authors of the first constitution.

My argument is based on the assumption that laws can indirectly authorize their own creation. It seems to me that the
objections to such laws are ill-conceived. Admitting such laws
presupposes the possibility of: (1) laws conferring legislative
power with retroactive effect; (2) partially self-referring laws.
These two assumptions I find unobjectionable (for the second

[1] Cf. Ch. V, sect. 3 above.   [2] Cf. Ch. II, sect. 1 above.

assumption cf. Hart, 'Self-Referring Laws'). Let us examine
two sets of laws. One set, consisting of the laws A, B, C, D, all
belong to the chain of validity represented in Fig. 6. The other
set, consisting of the laws E, F, G, and H, all belong to the chain
of validity represented in Fig. 7. Each of the laws of the first
group, and none of the laws of the second group, indirectly
authorizes its own creation. Assume further that this is the only
difference in content between the pairs of norms A and E, B and
F, C and G, and D and H. (The power designated as (1) is,
therefore, identical with the powers (2) and (3) together.)

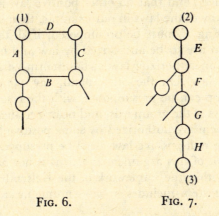

Fig. 6.   Fig. 7.

My claims are: (1) No contradiction results from assuming
that A, B, C, and D are valid laws. (2) It is true that the validity
of each of these laws can be proved only if, in the last resort, the
validity of one of the other laws is assumed and not proved, but
this is true also of E, F, G, and H. (3) Nor can it be argued that
that part of the content of A, B, C, and D, which authorizes
their own creation, is redundant or completely pointless, in the
sense in which a purely self-referring law, A_1, that 'This law is
valid', is pointless, because its existence or non-existence makes
no difference whatsoever; and that therefore the first group of
laws can be said to be identical in content with the second (non-
self-referring) group.

There are at least two differences between the two groups
resulting from the difference in their content: (1) The non-
existence of any one of the laws A, B, C, and D entails the
non-existence of the rest, for each of them entails the existence

of the rest. (We are assuming, of course, that the necessary legislative acts were performed.) The non-existence of any of the laws of the other group entails only the non-existence of the laws preceding it in the chain of validity. The laws which succeed it, if any, can be presupposed, or their validity proved, by reference to other norms (not represented in the chain of validity of Fig. 7), without entailing thereby the existence of the non-existing law. (2) Consequently, assuming, as Kelsen does, that the existence of norms can either be proved by reference to norms or presupposed (for reasons of theoretical expediency or personal belief), and that no other positive law authorizes the creation of any of the laws in our example, then a non-positive law authorizing E must be presupposed, if all the laws of the second group are to be authorized by law and be laws of one system. Such an authorizing law is a basic norm, i.e. a presupposed non-positive law. On the other hand, any one of the laws of the first group can be presupposed, with the result that it and the other laws of the group exist and belong to the same system, and all of them are authorized by some positive law. No basic norm, i.e. no non-positive law, need be presupposed.

The upshot of this argument is that it is not necessarily the case, even within the framework of the Kelsenite theory, that every legal system includes a basic norm, i.e. a non-positive norm.

VI.3: THE STRUCTURE OF A SYSTEM AND THE INDIVIDUATION OF ITS LAWS

The kinds and patterns of internal relations existing between laws in a legal system depend ultimately on two factors: (1) the principles of individuation; (2) the richness, complexity, and variety of the content of the legal system. Whatever the content of a system, if its laws are individuated according to Kelsen's principles the resulting pattern of internal relations (if any) will differ from the patterns of internal relations which will result from individuating the same system according to Bentham's principles. On the other hand, if the system is impoverished in certain respects, this may affect the pattern of its internal relations. If, for example, none of its laws is backed by sanction then there will be no punitive relations between its laws.

The principles of individuation are determined by legal theory, whereas the content of a system depends on contingent facts concerning that particular system. It can, therefore, be said that the principles of individuation make the existence of certain types of internal relations possible, whereas the complexity of the system determines whether relations of these types actually exist in the system concerned.

A normative system is a legal system only if it has a certain minimum degree of complexity. Thus it will be argued in Chapter VIII that every legal system must regulate the existence and operations of some courts, and that every legal system necessarily stipulates sanctions. This subject is closely related to the problem whether there is some minimum content common to all legal systems. The minimum content and the minimum complexity of all legal systems, together with the principles of individuation, determine the necessary internal relations existing in every legal system, that is the internal structure which is necessarily common to all legal systems.

Exploring the minimum complexity of legal systems would involve problems closely allied with the problem of the minimum content of legal systems, and therefore this task will not be undertaken here. Instead, this chapter and the following one examine the shape of acceptable principles of individuation, and the general characteristics of the major types of internal relations made possible by them.

It is not necessary for the purposes of this study to formulate the principles of individuation themselves. All that is needed is to lay down broad guidelines, in the form of general requirements by which the adequacy of every proposed set of individuating principles will be tested. These requirements are of two kinds: guiding and limiting. The guiding requirements set forth aims that the principles of individuation should attain; the limiting requirements specify pitfalls to be avoided. The limiting requirements determine the range of possible sets of individuating principles by excluding certain ill-conceived suggestions. The guiding requirements help us to choose the best of the sets of individuating principles that pass the test of the limiting requirements. None of the limiting requirements prescribes an accurate and absolute limit to the acceptability of sets of principles of individuation. Ultimately every such set is judged by its success in satisfying each of the requirements, balanced by its success in satisfying the rest. Yet it can be said that, whereas the limiting requirements are mainly principles of exclusion, the guiding requirements are mainly principles of selection.

A. *Limiting Requirements*

(1) The laws individuated by the principles of individuation should not deviate too much or without sound reasons from the ordinary concept of a law. This requirement, it will be remembered,[1] is based primarily on the desire to make the theoretical concept of a law the starting point for the explanation of the common-sense concept of a law; the common-sense concept will be elucidated by an explanation of its deviations from the theoretical concept, which is in its turn justified as being the best (or a good) tool in the analysis of the law.

(2) The laws individuated by the principles of individuation should not be over-repetitive. A law partly repeats another law when a legal provision which is part of it is also part of the other. For example, if every law includes a provision to the effect that parliament has unlimited legislative powers, then all laws repeat one another.

It may be thought that repetition, though perhaps inelegant, is not vitally important, for it causes no practical difficulties. After all, Kelsen does not suggest that law books should be re-written in order to present every law in his canonical form, a task which would increase the size of law books a thousand times. Bentham, with characteristic thoroughness, began outlining a system of cross-references which would solve most of the practical inconvenience caused by repetition.

It seems to me, however, that this possibility does not affect the importance of this requirement. The practical inconvenience can be avoided just because the inclusion of the repetitive provisions in many laws serves no useful purpose. It is precisely the acceptance of a theoretical concept of a law, yielding repetitive laws divorced from any real need or reason for repetition, which is objectionable. The concept of a law should be moulded in the way best designed to serve the activities and needs of the people

---

[1] See Ch. V, sect. 6 above.

who are concerned with the law (i.e. in various degrees—
everybody).

(3) The laws individuated by the principles of individuation
should not be redundant. That is, if the existence of one law
is a sufficient condition for the truth of certain normative
statements, then such a statement should not be regarded as
describing another complete law but rather as describing(part
of) the content of the first law.

This requirement can be regarded as a special case of the
more general requirement against repetition. It can perhaps be
further justified by the tendency not to allow unnecessary
abstract entities. This principle was recognized by Kelsen.[1] In
discussing his use of it we have already noticed that it has no
absolute force and that some redundancy may be allowed if
there are strong reasons for doing so.

B. *Guiding Requirements*

(1) The laws individuated by the principles of individuation
should be relatively simple. This is perhaps the most important
of the requirements. The whole purpose of dividing legal systems into laws is to create simple small units to facilitate discourse about and reference to various parts of the legal system,
as well as to promote the analysis of law.

At least two kinds of simplicity, of equal importance, should
be distinguished. One may be called conceptual simplicity: A
law should be conceptually simple; it should have a relatively
simple structure, easily grasped, and its meaning should be
relatively easily understood. Understanding the meaning of a
Kelsenite law is a task equal to understanding a legal textbook,
and, indeed, they are of roughly the same length. The structure and meaning of a norm like 'Do not steal' are much easier
to understand.

The other kind of simplicity is simplicity of identification: It
should be easy to discover the content of a law. The concept
of a law should be framed in such a way that the content of any
one law could in most cases be discovered by consulting a small
number of statutes, regulations, judgments, etc. It should not
be framed, as is the case with Bentham's and Kelsen's laws, in

---

[1] See Ch. IV, sect. 3 above.

such a way that a very large proportion of the legal material of
a system would have to be scrutinized in order to discover the
content of any one law.[1] Moreover, establishing that the content
of a law has indeed been completely discovered, though more
difficult than the discovery itself, should also be relatively easy.
According to Bentham and Kelsen the whole of the content of
a legal system has to be examined in order to establish that the
content of any one law has been completely discovered.

(2) The laws individuated by the principles of individuation
should be relatively self-contained (or self-explanatory). Every
law should contain a relatively complete part of the legal system. The legal system should be divided in a 'natural' way, i.e.
without combining unrelated ideas in one law, and without
dividing related ideas into several laws for no good reason. As
has been noticed,[2] this requirement competes with the previous
one. Laws should be simple but not too simple. Learning the
content of a law should be a meaningful contribution to learning
the content of the legal system.

(3) It is desirable that every act-situation (i.e. the performance of a certain act by certain persons in certain circumstances) that is guided by a legal system should be the core of a
law, unless it is an instance of, or unless it belongs to,[3] another
(generic) act-situation which is guided by that legal system in
an identical way and is itself the core of a law.

This requirement is a generalized and modified version of a
principle adopted by Bentham. The full significance of this
requirement will become clear only when the meaning of the
phrase 'an act-situation guided by law' is explained (in section
5 below). The general nature of the requirement can, however,
be explained by recalling Bentham's corresponding principle.[4]
Bentham thought that every act-situation commanded or prohibited by a legislator should be the core of a separate law.
Commanding and prohibiting act-situations are two ways
of guiding them. It will be argued later in this chapter that
they are not the only ways in which the law guides human behaviour.

[1] Bentham himself was aware of this fact: cf. *Limits*, p. 293. (The relevant
passage has been omitted in *OLG*.)
[2] In Ch. V, sect. 6 above.
[3] Here as elsewhere I am deliberately ambiguous on the question whether
generic acts and act-situations should be regarded as classes.
[4] Cf. Ch. IV, sects. 1 and 3 above.

An act-situation is the core of a law (which, as will be seen in Chapter VII, need not be a norm) if it is the object of a normative modality ('ought', 'must', 'may', etc.) or a normative predicate ('have a right', 'is a duty', etc.).

The justification of this requirement is quite obvious. Law is universally regarded as a special social method of regulating human behaviour by guiding it in various ways and directions. This function of the law, which is also the main reason for learning and referring to the law, should be made clear in its theoretical analysis. The way in which this function is pursued is best shown and brought to the forefront of the study of law by adopting this requirement.

(4) The laws individuated by the principles of individuation should, as far as possible, make clear important connections between various parts of a legal system.

This requirement plays a major role in the considerations advanced in the next chapter. Its general import and its objective can be exemplified by considering briefly a case which is not discussed in the next chapter. There is a good case for arguing that there are laws determining necessary conditions for the application of legal norms, laws like: 'All the legal norms of the system apply only to acts performed in a certain territory.' Such laws are not norms; they neither impose duties nor confer powers. They have, however, internal relations to at least some of the legal norms of the system, because they affect their interpretation and application. They specify some, though not all, of the performance-conditions of legal norms. A law imposing a duty not to steal applies, in consequence of the law in our example, only to thefts committed in a certain territory.

By allowing the existence of such laws the repetition of common performance-conditions in many laws separately is avoided, and many laws become correspondingly simpler. On the other hand the 'dependence' of these laws on other laws increases, they become less self-contained, less self-explanatory. These are considerations which are dealt with by some of the previous requirements. But there is a further consequence of allowing for laws determining conditions necessary for the application of groups of legal norms. Such laws isolate features common to many laws, thereby making clear certain connections between groups of laws. Not every connection between laws is of great legal significance, and only important connections should be singled out in separate laws. In such cases they assist understanding of the law. For example, such laws may serve as a basis for a classification of certain groups of laws within one legal system. In a certain legal system legal norms regarding the status and consequences of marriage may differ from all other legal norms of the system in that they distinguish between people according to their religion. This feature can serve as a basis for difference in jurisdiction, e.g. such laws will be adjudicated by religious courts. Thus a single feature of a group of laws serves to connect it in various ways with the operation of other laws of the system, and this may weigh in favour of representing this feature as the core of a separate law, with an internal relation to a certain group of laws that it characterizes. As will be seen in the next chapter, classification is just one of the purposes served by laws which point to important connections between laws.

The description of meta-theoretical requirements such as these is necessarily vague. There cannot be any clear-cut way of choosing between different theories. Such a choice is always a matter of tentative reasons, of weighing unmeasurable considerations one against the other. Nevertheless, the explicit formulation of meta-theoretical criteria is a condition for a rational and reasoned comparison of theories. Such a comparison was made in previous chapters between Bentham's and Kelsen's principles of individuation, and it has been argued [1] that Bentham's principles are better than Kelsen's.

Bentham's principles are, however, far from satisfactory. The laws individuated by them are over-repetitive, they are far removed from the ordinary concept of a law, and—most important of all—they are far too complex. Bentham is compelled to adopt them because his theory is based on two propositions: (1) Every law is a norm; (2) Every norm is a duty-imposing norm. Given these two propositions, Bentham's principles of individuation cannot be much improved. They could be somewhat improved by investigating and developing the concept of obedience laws as an explanation of laws conferring legislative powers. This would be a real but not a sufficient improvement. Any satisfactory account of the individuation of laws must reject both

---

[1] See Ch. IV, sect. 3 above, and cf. Ch. V, sect. 6.

these propositions. Much of the rest of this chapter is concerned with a critical examination of the second proposition. The next chapter examines the first proposition.

VI.4: DUTY-IMPOSING LAWS

Given the general desirability that every act-situation guided by law should be regarded as a core of a law,[1] it is clear that every acceptable set of individuation principles will allow for duty-imposing laws. Three of the four main ideas of the first stage of Kelsen's account of the nature of norms[2] (omitting his suggestion that all laws are created by acts intended to create laws) provide a sound starting point for an explanation of the nature of duty-imposing laws (or D-laws as they may be called). In this section it is attempted to supplement and slightly modify Kelsen's account by ideas borrowed from Hart.[3] The general problem to be considered is: When do law-creating acts impose duties, and in what circumstances should legal material be interpreted as giving rise to a D-law? Only very few general remarks can be made here.

The most appropriate starting-point for the analysis of D-laws is the examination of non-legal duty-imposing norms. The concepts of social obligation and of rules imposing such obligations have been studied in some detail by Hart. His explanation of a social duty-imposing rule can be briefly summarized as follows: A social rule that one ought to do A in C exists in a certain group if and only if:

(1) On most occasions members of the group do A in C; doing A in C is a regular pattern of behaviour in that group.

(2) Members of the group who do not conform to that pattern of behaviour usually encounter some critical reaction from other members of the group. Such reaction expresses itself in verbal criticism of their deviating behaviour, verbal or other manifestations of hostility or estrangement, or even acts of physical violence. Deviations from the pattern of behaviour are the occasion for critical reactions, though these need not always occur for the same reasons.[4]

---

[1] Cf. Ch. VI, sect. 3 above. [2] Cf. Ch. VI, sect. 1 above.

[3] Cf. *The Concept of Law*, pp. 79–88, 163–76, 211–15, and 'Legal and Moral Obligation' in A. I. Melden (ed.), *Essays in Moral Philosophy*.

[4] This condition seems to me too severe, in that it concerns only critical reactions on occasions of actual deviations from the pattern of behaviour. In fact,

(3) Such critical reactions are generally regarded as legitimate and unobjectionable by most members of the group, including the criticized person, i.e. persons manifesting such critical reactions are not subjected in turn to critical reactions from other members of the group. [1]

(4) The existence of the former conditions is widely known in the group. [2]

Such a rule imposes a duty if

(5) The social pressure manifested by the critical reactions is relatively serious, and

(6) The conduct prescribed by the rule usually conflicts with the wishes of the person who owes the duty. [3]

This is an analysis of a simple type of social rules. Most social rules are more complicated in two important respects:

(a) Many social rules allow for some control by individuals over the incidence of duty: Individuals can impose duties upon others who are under their authority (in parent-child, teacher-pupil relations, etc.). They may impose duties upon themselves (by promising, inviting guests, expressing intentions in certain

hypothetical or theoretical expressions of opinion and manifestations of attitude by the members of the group are also relevant to the existence of rules. I refer to views expressed in discussions of the rightness or wrongness of certain courses of conduct, to the education of the young, to expression of opinions in literature, etc. Lack of a proper balance between these abstract manifestations of attitude and manifestations of critical reaction in cases of deviation is one source and one form of social hypocrisy.

[1] This condition seems to me too severe in two respects. It stipulates that offenders must admit, in most cases, the wrongness of their own behaviour. It seems sufficient if they tend to participate in the critical attitude to other offenders in similar circumstances. Furthermore, Hart assumes that every member of the group has equal right to manifest a critical reaction. It is enough that for most cases of deviation there are some who have the *locus standi* to react critically, i.e. it is enough if critical reactions from specially placed individuals are regarded as legitimate. Often various peoples are permitted to manifest various degrees of critical reaction.

[2] This formulation of the conditions is an interpretation of *The Concept of Law*, pp. 54–5.

[3] *CL*, pp. 84–5. I have endeavoured to explain Hart's concept of a social rule without using his key phrase 'an internal point of view'. It seems that Hart uses this phrase for three different, though interrelated, purposes: (1) It designates certain facts which are part of the existence-condition of rules. (2) It designates certain truth-conditions of certain statements or certain implications of making them. (3) It designates a certain attitude to norms which can be called 'acceptance of norms'. To avoid possible confusion I have refrained from using the phrase altogether.

circumstances, etc.). A person may be absolved from a duty by the act of another's waiving his rights, releasing the first from his promise, etc. A person may by acts of compensation, etc., preclude completely or partly critical reaction for his violation of a duty. Another person can save the violator from all or some of the critical reactions by waiving his claim for compensation, etc.

(b) Hart's analysis applies primarily to rules addressed to all the members of the group in which they exist.[1] Many rules are addressed to a particular sub-class of the group in which they exist: to women only, to elderly bachelors only, to priests only, to the tribal chief only, etc. Other rules apply only to people who are *not* members of the group in which the rules exist (rules as to the behaviour of foreigners visiting the country, etc.).

In spite of, or perhaps because of, the simplicity of the rules analysed by Hart, they can be regarded as the basic type of rules because their analysis provides a starting-point for the analysis of other types of rules. Three features of Hart's analysis are particularly relevant to the understanding of D-laws:

(1) Whenever an act is imposed as a (social) duty on certain persons, there is a factor which makes the non-performance of the act less eligible than its performance (other things being equal), thus providing a standard reason for its performance. This factor is the likelihood of encountering critical reactions.

(2) The facts constituting the standard reason for performing the duty depend for their existence on voluntary human conduct, which is at least partly caused by or motivated by the fact that the duty-act has not been performed.

(3) The existence of the duty-imposing rule depends on persisting and complex patterns of behaviour encompassing a large proportion of the members of the group in which the rule exists, and consisting of critical reactions which are regarded as legitimate by bystanders.

The first feature exists whenever there is a persistent fact which makes a certain course of conduct less eligible for a certain group of persons. For example, the fact that one's fingers will be burnt if put into the fire is a reason for not putting one's

---

[1] Admittedly they are obligated to act only when in certain circumstances, but everyone can be found in such circumstances.

fingers into the fire.[1] Only when the second feature exists is it possible to talk about norms. When a standard reason for preferring the performance of an act to its non-performance is the foreseen voluntary human reaction to the non-performance of that act, there is room to employ the concept of a norm as explained in section 1 above. In this sense orders backed by threats are norms,[2] but they do not impose obligations. Obligations are imposed only if the third feature exists as well.

In the law the existence of the third feature can be taken for granted. The existence of every law depends on the existence of the legal system to which it belongs, and the existence of legal systems depends on persistent and pervasive patterns of behaviour on the part of a large proportion of the population to which they apply.

It is characteristic of the law that the function of the critical reactions is taken over to a considerable extent by organized sanctions. These clearly comply with the first two features mentioned above—they are applied by voluntary human acts as a result of the violation of legal duties, and they are generally to the disadvantage of the person against whom they are applied, thus constituting a standard reason for performing the duty.[3]

Sanctions differ from critical reactions in four important respects:

(1) Only deprivation of legal rights or of status, the imposition of legal duties, the deprivation of life, liberty, health, or possessions, and a small number of other similar measures, which may vary from one society to another, are sanctions. Critical reactions include these and many other manifestations, as explained above.

(2) It is characteristic of the law that the performance of a significant proportion of its sanctions is guaranteed by the use of force to prevent possible obstructions. This may be, but need not be, the case in social rules.

(3) The nature of the sanction is determined with relative

---

[1] Bentham called such facts 'natural sanctions'.

[2] Subject to the explanations in Ch. VI, sect. 2 above.

[3] See on sanctions Ch. IV, sect. 2 above. Kelsen often uses the term in a wider sense, which includes critical reaction. Following Hart, I use it in the narrow sense explained in Ch. IV, sect. 2 and here.

precision in the law, and only a small and predetermined number of sanctions are applied for each violation of a duty. It is characteristic of social rules that the nature of the critical reaction for the violation of every kind of duty is only vaguely determined by the rules, and that there is no fixed limit to the number of critical reactions to a violation of a duty. There are, of course, societies of which this is not true, and there are probably some rules in every society for which there are predetermined definite critical reactions (killing the culprit, a general social boycott, etc.).

(4) The application of legal sanctions is organized, in that the persons bound or permitted to apply the sanction are determined by the law with greater precision than is usually the case in social rules. More important still, the application of sanctions is characteristically (though not always) regulated by men whose office it is to regulate the application of sanctions (courts, police, etc.).[1] No such officers exist under social rules which entrust the application of punitive measures either to the injured party, or to persons who have a special relation to the injured party, or a special relation to the violator of the duty (his family, friends, etc.) or to the public at large.

It should be noted that none of these characteristics can distinguish every legal sanction from every critical reaction under social rules. No such distinction exists. They are distinguished because sanctions belong to legal systems the majority of the sanctions of which have these characteristics.

Though in the law sanctions replace to a large extent critical reactions as the characteristic fact giving rise to the existence of duties, they do not replace them completely. It is characteristic of the law that violations of legal duties are encountered by critical reactions just because they are violations of a legal duty. It is characteristic of the law that violations of legal duties are encountered by critical reactions even from people who regard the law as bad, though not atrocious.[2] No doubt, absence of such critical reaction does not mean that the legal duty does not exist. Nevertheless, the existence of the critical reaction of

---

[1] See Ch. VIII below.

[2] People may, of course, be taught that sometimes it is good to violate even good laws, for example, in order to bring down a bad government or to change the regime, i.e. to bring about the change of some important constitutional laws.

ordinary citizens may still be a factor in determining the character of the law as a D-law, e.g. by helping to distinguish between prohibiting an act and taxing it.

More important in this context is the critical reaction of the law-applying organs. This is a major factor in determining whether an act is sanctioned or taxed, in distinguishing between a sanction and coercive administrative measures, such as compulsory purchase, destruction for sanitary reasons, confinement for medical treatment, etc. In modern legal systems the critical reaction of law-applying organs is most characteristically expressed in the reasons given by courts for their decisions. It is through the importance attributed to them by the courts that other sources like parliamentary debates, the explanatory notes attached to government bills, etc., acquire their relevance in this context.

In referring to the critical attitude of law-applying organs one should be careful to note that there is more than one such attitude which will establish the existence of a duty and a sanction. Whenever a disadvantage of the appropriate kind is inflicted on an individual as a consequence of his behaviour, and is regarded as necessary, either as restoration of the *status quo* or as compensation for some damage caused by the behaviour of that individual or as punishment (i.e. as retribution, prevention, deterrent, correction, etc.), the disadvantage is a sanction and the act of the individual is a violation of a duty.[1] Thus both criminal punishment and a great variety of civil remedies are sanctions giving rise to duties.

The fact that the nature of a law as a D-law depends on the critical reactions of the courts and other law-applying organs means that the character and interpretation of legal material can be changed without any intervention by the original author of that legal material.

Can there be legal duties which are not backed by sanctions? In the nature of things, though the regulation of human

---

[1] The courts' attitude is not the only sign which helps to distinguish sanctions from other coercive legal measures. Nor is it the only sign which helps to distinguish between various types of sanctions. But it is an important factor in establishing these distinctions.

The courts' attitude is also one of the factors which determines which act among the conditions for a sanction is the violation of a duty (e.g. is it making a contract or breaking it?). See on these issues sects. 2 and 3 of Ch. IV above.

behaviour through the imposition of duties backed by sanctions is effective in many circumstances, it is not effective in all circumstances. (To what extent can labour relations be regulated in this way in present-day Britain?) One area which cannot be regulated effectively by the imposition of sanctions only is the behaviour of high-ranking law-applying and law-creating organs. This is not because of any logical impossibility, but because of the impracticability of such a method in these circumstances. In many communities it is accepted that persons in these positions need a relative immunity from the consequences of mistakes of judgment and from hasty, malicious, or trivial accusations of misuse of powers. Moreover, very often these officials have the power to ensure such an immunity for themselves. Consequently, in many legal systems only gross misconduct on the part of high-ranking officials is made subject to sanctions. This does not mean that they have a complete discretion in all matters concerning their office which do not involve such gross misconduct.

Thus in many legal systems whenever a person can, by legal procedure, produce the annulment or withdrawal of an official measure (a by-law, an expropriation order, a refusal to give a certain licence, etc.), and sometimes when he can get compensation from the state or some public body for damage caused by some official measure—in such cases it seems appropriate to speak of the official who took the measure as having violated a duty. This amounts to the assertion of the normative statements that in many legal systems law-applying and law-creating officials have a general duty not to purport to use powers which they do not possess, and that they have a duty to exercise their powers in accordance with some general principles (e.g. to investigate fully the relevant facts, to hear both sides to a dispute, to base their decision on all the relevant considerations, etc.).

That in some legal systems there are laws imposing duties on ministers and other officials not to make *ultra vires* regulations, invalid expulsion orders, etc. whereas there is no similar general duty not to make invalid wills, contracts, etc., is a consequence of the difference in the critical reactions to such acts. In many legal systems certain forms of misuse of powers and of *ultra vires* acts of officials encounter critical reactions from the public at large and its representatives in elected bodies, from the courts, and from the administrative hierarchy itself (by means of unofficial reprimands, difficulties in promotion, declarations to the press, etc.). When such critical reactions can be distinguished from criticisms of inefficiency, mistakes of judgment, or wrong policies, when acts are condemned as being 'against the rules', as reprehensible regardless of their success or utility, then the critical reactions and the existence of a legal remedy seem to me to indicate the existence of a legal duty-imposing law, though it is not backed by any sanction-stipulating law.

In the last four or five pages a few general observations have been made on the relation of legal duties and D-laws, and sanctions, legal remedies, and critical reactions. These are meant as a general indication of the kind of individuation principles relating to D-laws which would be acceptable, and as a general indication of the way in which the relevant legal material should be interpreted. Many problems have been overlooked and the observations made here are very general. A complete investigation of D-laws is an appropriate subject for a separate study. Among the complications which would have to be considered in a thorough investigation of the subject two can be briefly mentioned here:

(a) The problem of the necessary relation between the scope of D-laws and sanction-stipulating laws: Their scope need not be co-extensive. Sanctions are sometimes inapplicable because of some excusing circumstances or personal immunity (which can be renounced), because of the period of limitation, or because of a plea of estoppel, etc., none of which affects the scope of the D-law and of the duty it imposes. What is the relation between the scope of a law and a sanction-imposing law which warrants the interpretation of the first as a D-law?

(b) The somewhat similar problem of the relation between duty and responsibility; the examination of vicarious liability, absolute responsibility, etc.: How does joint action in undertaking an obligation, or committing a wrong, affect the ensuing duties, and how does it affect responsibility? There are many similar problems.

The application of sanctions can be prescribed (in which case it is itself a duty) or permitted. In either case it can be made dependent upon the consent, initiative, or discretion of various persons (the injured party, the public prosecutor, the courts, prison committees, etc.). In the next chapter it will be argued that permissions to apply sanctions constitute separate laws. Sanction-stipulating laws will be called S-laws. S-laws which make the application of a sanction a duty will be called DS-laws. S-laws which merely permit the application of a sanction will be called MS-laws.

A legal system may include among its S-laws only DS-laws and no MS-laws, without thereby creating an infinite regress. Firstly, because not every D-law has a corresponding S-law, and therefore not every DS-law need be supported by a corresponding S-law. Secondly, because a DS-law can prescribe a sanction for the violation of itself as well as of other laws.[1] And finally, because of the possibility of cross-reference between laws. Consider the following four laws of a legal system which distinguishes between A- and B-duties (e.g. according to the jurisdiction of the courts): (a) Everyone has an A-duty not to steal. (b) Everyone has a B-duty to maintain his children. (c) Every A-court has a B-duty to punish every violation of an A-duty. (d) Every B-court has an A-duty to punish every violation of a B-duty. Every one of the duties imposed by these laws is backed by sanction, and no law prescribes a sanction for violation of duties imposed by itself.

Given an acceptable set of principles of individuation, the following two theses concerning the structure of legal systems can be asserted:

(i) Every legal system contains D-laws.[2]
(ii) Every legal system contains S-laws.

The first thesis hardly needs justifying. Imposing duties is the primary, and in many respects the most important, way in which the law fulfils its function, which is to regulate and guide human behaviour. As will be explained in the next section, all the other ways in which the law fulfils its function depend on the imposition of duties. The second thesis follows from the

---

[1] Cf. Hart, *Self-Referring Laws*.
[2] *Theses*: The series is continued on pp. 156, 164, 169, 170 and 171, and is distinguished by roman numerals.

first on the basis of conclusions arrived at in this section, above. It is not the case that the existence of every D-law depends on the existence of a corresponding S-law (i.e. a law stipulating a sanction for the violation of the D-law). But the existence of every D-law the law-subjects of which are not officials depends on the existence of a corresponding S-law. And there can be no officials unless there are also D-laws directed to non-officials. Therefore, there must be in every legal system D-laws directed to non-officials, and there must exist in every legal system S-laws corresponding to such D-laws.

On the basis of these theses two further theses can be affirmed:

(iii) Punitive relations are internal relations.
(iv) In every legal system there are internal punitive relations.

As no S-law can exist without a corresponding D-law, every punitive relation is an internal relation. Therefore, and in virtue of thesis (ii), in every legal system there are internal punitive relations.

D-laws directed to officials and not supported by corresponding S-laws have internal relations to the laws, providing the remedies the existence of which is necessary for the existence of the D-laws. Such internal relations, however, need not exist in every legal system.

VI.5: POWER-CONFERRING LAWS

Norms are guides to behaviour. Bentham, Austin, and Kelsen thought that the only way in which laws guide behaviour is by prescribing it. The account of D-laws in the last section is an explanation of legal norms prescribing behaviour. D-laws are a species of prescriptive norms, they are prescriptive norms which are laws. I call D-laws and similar norms prescriptive, and not imperative, norms in order to indicate that they need not be created by acts done with the intention to create norms. Bentham, Austin, and Kelsen adopted an imperative theory of norms; they all thought that every norm is an imperative norm. Following Hart, we have outlined an explanation of prescriptive norms which are not necessarily imperative norms, but which, nevertheless, guide human behaviour in the same way as do imperative norms, namely, through the existence of certain standard reasons for compliance with them. The nature of these standard reasons, and the way in which, because of them, prescriptive norms guide behaviour and are standards for its evaluation, have been explained in the previous sections. In this section a concept of norms guiding behaviour without prescribing it will be outlined. Given the desirability that every act-situation guided by law should be regarded as the core of a separate law, the existence of such norms makes possible the existence of another type of laws, which will be called 'power-conferring laws' or P-laws. All P-laws are norms, i.e. they guide human behaviour. The account offered here of the nature of P-laws as norms is based on several remarks made by Hart in *The Concept of Law*.[1]

In discussing the existence of a type of norms two kinds of considerations should be distinguished. Ontological considerations determine whether there are sufficient grounds for postulating abstract entities. Normative considerations determine whether these entities are norms. For example, it has been argued in sections 2 and 3 above that, so far as the normative considerations are concerned, orders can be regarded as norms, but that it may be doubted whether there is an ontological justification for regarding them as entities of the relevant kind. Ontological and normative considerations should be supplemented by linguistic considerations that determine which terms are most appropriate for describing the norms concerned, and describe the appropriate occasions on which such norms are referred to in ordinary discourse. As throughout this study, I shall say very little about the linguistic considerations.

Hart explains that ' . . . there are important classes of laws where . . . (the) analogy with orders backed by threats altogether fails, since they perform quite a different social function. Legal rules defining the ways in which valid contracts or wills or marriages are made do not require persons to act in certain ways whether they wish to or not. Such laws do not impose duties or obligations. Instead, they provide individuals with *facilities* for realizing their wishes. . . . '[2] Hart is making here two very important points: There are laws which are power-conferring laws; and they are norms, they guide human

[1] See especially pp. 27–33, 40–1, 78–9, 92–4.   [2] *CL*, p. 27.

behaviour by providing individuals with facilities for realizing their wishes.

The second point is gravely undermined by Hart when he goes on to distinguish between rules determining capacities to exercise powers, rules specifying the forms and procedure of exercising powers, and rules delimiting the duration of the structure of rights and duties created by the exercise of such powers.[1] Later he mentions as of the same category rules specifying the subject-matter on which a certain legislator has power to legislate, rules specifying the qualifications and identity of members of legislative bodies, and rules specifying the form and procedure of legislation.[2] It seems to me that no law of these kinds is a norm, nor is it clear on what principles of individuation, and for what reasons, they should be considered as laws and not as parts of laws. If they are laws, they are laws which are not norms but have internal relations to legal norms (in these cases to P-laws), and derive, as it were, their legal relevance from their effect on the interpretation and application of these legal norms. Such laws will be discussed in the next chapter. This section is concerned exclusively with legal norms which are not D-laws.

Hart refers in the quoted passage to the 'social function' of laws. This phrase has at least two senses. According to the first, which I consider the more appropriate sense in which to employ the phrase, it refers to the social effects of a law (actual or designed). In this sense it may be said that the designed function of a law is to facilitate real-estate transactions or to discourage married women from continuing working. According to the second sense the phrase refers to the 'normative function' of laws. In this sense all D-laws have but one type of function—to prescribe a certain course of conduct. The normative function of P-laws is to provide individuals with facilities for realizing their wishes. Laws specifying a procedure in which certain powers (e.g. to make wills) can be used (e.g. only in writing) have social functions (e.g. to prevent deceit), but they do not have any normative function, for they do not in themselves provide facilities. They do not confer powers and are not norms. It is with the explanation of the normative function of P-laws that this section is concerned.

[1] *CL*, p. 28.   [2] Ibid, p. 31.

D-laws and other prescriptive norms guide behaviour by prescribing it. They prescribe behaviour because their existence entails the existence of facts which (a) constitute a reason for performing the prescribed behaviour on the occasions to which the norms apply, and (b) are caused by human reaction to the non-performance of the prescribed behaviour on these occasions; their existence, too, depends on the behaviour of a large proportion of the population. This characterization is true of every prescriptive norm, whether or not it imposes a duty.

Prescriptive norms can be regarded as a special kind of O-norms. The following is a crude outline of a three-stage partial analysis of O-norms. Let Z be the act-situation of some persons doing A_1 in C_1, and Y the act-situation of some persons doing A_2 in C_2; and let P be any generic state of affairs. The general form of an O-norm can be represented as $Z + P$. It can be read: By doing A_1 in C_1 an agent has an O-power over P (or to achieve P). An O-norm confers an O-power on the norm subjects.

First Stage: The existence of standard reasons: Suppose the following conditions are fulfilled:

(1) The occurrence of an instance of Z gives some considerable probability to the subsequent occurrence of an instance of P.

(2) The agent (i.e. the person performing Z on any occasion) usually knows of (1).

(3) The occurrence of a P following an instance of Z is very often either desirable or undesirable in the eyes of the agent.

When these three conditions obtain one may say that P is a standard reason for performing or not performing Z. It is significant that P is sometimes a reason for performing Z and sometimes for not performing it. For example, suppose that P is that a living-room is being heated and that Z is turning on an electric heater. That P is likely to follow Z is sometimes a reason for doing Z, sometimes for not doing it. This is a very simple example for two reasons: (1) Doing Z has no other consequences which are usually regarded by the agent as advantageous or disadvantageous. (2) The advantages and disadvantages of P in the eyes of most agents on most occasions are of a similar nature—the need of living beings for a certain degree of warmth in their environment. Other situations in which the conditions obtain, though more complex, are of similar nature.

Second Stage: Pre-normative situations: Suppose that the first three conditions as well as the following conditions are fulfilled:

(4) *P* is identical with or a consequence of the performance of every instance of *Y*, and an instance of *Y* is likely to follow every performance of a *Z*.

(5) The performance of a *Z* is a reason for or part of the motive for the performance of a *Y*.

(6) That conditions (4) and (5) are fulfilled is known to the agent (of *Z*).

When these conditions obtain, it can be said that performing *Z* causes the performance of *Y*, and therefore that it causes *P*. The performance of a *Y* has some advantage to the agent of *Z* when *P* is thought by him to be advantageous, and it has some disadvantage for him when *P* is to his disadvantage. That *Y* and that *P* are likely to follow the performance of *Z* is a reason sometimes for performing and sometimes for not performing *Z*. It can be said that in virtue of his ability to perform or not to perform *Z* an agent has some control over the occurrence of a *Y* and of *P*; in such cases it will be said that the agent has an O-power over *Y* and over *P*. Such pre-normative situations exist when, for example, a person asks another to turn on the heater, or orders him to do so, in circumstances which make compliance likely. Another example would be a case where a guest put on his overcoat in his host's room, knowing that this would move the host to turn on the heater.

Third Stage: The existence of norms: Suppose that in addition to the first six conditions the following ones are fulfilled:

(7) The performance of instances of *Y* in consequence of the performance of instances of *Z* involves on various occasions the active participation or the acquiescence of a large proportion of the members of a certain population.

(8) That condition (7) is fulfilled is widely known in that population.

When all eight conditions are fulfilled normative considerations justify talking about the existence of a norm. Thus it can be said that in a certain population there is a norm conferring on members of the population O-power to obtain food by asking for it for their children, provided that usually such requests are fulfilled and the rest of the conditions obtain, and even if there is no duty on the population to give charity in these circumstances. That we do not often talk of the existence of norms in such circumstances is due to ontological and linguistic and not to normative considerations.[1]

Prescriptive norms can be defined on the basis of O-norms as follows:

Let ' $-Z$ ' mean the non-performance of Z, ' $Z!P$ ' be read ' Z is prescribed on pain of P ', and ' $Z!$ ' be read ' Z is prescribed':

Definition: ' $Z!P$ ' means the same as ' $-Z+P$ ' provided that P is standardly regarded by the norm-subject to his disadvantage when it occurs in consequence of his not performing Z.

Definition: ' $Z!$ ' means the same as ' $(\exists P)\ Z!P$ '.

Thus explained, prescriptive norms are seen to be only a special case of O-norms. O-norms guide behaviour but some of them do not guide it in a definite direction. The existence of an O-norm is sometimes a reason for performing the norm-act, sometimes a reason for not performing it, for its likely consequences are sometimes advantageous and sometimes disadvantageous. When the likely consequences of performing the norm-act are on all occasions disadvantageous then its non-performance is prescribed.

This rough outline of the analysis of O-norms and of their relations to prescribing norms needs to be refined and developed in many points. This is, however, a task for a general theory of

---

[1] My claim to have analysed an important type of norms, which I call O-norms, is certain to raise certain doubts, which, I believe, cannot be resolved without attempting to make more precise the very general points made here. It should, however, be noted that for the purposes of the study of legal norms it is enough to accept these points as forming only a partial characterization of O-norms. It is enough to consider them as necessary, though not sufficient, conditions for the existence of norms of a certain type. The explanation given below of PR- and PL-laws includes further conditions (i.e. certain internal relations to D-laws) which in any case justify regarding laws of these types as O-norms.

norms. For the purposes of this study it is enough to present the concept in crude outline. O-norms depend on widespread known and uniform human reaction to human behaviour. It is natural to suppose that the uniformity of reactions pre-supposed by O-norms is not a mere coincidence. When people usually react in the same way in the same circumstances it is likely that they do so for similar reasons. Such reasons can be their opinions of right and wrong, their views on the good of the community or of their own good, etc.

One possible reason for a uniformity of reaction can be that the reaction is itself a duty. That by doing Z some persons have the O-power over P can be due to the fact that Y, which produces P, is itself prescribed by another norm, i.e. that $Y!$ *when Z* is a norm. When this is the case there is an internal relation between the two norms, for, on the one hand, the O-norm exists because of the existence of the prescriptive norm, and, on the other hand, it regulates the application of the prescribing norm. In other words, the identity of the persons who are obliged to behave in a certain manner by the prescribing norm, and the circumstances in which they are obliged to do so, can be affected by the exercise of the O-powers conferred by the O-norm. Such an internal relation of an O-norm to a pre-scribing norm will be called a 'regulative relation'. Whenever an O-norm has a regulative relation to a prescriptive norm the O-norm is properly described as conferring power to regulate the application of certain duties by instances of a certain act-situation. O-norms of these types will be called PR-norms (and if they are legal norms—PR-laws), and the powers they confer will be called PR-powers or regulative powers.

PR-laws stand in regulative relations to D-laws the applica-tion of which they regulate. Like other non-prescriptive O-norms, they guide behaviour not by making one course of behaviour more eligible than its avoidance whenever certain circumstances are the case, but by stipulating certain conse-quences of certain acts, which sometimes make it advantageous to perform these acts and sometimes make it advantageous not to perform them.

PR-laws are of great importance in the law, but usually they are of much greater complexity than the PR-laws already described. Usually, too, they regulate the application of more than one D-law, and they often regulate the application of D-laws at one remove, i.e. by regulating the application of other PR-laws, which in turn regulate the application of D-laws. Consider, for example, laws conferring powers on officials to marry people. They depend for their legal effect on other laws creating the status of marriage, namely, laws imposing duties and conferring powers on married people. These power-conferring laws in turn depend for their legal effects on other laws the application of which they regulate.

Laws conferring powers to transfer the ownership of property, or to declare a state of emergency, operate in similar fashion; they bring certain people under the application of certain laws, thereby conferring upon them powers or depriving them of powers, imposing on them duties or releasing them from duties, etc.

Regulative relations will be further discussed in the next chapter, where the relations of PR-laws to other laws will be further examined. The above discussion substantiates the claim that PR-laws are norms, for they guide behaviour. The fact that by doing certain acts one transfers one's property is sometimes a reason for doing these acts; at other times it is just as good a reason not to do them.

PR-laws are just one kind of O-norms. They are characterized by the fact that the reaction to the performance of the norm-act is prescribed by another norm which must co-exist with the PR-law if the latter is to have any effect at all. There is another kind of O-norms that should be mentioned. These are norms conferring legislative powers, or PL-norms as they will be called. They are characterized by the fact that the reaction to the performance of the norm-act is prescribed by other norms, but these do not exist when the PL-norm is created; they are created by the norm-acts of the PL-norm themselves. The D-laws imposing the duties which are transferred from one person to another when ownership is transferred exist before the transfer of ownership, and only because they exist does the PR-law that confers powers to transfer ownership have any legal significance. The duties imposed on a person when he concludes a contract are prescribed only by the contract itself, by a norm created by his act, not by a pre-existing norm. The PL-law conferring PL-powers to make contracts does not depend for its significance on the existence of other laws. It has relevance even before any laws have been created on its basis. Its relevance is that it confers powers to create new laws.

Similarly, by declaring a state of emergency the competent minister regulates the application of laws that he does not thereby create, and that must have existed before his declaration if it is to have any effect. By making a regulation, on the other hand, a minister does not regulate the application of any previously existing laws; he is creating a new law. The duties he imposes are prescribed by a law created by him on this occasion, not by a previously existing law.

Laws enacted by the exercise of legislative powers conferred by a PL-law have an internal relation to that law, of a kind which will be called 'genetic relations'. The following two theses can be asserted, though, as they concern the minimum content or complexity of legal systems, they will not be defended here:

(v) In every legal system there are PL-laws.
(vi) In every legal system there are PR-laws.

The first of these theses will be further considered in Chapter VIII, where it will be argued that every legal system contains courts with legislative powers. It follows from theses (v) and (vi) that:

(vii) In every legal system there are genetic relations between laws.
(viii) In every legal system there are regulative relations between laws.

Thesis (viii) follows directly from (vi). Thesis (vii) follows from (v), and the fact that, although it is not the case that for every PL-law there are other laws enacted by the exercise of powers it confers, there are some PL-laws for which there are such laws, having genetic relations to them.

PL- and PR-laws have this in common, that both guide behaviour, but not in the same direction on every occasion to which they apply. Sometimes their existence is a reason for performing the norm-act, sometimes it is a reason for not performing it. Therefore they are both called power-conferring or P-laws. Legal systems contain only two kinds of norms, P-laws and D-laws. Understanding their function and interrelations is an important part of understanding the structure and function of legal systems. It is essentially this claim that Hart is making when he says that in the combination of primary and secondary rules lies the key to the science of jurisprudence.[1] The explanation suggested above of D-laws and P-laws and their relations is an explanation of that dictum. In a few respects this explanation differs from Hart's account of secondary rules and their relations to primary rules:

(1) Hart considers that all the laws in a legal system are either primary or secondary rules. It will be argued in the next chapter that though D- and P-laws are the only types of legal norms there are other types of laws which are not norms.

(2) It will be argued in Chapter VIII below that the rule of recognition is not a P-law but a D-law, hence it is incorrect to say that P-laws correspond to Hart's secondary rules.

(3) Hart says that secondary rules may 'be said to be on a different level from primary rules, for they are all *about* such rules; in the sense that while primary rules are concerned with the actions that individuals must or must not do, these secondary rules are all concerned with the primary rules themselves'.[2] This seems a rather unfortunate way of describing the situation. Though secondary rules and P-laws have internal relations to primary rules and D-laws respectively, they are not about them but 'about' human behaviour which they guide as primary rules and D-laws do, though in an indefinite direction.

(4) Hart does not distinguish between PL-laws and PR-laws, a distinction which is of the utmost importance. He says for example that operations of making a contract or transferring property can profitably be regarded as legislative acts of a limited range.[3] I have argued above that only powers to make contracts are legislative powers, whereas powers to transfer property are regulative powers or PR-powers.

The full importance of the distinction between legislative and regulative powers was realized only by Bentham (he called them legislative and aggregative powers), though he did not attempt to draw a corresponding distinction between types of laws. Even Bentham failed in providing an exact criterion for

---

[1] *CL*, p. 78.   [2] Ibid, p. 92.   [3] Ibid, p. 94.

deciding for each power of which kind it is. I have not tried here to tackle this problem, for it admits of no easy solution and its discussion does not belong to an introductory study like this.

(5) Hart's concept of rules of adjudication will be examined in Chapter VIII below. It can be best treated not as a special type of secondary rules on a par with rules of change, but as a special subclass of PL-laws or of rules of change.

A.   *Note on Obedience Laws*

Bentham and Austin regard at least some laws authorizing legislation as obedience laws.[1] I have suggested above that all these laws should be regarded as PL-laws. The reasons for preferring PL-laws to obedience laws as an explication of the concept of laws authorizing legislation are outlined here.

Whenever a statement of the form (1) 'x has legislative powers to legislate laws by doing A in C' is true, there is a statement of the form (2) 'y has a duty to (or ought to) obey x if he does A in C' that is true, and is entailed by the first statement, and entails it. Statements of the form (1) can be regarded as the standard description of PL-laws, if it is decided to accept this category of laws. Statements of the form (2) can be regarded as the standard description of obedience laws, if it is decided to accept this category of laws.

The fact that statements of these types can be arranged in pairs of mutually entailing statements means that if PL-laws are, as I have claimed, an explication of laws authorizing legislation, so are obedience laws, and vice versa. What are the reasons for preferring PL-laws as an explication of laws authorizing legislation? And why should not both PL-laws and obedience laws be postulated?

The wish to avoid redundancy and to be faithful to the ordinary conception of the law point to the rejection of the last possibility. We usually think that the authorization of legislation involves only one and not two laws. Furthermore, as any of the pair of statements can be derived from the other it is enough to postulate the existence of one law in order to establish the truth of both statements. On the other hand, it is desirable that every act-situation guided by law should be the

---

[1] Cf. Ch. I, sect. 3 above.

core of a separate law. Laws authorizing legislation guide both
the behaviour of the authorized legislator and the behaviour
of the potential subjects of his laws. Statements of the first form
describe the way in which the legislator's behaviour is guided,
whereas statements of the second form describe how the behaviour of the potential subjects of his laws is affected. There
is therefore a case for postulating both obedience and PL-
laws.

Here is a conflict of general requirements which can be
solved only by weighing the conflicting considerations one
against the other.

Because the redundancy in this case is very far reaching—one
statement alone entails the other and the entailment is mutual—
I suggest that only one type of laws should be postulated. I
prefer to postulate PL-laws for two reasons: First, this is the
usual way in which we are accustomed to think about the law.
Second, it seems that the behaviour of the authorized legislator
is guided by authorizing legislation in a more direct and
immediate way than the behaviour of the potential subjects of
his laws; for in a sense they are affected only if he uses his powers
and makes laws.

The discussion in this section centred on laws authorizing
legislation, i.e. the creation of laws by acts intended to create
laws. Other human acts may also create law if authorized by
law,[1] and the authorizing law can be similarly treated.

---

[1] Cf. Ch. III, sect. 3 above.

VII

LEGAL SYSTEMS AS SYSTEMS OF LAWS

VII.1: ON THE NORMATIVITY OF THE LAW

All the philosophers hitherto considered are united on one crucial issue; they all think that every law is a norm. In this chapter I shall put forward the view that, though, in the sense explained later, normativity is an important characteristic of the law, some laws are not norms; or, more precisely, that, given the minimum content and minimum complexity of legal systems, and given an acceptable set of principles of individuation, there are in any legal system some laws which are not norms. As the minimum content and complexity of legal systems is not discussed in this study, all that can be actually established here is the possibility of laws which are not norms.

The case for such laws rests on the general requirements of avoiding repetition and of not deviating without sufficient reason from ordinary discourse, and, most important of all, the case for such laws rests on the requirements of simplicity and clarity in the exposition of important connections between various parts of a legal system. This chapter is concerned only with the general case for the existence of laws which are not norms. Therefore no attempt will be made to enumerate and analyse all the types of laws which are not norms. Only two types of such laws and the advantages gained by postulating them will be explored in the next two sections.

There is, however, one point of principle which should be dealt with in advance. As has been stated in the Introduction, the three most important characteristics of the law are that it is coercive, institutionalized, and normative. And the differences between many legal philosophers can be regarded as stemming from their different explanations of these features of the law. In the previous chapter a partial explanation of the normativity of the law has been offered. It has been suggested that the law is normative because its function is to guide human behaviour, and that it guides human behaviour in two ways: either by affecting the consequences of a certain course of conduct in a way which constitutes a standard reason for avoiding that course of conduct, or by affecting the consequences of a certain course of conduct in a way which constitutes a reason for pursuing or avoiding it, depending upon one's wishes. This view differs from the theories of Bentham, Austin, and Kelsen, who considered only the first way of guiding behaviour. It accords with Hart's view that law guides human behaviour also by providing facilities for fulfilling certain human wishes.

Hart seems, however, to agree with the other philosophers considered in thinking that the normativity of the law means that every law is a norm. According to Bentham, Austin, Hart, and, in his own distorted way, according to Kelsen as well, the most important consideration in the individuation of law is to guarantee that every law is a norm. Thereby they make the principles of individuation, and the concept of *a law* which they define, the only key to the explanation of the normativity of the law.

As against this view it has been suggested in Chapter VI, section 3 above that there are many other considerations affecting the individuation of laws and the concept of a law, and consequently that there are laws which are not norms. The normativity of the law is explained by two theses:

    (ix) In every legal system there are norms.[1]

    (x) All the laws of a legal system which are not norms have internal relations to legal norms,[2] i.e. they affect the existence or application of legal norms. Moreover, their sole legal relevance is in the way in which they affect the existence and application of legal norms.

Substituting this explanation of the normativity of the law for the prevalent explanation, which consists in the thesis that every law is a norm, produces two results:

(1) The explanation of the normativity of the law, being dependent on the internal relations between laws, turns out

---

[1] Cf. Ch. VI, sects. 4 and 5 above.

[2] Internal relations are at least sometimes transitive, for by affecting the existence or application of one law they also affect the existence or application of the laws which depend on it for their existence or application.

to be based on the concept of a legal system rather than on the concept of a law.

(2) The analysis of the concept of a law depends on the analysis of the concept of a legal system. For the understanding of some types of laws depends on their internal relation with some other laws. They derive their legal relevance from their relations to other laws. The analysis of the structure of legal system is therefore indispensable for the definition of 'a law'.[1]

VII.2: ON PERMISSIONS

The following thesis can be added to the ten hitherto asserted:

> (xi) According to every momentary legal system, every act-situation which is not prohibited by a specific law of the system is permitted.

Thesis (xi) is true whatever the content of the legal systems may be. If a momentary system contains a law prohibiting the performance of any act which is not expressly permitted by law, the thesis is still true, though, with regard to that system, it is vacuously true; for as a matter of fact all the act-situations are either expressly permitted or expressly prohibited by the system. The thesis is also vacuously true so far as it regards a legal system which contains a law permitting all acts other than those expressly prohibited by other laws.

As formulated, the thesis applies to momentary legal systems only. In order to apply to non-momentary systems the thesis should be modified to account for the possibility of retroactive laws. An act-situation can always be prohibited after the event by retroactive legislation. A court's decision that a particular act was an offence, though there was no previous law which made it an offence, is such retroactive legislation; sometimes it applies to that particular act only, sometimes it amounts to the creation of a general law with (at least partial) retroactive effect.

Given that the truth of thesis (xi) is independent of the content of particular legal systems, and that it should be distinguished from laws of particular systems prohibiting or permitting all the acts which are not otherwise regulated by

[1] Cf. Introduction.

the system, what is the significance of the thesis? It reflects the conception of the law as regulating human behaviour by prescribing conduct, and it expresses the decision to regard legal systems as independent normative systems, i.e. as normative systems which can be and are studied separately from other norms.

From the legal point of view all such acts are permitted unless prohibited by a law. Thereby is reflected the fact that the law guides behaviour by prescribing or prohibiting it. If it does not prescribe or prohibit it, then it is not guided in that way. To say that an act is permitted is to say that it is not guided in a certain way, it is not prohibited. The principle that acts are permitted unless prohibited by a law expresses a decision to consider the way in which the law guides behaviour in a certain manner, without reference to the possibility that it may be guided by other factors.

Thesis (xi) should be supplemented by the following thesis:

(xii) According to every momentary legal system, no *future* act can create laws or affect the application of laws unless there is in that momentary system a law conferring upon it that power.

Some acts which were performed before the moment in which a particular momentary system exists can be recognized as the exercise of legislative powers according to that system, even though the system contains no law authorizing such acts of legislation. This is the case, for example, if the system contains laws which were enacted without any legal authorization.[1] These acts of legislation were not guided by law, for their character as the exercise of legal powers is derived only from the fact that a subsequent momentary system contains laws enacted by them.

Thesis (xii) is analogous to thesis (xi). Thesis (xi) expresses the decision to consider the law in one isolated function, as guiding behaviour by imposing duties. Thesis (xii) expresses the decision to consider the law in one function in isolation, that of guiding behaviour by conferring powers.

Because of thesis (xi) it might seem that every act-situation which is not prohibited by law can be regarded as the core of a

---

[1] Cf. Ch. II, sect. I and Ch. VI, sect. 3 above.

law permitting it. No such general doctrine can be accepted, because it conflicts with the normativity of law in general for (a) to say that an act is permitted is not to give a description of a norm—it means not that the act is guided but that it is not guided, and (b) statements describing such permissions are not, generally, descriptions of laws which are not norms, for such putative laws have no internal relations to any legal norms.

Nevertheless, some statements of the form 'x is permitted to (or may) do A in C' will be regarded as describing laws that are not norms, and these will be called permission-granting or M-laws. Postulating the existence of M-laws presupposes the following convention:

A Convention of the Interpretation of M-laws: When an M-law partly contradicts a D-law of the same momentary system, both are valid and the M-law represents an exception to the D-law: the D-law, in spite of its express content, does not apply to cases falling under the M-law.

Any acceptable principles of individuation governing the individuation of M-laws must ensure that every M-law fulfils the following three conditions:

(1) The act-situation permitted by an M-law belonging to a given momentary legal system is an instance of an act-situation prohibited by one or more D-laws belonging to the same momentary system; but the act-situation permitted by the M-law is not co-extensive with (equivalent to) the act-situation prohibited by any of these D-laws.

(2) There are reasons for regarding the permission granted by the M-law as an exception to prohibitions imposed by one or more D-laws.

(3) There are reasons for regarding the exception to the prohibitions as a separate law.

The convention of interpretation and the first condition determine the formal relations between M-laws and D-laws. They guarantee that every M-law will have an internal relation to one or more D-laws. Every M-law modifies the application of at least one D-law. The second and third conditions provide a justification for postulating laws with these relations to D-laws.

Suppose, for example, that the following statements are true:

(1) Everyone may use force in self-defence. (2) Everyone may carry a walking stick. (3) It is prohibited to carry a gun. Why do we regard the first but not the second as an exception to a general prohibition? Not because there is no true statement describing a prohibition which (2) partly contradicts. For given (3) the following statement is true: (4) It is prohibited to carry stipons ('stipon' is defined as 'a walking-stick or a gun'). (2) partly contradicts (4), yet it should not be regarded as describing an exception to it. There are no reasons for regarding (2) as describing an exception to (4).

The reasons for regarding a normative statement of this form as describing an exception to a general prohibition are in the critical reactions of the population at large, and particularly of the law-applying and law-creating organs. In other words, whether or not a permission is an exception to a prohibition depends upon the reasons given for the prohibition and for the permission. For example, a permission is an exception to one or more prohibitions if the reasons for the prohibitions apply also to the permitted cases (in the sense that they apply to a general class including both the prohibited and the permitted cases), and also if these cases are exempted from the prohibition because of the presence in them of some features that are reasons for permitting them and outweigh the more general reasons for prohibiting them.

But the fact that a true statement describing a permission describes an exception to a prohibition is only a necessary, and not a sufficient, condition for regarding it as describing a separate law. It may be regarded as a consequence of a statement describing a more narrowly defined prohibition. For example, that one may drive any Rolls Royce is an exception to a prohibition to drive cars manufactured before 1935. Yet it should not be regarded as describing a separate law, but rather as a consequence of a statement to the effect that one may not drive any car manufactured before 1935 other than a Rolls Royce. This last statement, if it describes a complete law, describes a D-law.

One reason for regarding a statement which describes a permission as describing an M-law, i.e. one reason for postulating an M-law, is that the permission is an exception to each one of a group of D-laws, and that it reveals an important feature common to them, thereby pointing out an important connection between laws.[1] This is the reason why there can be laws permitting self-defence and other forms of self-help. Similar reasons justify postulating, in legal systems with an appropriate content, laws permitting interference with somebody else's property in circumstances of emergency, in order to save it, etc.

There may be other reasons for postulating M-laws; one type of M-laws, already mentioned, is the group called MS-laws, laws permitting the application of sanctions. A law is an S-law, even if it only permits and does not prescribe the performance of acts which constitute the application of sanctions, but only if it is an exception to a general prohibition. The reason for postulating MS-laws is not that they single out a feature common to many laws, but that they clarify the relation between D-laws and S-laws, which is of major importance in the understanding of the law.

Suppose, for example, that a sanction for breaking a D-law forbidding adultery is that (1) the betrayed spouse or his next of kin may whip the adulterous spouse in the market-place, etc. It is better to regard (1) as a description of an MS-law rather than as describing part of the law against assault: (2) Assault is prohibited unless it is whipping an adulterous spouse, etc. It would be awkward to regard (2) as both a law prohibiting assault and a law stipulating a sanction against adultery; all the more so, because the law will then turn out both to impose a duty and to grant a permission. The two functions should be separated and assigned to two laws, a D-law against assault and an MS-law regarding adulterous spouses.

A full analysis of these types of M-laws demands a detailed exploration that cannot be undertaken here. Further examination will, undoubtedly, reveal a need for other types of M-laws. The aims of this section, however, have been served by outlining what governs the individuation of M-laws. By doing this the necessity for postulating, in certain circumstances, one type of laws that are not norms has been proved.

It is not clear whether M-laws exist in every legal system,

[1] Cf. Ch. VI, sect. 3 above.

although they probably exist in all of them. But it was established that whenever an M-law exists it has an internal relation with at least one D-law, thus contributing its share to the internal structure of the legal system to which it belongs.

In accepting a conception of law which allows for the possibility of laws which are permissions I am following Bentham's view,[1] but with two important differences:

(1) By insisting that every M-law modifies existing D-laws the possibility that an M-law will continue to exist after the D-laws it modified were repealed, by it or by other laws, is ruled out, and conformity to the thesis of normativity explained in the previous section is guaranteed.[2]

(2) The existence of any particular M-law is determined not by regard to the circumstances in which the relevant legal material was created,[3] but by judging whether admitting its existence will—while reflecting correctly the content of the legal system—promote any of the general aims determining the principles of individuation.[4]

VII.3: ON LAWS INSTITUTING RIGHTS

Many of the laws of every legal system are concerned with the institution, or presuppose the existence, of rights, and among them there are certain laws which are not norms. In this section a few remarks will be made on the nature of laws instituting rights and on the role of D-laws and P-laws in the institution of rights. No classification of, or distinctions between, various types of rights will be attempted, and the remarks will be confined to those features common to laws concerning any type of rights. It should be emphasized that this section is not concerned with the analysis of the concept of a right, but with the analysis of laws instituting rights. Such an analysis is a precondition for a definition of 'a legal right', and some points concerning a few suggested definitions of this phrase will be made later in this section.

Persons have rights of certain types in certain objects or

---

[1] See Ch. III, sect. 2 above.
[2] For Bentham's different view see Ch. III, sect. 2 above.
[3] This is Bentham's position; cf. Ch. III, sect. 2 and Ch. IV, sect. 1 above.
[4] See Ch. VI, sect. 3 above.

towards certain persons. The right of an owner differs from the right of a mortgagor, and from the right of a wife to maintenance. The right of ownership in immovable property differs in certain respects from the ownership of movable property. Similarly the right of a wife to maintenance differs from the right of a child to maintenance. One must distinguish, therefore, not only between various types of rights (ownership, maintenance, etc.) but also between various classes of right-subjects (i.e. right-holders) and right-objects.

Rights are relations between right-subjects, which are always persons, though not always natural persons, and right-objects, which are either persons, or physical objects, or abstract legal entities (e.g. shares). Some rights are three-place relations, etc., but the laws instituting such rights do not differ substantially from laws instituting other rights.

Every atomic statement of a right relation, i.e every statement that certain persons have a certain right in certain physical objects or over or against certain persons, will be called a 'key statement'. Every law the proper description of which includes a key statement, or is logically equivalent to a statement which includes a key statement, is a law instituting the right described by the key statement.

Laws instituting rights fall into three categories: they are either investitive laws, or divestitive laws, or constitutive laws. Investitive laws specify the ways in which rights can be acquired. Divestitive laws determine the ways in which rights can be disposed of. Constitutive laws specify the consequences of being a right-holder.

An investitive law is a law which determines that when certain conditions obtain a certain person who did not have a certain right acquires it. If 'P' designates any state of affairs, 'K_{t1}' means that a key statement is true at time t_1, then the general form of investitive laws can be said to be: When $\sim K_{t1}$ and P, then K_{t2}. A divestitive law is a law which determines that when certain conditions obtain a certain person who has a certain right loses it. Its general form can be said to be: When K_{t1} and P, then $\sim K_{t2}$. A constitutive law is a law which determines that if a certain person has a certain right, and certain further conditions obtain, then he has a certain other right or a certain duty or a certain power. The general form of constitutive laws can be said to be: When K_{t1} and P, then Q, where Q designates either another key statement or the existence of a duty or a power.

The conditions specified by such laws (and designated by 'P' in their general form) can be divided into three types:

(1) The existence of any legal right, duty, or power in the hands of a certain person.

(2) The performance of some acts by a certain person.

(3) The occurrence of a certain other event.

A law instituting a right can stipulate conditions of any one of these types or of any number of them.

For example, a law can stipulate that ownership is acquired by gift, i.e. by certain acts of a previous owner. Such a law is both a divestitive and an investitive law of ownership. It determines a way in which ownership can be acquired by the act of another man, and a way in which it can be lost by the act of the owner. Another law can determine that ownership in property of a certain type (which cannot be left by will) is acquired by a person upon the death of his spouse, who was the previous owner. Such a law makes the acquisition of ownership dependent not upon the performance of any act but upon the occurrence of an event.

Other laws may determine, for example, that every person who owns land has a certain duty to pay certain taxes. A law may determine that owners of land have powers to grant licences to other persons to visit the land or to use it. A law may determine that owners of land are the owners of any crops growing on the land. All these laws are constitutive laws. They determine the consequences of having rights. The last mentioned is also an investitive law, for it determines also a way of acquiring rights.

It can be said that all the investitive, divestitive, and constitutive laws concerning one legal right, all the laws instituting one legal right in one legal system, define that right in that legal system. Such a definition, however, is not what may be called the 'jurisprudential definition' of that right. A jurisprudential definition of a right aims at picking out the most important features of the various types of laws that institute that right. The considerations determining what should count as an important feature in the law instituting a right cannot be examined here. It should, however, be clearly understood that a jurisprudential definition of any right presupposes some knowledge of the laws instituting that right in some legal systems.

Jurisprudential definitions of rights presuppose not only the content of laws instituting the rights defined, but also their structure. It is essential for an adequate analysis of the concept of any right to take into account the fact that rights are instituted by investitive, divestitive, and constitutive laws, and to understand their function and structure. Therefore a general theory of the structure of legal systems is a prerequisite for an adequate analysis of rights.

It seems to me that the attempts to investigate the concepts of rights have neglected the relations between rights and the laws instituting them, and that this accounts to a considerable extent for the shortcomings of these attempted elucidations of concepts of rights.

One reason for the neglect of laws instituting rights in the analysis of rights has been the view that right terms should not be used in the proper description of laws. This view should be distinguished from another, namely the view that legislators do not usually use right terms in formulating laws as part of the process of their enactment. The fact, if it is a fact, that legislators do not often use right terms in enacting laws is no reason why jurists in describing these laws should not use right terms.

Two different reasons are sometimes given for excluding right terms from the proper description of laws. Hart, for example, thinks that 'a statement of the form "X has a right" is used to draw a conclusion of law in a particular case which falls under such rules',[1] and the rules themselves do not refer to rights. The same is presumably true, in his opinion, about other right terms (like 'is the owner of', etc.). It seems to me that right terms are used in making applicative normative statements just because these apply laws which are properly described by the use of right terms. In fact, the reasons which make it advantageous to describe laws by the use of right terms are also the reasons which make it advantageous to describe, on occasions, particular cases falling under such laws by the use of right terms.

[1] *Definition and Theory in Jurisprudence*, p. 17.

Another line is adopted by Alf Ross. He regards statements including key statements primarily as a convenient method of describing parts of laws. Ross admits that the representation of the law is much simplified when the law is described by statements referring to rights. He admits that many 'legal rules can be stated more simply and more manageably' by statements including key statements.[1] Nevertheless, he does not regard such statements as proper descriptions of laws, for many such laws would not be norms, and all of them would not be laws of the only form recognized by Ross. Ross inherited from Kelsen the belief that all laws are addressed to the judges, and he thinks that all laws are prescriptive laws.[2] All these views have already been examined and rejected, and Ross has no new and valid arguments to offer in their support.

Ross speaks of 'a technique of representation . . . expressed . . . by stating in one series of rules the facts that "create ownership", and in another series the legal consequences that "ownership" entails'.[3] Assuming that these are laws, and not parts of laws, as they are according to Ross's theory, one can, perhaps, equate Ross's first series of 'rules' with my investitive laws, and his second series with my constitutive laws. Ross overlooked the necessity of divestitive laws.

In some respects Hohfeld's analysis[4] advanced our understanding of rights considerably, but in other respects it was completely erroneous, and its influence retarded the proper understanding of rights. Four particularly grave mistakes of Hohfeld should be briefly mentioned here:

(1) He considered all rights as sets of any number of his four elementary rights, namely claim, privilege, power, and immunity.

(2) He thought that every right is a relation between no more than two persons.

(3) He thought that all rights are relations between persons.

(4) He considered his four elementary rights to be indefinable.

---

[1] *On Law and Justice*, p. 171. Cf. 'Tû Tû' 70 *H.L.R.* (1) 819. Much of the oddity of Ross's views results from his peculiar angle on ontological problems. Many of his mistakes are exposed by Simpson: 'The Analysis of Legal Concepts', 80 *L.Q.R.* 535.

[2] *On Law and Justice*, pp. 32–3.			[3] Ibid., p. 171.

[4] In *Fundamental Legal Conceptions*.

As is clear from the foregoing analysis, rights are not sets of claims, powers, etc. Their possession (often in combination with the occurrence of some event or the performance of some act) entails the possession of other rights, or of powers or duties. The same point is made by Honoré:

> . . . the 'right to £100 under the contract' might seem to be identical with a claim for £100 against the debtor. But even this is plausible only as a description of the momentary position of the right holder. Since there are rules of law by which duties under contracts are transferred on death or insolvency to persons other than the debtor, we shall sometimes be compelled to say that the right to £100 under the contract remains but that the claim securing it is not now against the debtor but against his trustee in insolvency or executor.[1]

Hence even simple rights are not identical with claims. Nor are they sets of claims, powers, etc., though unlike Honoré I do not claim that they cannot be represented as such sets. My claim is only that such a representation obscures the way in which they are instituted by laws, and in particular it obscures the interrelations between investitive, divestitive, and constitutive laws.

Honoré prefers to say that rights are 'protected by certain claims and give rise to certain liberties'. The concept of constitutive laws is intended to make possible an explanation of the way in which rights are protected by claims and give rise to liberties. The concept of constitutive laws is, however, wider, and takes into account the possibility that rights give rise also to duties and powers.

Hohfeld's insistence that every right is a relation between no more than two persons is completely unfounded and makes the explanation of rights *in rem* impossible, as has often been noted. But Hohfeld is also mistaken in thinking that rights cannot be relations between a person and an object. Here Honoré's argument is decisive:

> To argue that legal relations can only subsist between persons is either arbitrarily to restrict the definition of 'legal relation' or obscurely to reflect the truism that legal claims can only be enforced by proceedings brought against persons. When a person has a right

---

[1] 'Rights of Exclusion and Immunities against Divesting', 34 *T.L.R.* 456–7.

to exclude others generally from tangible property he stands, legally, in a special relation to the property. It is entirely natural and unobjectionable to call his right a right *to* the thing or *to the use* of a thing or *over* a thing. Yet we would not say a person had a right to a thing unless he was protected by claims excluding persons generally from interfering with it. A right to a thing or its use or over a thing is *protected by* claims against persons but is not to be identified with them.[1]

Hohfeld's view that his four elementary rights are indefinable is a consequence of a misconception of the nature and function of definitions. For Hohfeld himself defined 'privilege' in terms of 'no duty not to do', and immunity as the absence of liability. Hart has further shown that claims can be defined as a power to enforce a duty coupled with the power to abolish it.[2] The analysis of P-laws in Chapter VI, section 5 above suggests that powers can be defined ultimately in terms of duties.

The possibility of analysing rights, and therefore also laws instituting them, in terms of duties and powers, and therefore in terms of P-laws and D-laws, is of the utmost importance. It is a result of theses (ix) and (x),[3] which state that all the laws of a legal system are either P-laws or D-laws, or laws the sole legal relevance of which is in their internal relations to P-laws and D-laws.

Right-concepts serve two functions in the representation of the law, both of which are of paramount importance in simplifying the structure of laws and in pointing to important connections between various parts of a legal system:

(1) They are a means of relating PR-laws to P-laws and D-laws regulated by them.

(2) They provide a way of detaching certain conditions which are common to many duties or powers from the D- or P-laws establishing the duties and powers, and isolating them in laws which are not norms but are internally related to these D- or P-laws.

In examining these two functions of right-concepts two levels of complexity of laws instituting rights can be distinguished.

---

[1] 'Rights of Exclusion and Immunities against Divesting', 34 *T.L.R.* 463.

[2] *Definition and Theory in Jurisprudence*, p. 16. These ideas were further developed by Hart in his lectures on 'Rights and Duties'.

[3] Cf. Ch. VII, sect. 1 above.

First, let us suppose that all the constitutive laws concerning one right, say R, either impose duties or confer PL-powers, that is that the consequences of having a right are that (given some further conditions) one has some legislative powers or is under some duties. This means that all the constitutive laws regarding R are either PL-laws or D-laws.

Such constitutive laws have internal relations to the investitive and divestitive laws concerning R. The investitive laws concerning R are either PR-laws, i.e. laws making the acquisition of R dependent upon a voluntary human act (among other conditions), such as laws conferring powers to transfer ownership by sale or by gift; or they are laws which are not norms, laws which make the acquisition of the right dependent only upon events which do not include voluntary human acts (e.g. the transfer of ownership upon the death of the owner, in property which cannot be left by will).

PR-investitive laws of R regulate the constitutive laws concerning R. In such laws rights fulfil their first function, that of relating PR-laws and PL- and D-laws regulated by them. Investitive laws of R which are not norms single out conditions that are common conditions of many legal norms, i.e. of all the constitutive laws of R, thus simplifying these constitutive laws as well as pointing to connections between them. Hence, in investitive laws which are not norms rights fulfil their second function mentioned above.

Divestitive laws are also either PR-laws or laws which are not norms, and they, too, affect the constitutive laws in the same ways as do investitive laws; but whereas the latter determine, as it were, positive conditions for the application of constitutive laws, divestitive laws determine negative conditions for their application. They determine when they no longer apply. Rights fulfil their two functions in divestitive laws just as they do in investitive laws.

By allowing for constitutive laws in which the possession of rights is made a condition for having a PR-power or another right we add to the structural complexity of legal systems, but their functioning remains unaltered. Constitutive laws which confer PR-powers or rights relate, directly or indirectly, one right to another. Thereby they create indirect relations between the acquisition of the first right and the consequences of the second right. Ultimately they all either connect PR-laws with other legal norms, or simplify the structure of laws and point to important connections between them.

The structure of legal systems is further complicated by laws concerning status and juristic persons. PR-laws regulate other laws not only through being ways for the acquisition or loss of rights but also through affecting status (power to marry and power to get married, etc.) and through affecting juristic persons (power to vote in a parliamentary election, power to appoint a company director, power to establish a limited company, etc.). These topics cannot be discussed here beyond saying that laws instituting status and juristic persons are also explained by their relations to P- and D-laws.

Though the point will not be argued here, every legal system institutes some rights and contains laws instituting rights which are not norms. The number of necessary internal relations is correspondingly greater. Their necessary patterns are a subject for further investigation which cannot be undertaken here.

VII.4: GENETIC AND OPERATIVE STRUCTURE

In the last chapter the variety of legal norms and the necessary relations between them were considered. In this chapter the possibility and necessity of laws which are not norms was argued for, and it was claimed that they derive their legal relevance from their internal relations with legal norms. In demonstrating these points a few types of laws which are not norms were briefly discussed. The general aim of these chapters was to replace the picture of the structure of legal system adopted by Bentham, Austin, and Kelsen by a new picture.

They conceived of legal systems basically as sets of independent laws, sets of laws with no necessary relations between them. Hart has argued that this notion is fundamentally mistaken, but he did not go far enough. It has been suggested here that legal systems should be regarded as intricate webs of interconnected laws.

The considerations advanced in this and the previous chapter did no more than lay the foundation for exploration of the structure of legal systems. I would like to finish this discussion by suggesting that it is best to distinguish between two kinds of structure of legal systems: a genetic structure and an operative structure.[1]

The fundamental relation of the genetic structure is the genetic relation, namely the relation between a law and another law authorizing its existence. Genetic relations should be subdivided, taking into account several more factors hitherto disregarded. Among such factors are:

(1) The date of creating a law (where such a date can be determined).

(2) The function and general authority of the body which created the law.

(3) The nature of its particular authority to create the particular law (is its power derived from the constitution or from a municipal by-law? etc.).

(4) In certain cases, the reasons given to justify creating the law.

(5) Laws determining ways of modifying or repealing laws.

(6) The existence or otherwise of facts repealing or modifying laws.

A fully developed theory of the genetic structure of a system will establish a hierarchy of 'resistance to change' among laws, i.e. resistance to modification by conflict with other laws, etc., and will provide ways of representing the time during which a law has been valid or will be valid, both where this period is determined in the law itself, and where it is determined later in one way or another. Such a system of relations will account for various possibilities of conflicts of laws and ways of resolving them, for various degrees of voidability of laws. It will also explain the various ways in which laws can be retroactive.

The genetic structure of a legal system reveals which of its laws are or were valid at any given moment, and what powers for the future creation of laws various bodies enjoyed at any moment. It also reveals how legal systems underwent change during their existence. The development of the theory of the genetic structure is essential for the understanding of the structure of non-momentary legal systems, i.e. of legal systems

---

[1] The distinction between genetic and operative structures is analogous, in certain respects, to Kelsen's distinction between dynamic and static theories of law. Cf., e.g., *PTL*, p. 70.

existing in a period of time. Indeed, it is tempting to say that the genetic structure is the structure of non-momentary legal systems.

The operative structure is particularly relevant to the understanding of momentary legal systems. We should like to consider it as the structure of momentary systems. It is not concerned with the way laws were created but with the effects of the laws existing at any given moment. Various parts of one law can have different degrees of 'resistance to change' (if they were, for example, created by the exercise of different powers), and different durability (one part may have been enacted for a year only, while another part was for an indefinite period, etc.). The operative structure of a system takes no account of these facts. It is concerned only with the effect of the laws while they exist.

The operative structure of a legal system is based on its punitive and regulative relations. Virtually all the discussion in the last two chapters was concerned with the operative structure of legal systems.

A. *Note on Coercive Sanctions*

It was argued above[1] that not every legal sanction is coercive. It has been further argued that not every legal duty is backed by sanction,[2] and yet it has been conceded that coercion has a special importance in the law.[3] The foundations of a theory of the structure of legal systems laid above make it possible to analyse the role of coercion in the law.

Though laws imposing duties on law-creating and law-applying organs can exist without corresponding S-laws, they presuppose the existence of D-laws addressed to ordinary citizens which are backed by S-laws. In this sense duties which are not backed by sanctions are secondary to, and presuppose the existence of, duties backed by sanctions.

Sanctions which are not coercive sanctions consist in the withdrawal of rights, powers, or status, etc. It has been established that laws instituting rights, status, etc., ultimately presuppose D-laws and PL-laws, which in turn do not presuppose any other rights, status, etc. In every legal system some of these

---

[1] Cf. Ch. IV, sect. 2 above.   [2] Cf. Ch. VI, sect. 4 above.
[3] Cf. Introduction.

D-laws are addressed to ordinary citizens, and therefore pre-suppose some S-laws; at least some of these do not presuppose any other rights, status, etc. Some stipulate coercive sanctions, possibly by permitting the use of force if resistance is offered, or at the very least because they are themselves backed by other laws making it an offence to obstruct the execution of the sanctions, and these laws are backed by coercive sanctions.

In this way all the laws apart from PL-laws are related in necessary operative relations to laws stipulating coercive sanctions. PL-laws are not similarly related to coercive sanctions. Moreover, they may exist, even if no use is made of the powers they confer, that is even if they have no genetic relation to any law stipulating a coercive sanction or presupposing such a law. Nevertheless, it is clear that ultimately the point in having PL-laws is that they provide a way of changing laws which are not themselves PL-laws. Thus even PL-laws conceptually presuppose in a very indirect way the existence of some coercive sanctions at some time in the life of a legal system.

The upshot of this discussion is that Bentham, Austin, and Kelsen misunderstood the function of coercion in the law. Its function is not as the standard motive for any act guided by the laws. It is much more complicated and indirect, though no less essential. Coercion is the ultimate foundation of the law, in the sense of being (part of) the standard reason for obedience to some D-laws that are presupposed in many enormously varied ways by all the other legal norms, and, through them, by all the other laws of the system.

VIII

THE IDENTITY OF LEGAL SYSTEMS

VIII.1: THE IDENTITY OF NON-MOMENTARY LEGAL SYSTEMS

Discussion of the structure of legal systems in the previous two chapters has assumed that the content of a given legal system is known, and the proper way to represent it as a system of interrelated laws has been explored. This chapter is concerned with the criterion for determining the content of legal systems, i.e. with the criterion of identity of legal systems. The key to the problem of structure is the criterion determining which of the complete descriptions of a legal system is its proper description. The problem of identity is the problem of finding a criterion determining whether a given set of normative statements is a complete description of a legal system.

Corresponding to the distinction between a legal system and a momentary legal system there are two criteria of identity—one specifying the way in which the identity of legal systems can be ascertained, the other providing a way in which the identity of momentary legal systems can be ascertained.

Apart from a few remarks in this section, this chapter is concerned only with the problem of identity of momentary systems. The crux of the problem of the identity of (non-momentary) legal systems is the question of continuity, namely what events disrupt the continuous existence of a legal system, bring about its disappearance, and, perhaps, result in the creation of a new legal system in its stead. In other words, the crucial problem is the problem of deciding whether two given momentary systems belong to the same legal system.

In previous chapters the solutions of this problem implied by the theories of both Austin and Kelsen were considered and rejected. They admit that the fact that two momentary systems contain many laws which are identical in content is no proof that they belong to the same legal system. Austin implies that the identity of the ultimate legislator of the laws of the two momentary systems is both necessary and sufficient for them to belong to one legal system.

Kelsen avoids some of the weaknesses of this position; for him the constitutionality of the creation of the laws of the one momentary system relative to the other is the deciding factor. According to his theory, two momentary systems A and B belong to the same legal system if, and only if, the creation of all the laws of B which are not identical with laws of A was authorized by the laws of A. The creation of a law is authorized by another if the law-creating acts creating the first amount to the exercise of legislative powers conferred by the second, or by another law the creation of which is authorized by the second.

If the creation of a law is not authorized by another law it can be called an 'original law'. Kelsen's criterion for the identity of legal systems presupposes that no momentary system contains an original law which does not belong also to the first momentary system of the same legal system. But this presupposition, as has been argued in Chapter V, section 4 above, is not justified. The continuity of a legal system is not necessarily disrupted by the creation of new original laws. Nor is the fact that the creation of a law is authorized by a law belonging to a certain legal system a sufficient proof that the authorized law belongs to that system. A country may be granted independence by a law of another country authorizing all its laws; nevertheless, its laws form a separate legal system.

The 'constitutional continuity' of the laws is only one, and not the most important, factor in determining whether two momentary systems belong to the same legal system. Another factor is the content of the non-authorized law. The creation of a new original law disrupts the continuity of a legal system only if it is a constitutional law of great importance.

But neither the 'constitutional continuity' of the new laws nor their content are necessary or sufficient conditions for establishing the continuity or lack of continuity of legal systems. Legal systems are always legal systems of complex forms of social life, such as religions, states, regimes, tribes, etc. Legal systems serve as one, but only one, of the defining features of these.

Significant and unconstitutional changes of law may be

important enough to establish an alteration in the identity of
the social entity of which the legal system is a part, but other
factors have to be taken into account as well. The identity of
legal systems depends on the identity of the social forms to
which they belong. The criterion of identity of legal systems is
therefore determined not only by jurisprudential or legal
considerations but by other considerations as well, considerations belonging to other social sciences.

Not wishing to trespass on other fields, I shall confine myself
henceforth to the problem of the identity of momentary systems.
It should not, however, be assumed that momentary systems can
be analysed independently of the legal systems to which they
belong. It will become clear from the arguments of this and
of the next chapter that both the identity and the existence of
momentary systems can be determined only by reference to
other momentary systems of the same legal system. But the
solution of these problems does not presuppose an ability to
determine the *precise* boundaries of legal systems.

VIII.2: IDENTITY AND MEMBERSHIP IN MOMENTARY LEGAL SYSTEMS

The criterion of identity of momentary systems can be
formulated as follows: A set of normative statements is a
complete description of a momentary legal system if, and only
if, (1) every one of the statements in it describes (part of) the
same momentary system as all the others, and (2) every normative statement which describes (part of) the same momentary
system is entailed by that set.

This formulation presupposes a criterion of membership in
momentary systems, i.e. a criterion for ascertaining whether a
given normative statement describes (part of) the same momentary system as the one which is described by a given set of
normative statements. It is with the problem of membership in
momentary legal systems that the rest of this section is concerned.

The definition of 'a complete description' of a momentary
system[1] makes it clear that, if a normative statement is entailed
by a set of normative statements, then it describes the same
system as is described by the set. The difficulty in finding a

---

[1] Cf. Ch. III, sect. 1 above.

criterion of membership is in discovering a condition for a given normative statement partly describing the same system as a given set of normative statements, even though it is not entailed by it. There are various ways in which one may try to tackle this problem. In Chapters II and V we have criticized two attempted solutions based on the principle of origin, i.e. making the facts creating laws the sole factor determining the legal system to which they belong. Here we shall attempt to sketch a more hopeful line of approach, which can be said to be based on the principle of authoritative recognition.

The defects of Austin's criterion of membership were soon discovered by other legal theorists. Some attempted, without much success, to perfect his criterion, and remained faithful to the principle of origin. Others abandoned this principle altogether. One of the latter was Holland, who defined laws as 'a general rule of external human action enforced by a sovereign political authority'.[1] Holland, as opposed to Austin, thinks that it is not the way in which laws are created but the way in which they are enforced that determines their nature as 'positive' laws, as distinguished from non-legal custom, etc.; and, by implication, it is this that determines also to which legal system a law belongs.

His definition, however, is deficient in many respects. Not least among them is that it accepts Austin's theory of sovereignty in only slightly modified form, and that it assumes that every law can meaningfully be said to be enforced. It is clear from the discussion in the previous two chapters that: (a) Not every law which is a 'rule of behaviour', i.e. a norm, can be enforced. Power conferring laws cannot be enforced. (b) No law which is not a norm can be enforced.

Both these shortcomings are avoided by Salmond's definition of a law. Salmond explains that, whereas there are various ways in which laws are created, 'all law, however made, is recognized and administered by the courts, and no rules are recognized by the courts which are not rules of law. It is, therefore, to the courts and not to the legislature that we must go in order to ascertain the true nature of the law.'[2] Accordingly he defines law as follows: 'The law consists of the rules recognized and acted on by courts of justice.'[2]

[1] *Jurisprudence*, p. 40.   [2] *Salmond on Jurisprudence*, p. 41.

Unlike Austin's definition of law, Salmond's definition does not include an embryonic theory of legal system. Salmond's aim is merely to point to the difference between legal systems and other norms and normative systems. He therefore assumes the normativity of the law, disregards its coercive nature, and bases his definition on the fact that legal systems are institutionalized. It is this that distinguishes them from other normative systems. The institutionalized nature of the law is manifested, according to Salmond, in the existence and operations of the courts, i.e. of certain law-applying organs. In this he differs from Bentham, Austin, and Kelsen, who all concentrate on and emphasize the importance of the law-creating organs, and regard their particular mode of creating laws as one of the distinguishing features of legal systems.

Salmond's main contention is sound. Not every law is created by law-creating organs, and though the importance of legislation as a law-creating method is characteristic of modern legal systems, it is not characteristic of every legal system, nor is any other law-creating method. On the other hand, it can be said that every legal system institutes law-applying organs which recognize every law of the system. Having said this, we must admit that there are many borderline cases. Some such cases will be mentioned in the sequel. But borderline cases are unavoidable in problems like this, and their existence does not in itself detract from the value of general statements on the subject, though these should not be interpreted too dogmatically.

The importance of law-applying organs in the law is manifested in various ways which should be carefully separated. One of the most important aspects of their role, the aspect which more than any other can be connected with a 'definition of law', is the relevance of law-applying organs to the criterion of membership in momentary legal systems. The criterion formulated below follows the philosophical tradition established by Salmond, but it deviates from the particulars of his position to a considerable extent. A statement will be said to describe a primary organ if it identifies it and ascribes to it primary legal powers.

A given normative statement describes (part of) the same momentary system as is described by a given set of normative statements, if it describes a primary law-applying organ that recognizes[1] the laws described by this set of normative statements; or if a primary law-applying organ described by the set of normative statements recognizes the law which the given statement describes. Accordingly, it can be said that a momentary legal system contains all, and only all, the laws recognized by a primary law-applying organ which it institutes.

It may be found necessary to conceive of a legal system not as a set of laws recognized by all the primary law-applying organs instituted under it—as is implied in this criterion—but as a set of substantially, but only partly overlapping, sets of laws, each recognized by one or more of the organs instituted under it. The proposed criterion of membership can be relaxed to take account of that need. The various ways in which this can be done will not be explored here.

The meaning and implication of this criterion of membership should be carefully scrutinized. It assumes that every momentary legal system institutes at least one law-applying organ of a type the nature of which will be explained below. The criterion thereby presupposes and manifests a certain view of the institutional nature of law. Furthermore, the criterion assumes that the identity and actions of primary law-applying organs are essential in establishing the membership of a legal system. Given only two normative statements, neither of which describes a primary law-applying organ, it is impossible to determine whether or not they describe part of the same momentary legal system.

The criterion is based on two key concepts, 'primary law-applying organs' and 'recognizing a law'. The following remarks are only the beginning of an explanation of these concepts. A primary law-applying organ ('primary organ' for short) is an organ which is authorized to decide whether the use of force in certain circumstances is forbidden or permitted by law. This concept is indeed the key to the criterion. It was argued in Chapter VII, section 4 that:

(1) Every legal system prohibits the use of force in certain conditions (at least when force is used to obstruct the execution

[1] 'Recognizes' here means 'is certain to recognize, if the question be raised before it'. Or, in so far as the system described no longer exists, it means that the organ did recognize the laws in question when it existed.

of sanctions) and permits (or prescribes) the use of force in certain other circumstances, i.e. in the course of executing certain sanctions.

(2) In every legal system all the laws have internal relations to the laws forbidding the use of force or to the laws permitting or prescribing the use of force in the execution of sanctions.

A primary organ may be authorized to decide only whether a certain specific law forbidding the use of force was violated; but in deciding this, it is liable to have to decide whether the use of force was justified as being the execution of some sanction or other, or whether it was justified on other grounds (mistake, etc.). In recognizing certain acts as the execution of sanctions, the organ, explicitly or implicitly, also recognizes other laws forbidding the use of force, namely those laws for the violation of which the sanctions were prescribed. Similarly, by admitting a defence of mistake (e.g. accepting that the agent acted under a misapprehension as to his rights or the rights of other people) other laws may be recognized.

Thus a primary organ, an organ which is authorized to decide whether certain acts using force were a violation of a certain law, is liable to recognize in the exercise of its powers other laws permitting the use of force in the execution of sanctions, and other laws prohibiting the use of force which belong to the same momentary system. A primary organ may also recognize the existence of other law-applying or law-creating organs, and the validity of their actions and of the laws regulating their actions. Thus a primary organ recognizes, directly or indirectly, explicitly or implicitly, all the laws of the momentary system.

For the purposes of this criterion of membership an organ can be said to be authorized to decide whether a law forbidding the use of force was violated, if in certain circumstances its decision is a condition for the execution of a sanction against the violator, either by that organ itself or by others.

One can imagine a society in which there exist certain rules prescribing behaviour and backed by coercive sanctions, but in which there exist no primary law-applying organs. The decision that a law was violated and the application of sanctions may be entrusted to the injured party or his family or to any one in the society, provided that the violator has not already been punished by another person, etc. Primary organs make their appearance the moment the power to decide upon the application of such sanctions is concentrated in the hands of relatively few people, who are appointed to or otherwise entrusted with this task primarily because of their supposed abilities, or because they deserve it, and not because of their relation to the injured party or to the violator of the law, provided that they have such powers for a relatively long period and may use them in an indefinite number of cases. Primary organs may be the organs executing the sanctions, or their decision that the law was violated may be in certain circumstances a necessary condition for the application of the sanctions.

The study of elementary forms of primary organ may shed much light on normative systems which are on the border between a legal and a pre-legal status. Understanding the various types of such transitory normative systems is more important than deciding for each of them whether it is a legal system or not, a question which in many cases is completely barren. The exploration of various forms of primary organ is, however, clearly beyond the scope of this study.

The moment one primary organ exists, even if it is empowered to decide upon the violation of only one norm, it is possible to distinguish between the norms recognized by it and other norms which are not recognized, either because they have no bearing on the use of force or for some other reason. The fact that the organ's decisions are based, however remotely or indirectly, on a certain group of norms justifies regarding them as constituting a normative system. It is this sense of 'normative system' which is determined by the criterion of membership formulated above.

It is arguable that not every such normative system is a legal system; that in a legal system the decision on the violation of more than one norm should be entrusted to primary organs. As has been pointed out above, the essential role of institutions in the law is not confined to their role in the criterion of membership. We need not, however, concern ourselves here with this problem, for, whatever its solution, the correctness of the proposed criterion of membership is not affected by it.

A primary organ's decision can be declared, and is sometimes accompanied by an order or a permission to apply a sanction, or do some other acts. The decision may not even be declared. Upon reaching it the organ may simply proceed to act accordingly, i.e. to apply the sanction or abstain from applying it. In developed legal systems primary organs arrive at their decisions usually after a process of litigation regulated by law, and the decision itself is often accompanied by an explanation of the reasons which led to it. In such circumstances it is relatively easy to find which are the laws recognized and acted on by the organs. It is more difficult to do this when the decision is not explained or justified by the organ.

It is, however, possible to tell a person's reasons for an act or a decision, even if they are not revealed by that person himself. Where legal organs are concerned, the task is made easier by the fact that laws exist only as part of legal systems that are widely accepted by a certain population. Thus the primary organ is usually expected by the population or the legal profession to recognize certain laws, and if its decisions do not conflict with them it may be assumed to have acted on their basis.

It goes without saying that laws are only part of the reasons for the decisions of primary organs. Other reasons may be certain findings of fact, considerations of justice, etc.

Primary organs may not only act on previously existing laws, they may sometimes create new laws and apply them. As they recognize the laws which they create, the distinction between laws which exist prior to their recognition by the primary organs and laws which are created and applied by the primary organs is not essential to the understanding of the criterion of membership. It is, however, of the utmost importance to understand that the view that all the laws are recognized by primary organs (or the view that they are all recognized by courts), or that their membership in a legal system is determined by this fact, does not entail the view that primary organs create all the laws (or that the courts do this).

Whether their creation can be attributed to the primary organs (or to the courts) depends upon various factors. Thus, if a law was created by the exercise of powers conferred by another PL-law recognized by the primary organs or the courts, then it is recognized by them as made by whoever has these powers. Furthermore, if the reasons given for recognizing a law are reasons justifying its content, then we shall tend to think that it was created by the courts or the primary organs. If, on the other hand, the reasons for recognizing a law concern the authority of some person or body of persons who laid it down, then it is likely that the court or the primary organ is applying a previously existing law. This view will be strengthened if the law is held to be valid from the time it was laid down by that person or group, and even more so if it was practically certain before the organ's decision to act on this law. When these conditions obtain, the law recognized can be an original law, i.e. a law created by a person or group who were not authorized by law to create it.

Saying of a primary organ that it recognizes a law means that, had the question been raised before it, in the proper exercise of its powers it would have acted on that law. It is a counter-factual statement which raises many philosophical questions that need not concern us here. The evidence for such statements is the past behaviour of the primary organ, the attitudes and opinions of the population and of the legal profession, etc. The evidence can be and is largely indirect. Of special importance is the fact that recognizing a PL-law logically entails recognizing all the laws created by the exercise of powers conferred by it. This fact is responsible for the importance often attached to PL-laws in discussions of the problem of membership. Of equal importance is the fact that one primary organ's recognition of the norms creating another primary organ (or a court) gives considerable support to the supposition that the first organ will recognize all the laws recognized by the second, though it does not entail it.

This short explanation of the criterion of membership leaves many unanswered questions, though I believe that all of them can be satisfactorily answered. We may conclude this section by enumerating some of them.

Some further explorations need be made of the structure of legal systems, to prove that the degree of interdependence of laws presupposed by the criterion proposed here really exists. The following are some of the main problems:

There is the question of certain pleas or defences like personal immunity, and their effects on the content of legal systems. Total immunity from sanctions can sometimes prevent primary organs from considering certain norms, in which case they must be regarded as not belonging to the legal system that consists of the laws recognized by the primary organs. Thus religious bodies can be immune from state control and be subject to a separate legal system. When the immunity is not complete it does not suffice to isolate the norms governing the behaviour of the immune persons, if there are such norms. But the precise effects of immunity and similar defences need looking into precisely and in much greater detail.

Another problem is the question of a 'conflict' between the acts of various primary organs. Can one such organ, A, recognize another organ, B, and recognize all the laws applied by B, while B does not recognize A and some of its laws? And how should one account for such a situation?

Yet another difficult problem is to distinguish between an organ's recognition of the laws of its own legal system and its recognition of laws of other legal systems in virtue of the directions of its private international laws.

Finally, there is the problem of distinguishing law from fact— Are companies' regulations recognized by courts as law or as fact? What is the status of a father's order to his child, disobedience to which is punishable by law? etc.

VIII.3: ON THE RULE OF RECOGNITION

Many legal theorists based their explanations of law on the activities of law-applying organs. None of them succeeded in offering a satisfactory criterion of membership. This is due, no doubt, at least partly to their failure to formulate clearly the problem, and to separate it from other problems. This feature is so marked that it is often questionable whether they were at all interested in the problems of membership and identity. The criterion formulated in the previous section expresses a difference from the views of most other theorists who share Salmond's approach in two important respects:

(1) It is concerned not with the activities of the courts or of law-applying organs in general but with primary organs only.

(2) It is concerned with the actual behaviour of primary organs, not with what they ought to do, yet it is concerned with the activity of these organs as guided by normative considerations.

This second point, and the nature of the proposed criterion of membership in general, can be made clearer by reference to Hart's position on the subject, i.e. to his doctrine of the rule of recognition.

The relevance of the rule of recognition to the problem of membership is made clear in the very first passage in which the concept is introduced. Rules of recognition, Hart explains, 'specify some feature or features possession of which by a suggested rule is taken as a conclusive affirmative indication that it is a rule of the group'.[1] A rule of recognition is 'a rule for conclusive identification of the primary rules of obligation'.[2]

The rule of recognition is a legal rule and belongs to the legal system. It differs from other laws in that its existence is not determined by criteria laid down in other laws but by the fact that it is actually applied:

... whereas a subordinate rule of a system may be valid and in that sense 'exist' even if it is generally disregarded, the rule of recognition exists only as a complex, but normally concordant, practice of the courts, officials, and private persons in identifying the law by reference to certain criteria. Its existence is a matter of fact.[3]

This seems to imply that the rule of recognition is always a customary and not a legislated rule. On the other hand, Hart says:

If a constitution specifying the various sources of law is a living reality in the sense that the courts and officials of the system actually identify the law in accordance with the criteria it provides, then the constitution is accepted and actually exists. It seems a needless reduplication to suggest that there is a further rule to the effect that the constitution (or those who 'laid it down') are to be obeyed.[4]

The constitution, in such cases, should presumably be regarded as created both by legislation and by custom, a position which is perhaps not impossible, but needs some explaining.

This is a minor difficulty. Of much greater consequence is the difficulty of finding who are the norm-subjects of the rule

---

[1] *CL*, p. 92.   [2] *CL*, p. 92.   [3] *CL*, p. 107.   [4] *CL*, p. 246.

of recognition and the doubt as to whether it is a duty-imposing or a power-conferring law. (It should be remembered that, according to Hart, all norms are either duty-imposing or power-conferring norms, and that he assumes that all laws are norms.) Hart says that 'wherever such a rule of recognition is accepted, both private persons and officials are provided with authoritative criteria for identifying primary rules of obligation.'[1] This suggests that the rule of recognition is directed to the population at large. Does it mean that all the law-subjects of all the laws which are to be identified by it are its law-subjects?

Hart often contrasts the rule of recognition and other secondary rules with primary rules which are rules of obligation. So presumably rules of recognition do not impose obligations but confer powers. This hypothesis is strengthened by the following half sentence: in certain circumstances ' . . . the rule which confers jurisdiction will also be a rule of recognition'.[2] But it is quite clear that this is not Hart's intention, as he himself confirmed to me. In his book Hart explains only that duty-imposing laws can be customary laws. There is no sense, according to his theory, in which power-conferring laws can be customary laws,[3] unless they are part of a legal system of which they are not the rule of recognition.

Consequently it must be concluded that the rule of recognition is a duty-imposing law. This means, however, that its law-subjects cannot be the population at large, for there is no duty on ordinary people to identify certain laws and no others (nor, for that matter, do they have a legal power to do so).

The rule of recognition should, therefore, be interpreted as a D-law addressed to the officials, directing them to apply or act on certain laws. Hence only the behaviour of the officials and not the behaviour of the population as a whole determines whether the rule of recognition exists.

The fundamental reason which moved Hart to adopt his doctrine of the rule of recognition is expressed in the following sentence: 'If the question is raised whether some suggested

---

[1] *CL*, p. 97.   [2] *CL*, p. 95.

[3] The explanation of P-laws in Ch. VI, sect. 5 above admits the possibility of customary P-laws. But the existence of P-laws in general depends on the existence or the possible creation of certain D-laws, and there are no such D-laws to make possible the interpretation of the rule of recognition as a P-law.

rule is legally valid, we must, in order to answer the question, use a criterion of validity *provided by some other rule*.'[1] It is this assumption that is questionable. It seems to me that to answer the question whether a certain suggested law exists as a law in a certain legal system one must ultimately refer not to a law but to a jurisprudential criterion.[2] Ultimately one must refer to a general statement that does not describe a law but a general truth about law.

In some legal systems there may be laws which oblige certain organs to apply all the laws fulfilling a certain condition, and it may be that these laws are in fact all the laws of the system. But even when such laws exist, which is not always the case, the laws of the system belong to the system not because of this rule of recognition, but because they are all recognized by the primary organs.

That it is not the case that in every legal system there is one such rule of recognition can be seen by considering the following two points:

(1) It is not clear on what Hart bases his view that there is only one rule of recognition in every legal system. Why not say that there are various rules of recognition, each addressed to a different kind of officials? Why not say that various rules of recognition prescribe the recognition of various types of laws?

(2) Though, as has been suggested in the previous section, the behaviour of primary organs is the key to the criterion of membership, there is no reason to think that they always act in fulfilment of duties, as Hart's theory entails. They may be under a duty to recognize some laws and yet be legally free to recognize or not recognize certain others.[3] Suppose, as Hart does, that legal laws can be D-laws merely in virtue of diffused critical reactions, without being backed by sanctions or other legal remedies. Even so, it need not be the case that primary organs will meet with critical reactions if they stop recognizing certain laws or begin recognizing certain other laws.

---

[1] *CL*, p. 103. My italics.

[2] It should be remembered that we are concerned with the ordinary man's point of view, not with that of a judge faced with the question 'which law ought to be recognized?'.

[3] Cf. Ch. II, sect. 4 above.

A.   *Note on Laws and Paper Laws*

This chapter is concerned with the way in which the fact that the law is institutionalized helps to solve the problem of membership. The proposed solution accords special importance to certain law-applying organs, without thereby assuming (1) that laws are predictions or descriptions of the acts of these organs; (2) that the laws are directed only to these organs; they are directed to various classes of persons and are simply recognized by these organs; (3) that all the laws are created by these organs; or (4) that the organs are always under a duty to recognize them.

The proposed criterion of membership points the way to the solution of another problem. Kelsen thinks that minimum efficacy is a necessary condition to the validity of every law.[1] This is his solution to the problem of 'paper laws'. The proposed criterion of membership suggests a different approach to the problem: The laws of a system are those recognized by the primary organs. Statutes or regulations, etc., which are disregarded by the law-applying organs are not really part of the legal system. If they are recognized in a modified form they are laws in this modified form. But the fact that they are disregarded by the population is irrelevant to their existence. Moreover, even if they are disregarded by the police, even if no prosecutions are brought for their violation (if they are D-laws), and if interested parties do not invoke them before the law-applying organs, they are still valid laws, provided that if raised before primary organs in the proper exercise of their powers they would recognize and act on them.

It must be admitted that ordinary prevalent opinion on the subject is divided, and the view suggested here cannot be justified as explicating current opinion. Its justification is indirect. Firstly, it accords with the views expressed on the problems of membership and identity, which in their turn are explications of common sense and professional opinion on these subjects. Secondly, it expresses another aspect of the decision to attribute a central role to the law-applying organs.

It is true that one of the distinguishing features of norms is that they constitute certain types of reasons for action. But

---

[1] Cf. Ch. III, sect. 3 above.

norms are always only one of the reasons for action in every situation; their effect and their weight are affected by many other facts that are also reasons for action, and which sometimes enhance and sometimes diminish or even contradict the effect of norms. The fact that the existence of certain laws is not always a decisive reason for acting as they prescribe is generally accepted. An important moral rule contradicting a law may cause the population to disregard the latter, but neither the contradiction nor its effect on the population mean that the law does not exist. Similarly, a low rate of crime detection may cause people to attribute a smaller weight to certain laws, though this does not mean that the laws do not exist.

It is characteristic of norms that the type of reasons for action which they constitute are in general weighty and important reasons for action. Hence the tendency to think that if a law has lost much of its importance as a reason for action, because of its general disregard, it is no longer a law. But where normative systems are concerned it seems reasonable to allow this consideration of the weight of individual norms as reasons for action to be overridden by consideration of the systematic nature of the norms. Because they belong to a system characterized by the organized application of laws by specially appointed organs, even laws largely disregarded and neglected are laws so long as they are recognized by these organs.

IX

ON THE EXISTENCE OF LEGAL
SYSTEMS

IX.1: ON THE PRINCIPLE OF EFFICACY

The problem of existence is the quest for a criterion to determine whether a certain suggested legal system exists, i.e. whether a given set of normative statements, which, if true, is a complete description of a legal system, is true.

Some legal theorists based their views on this problem on the principle of efficacy, i.e. on the assumption that the existence of legal systems depends only on their efficacy, on the obedience to their laws.[1] None of the exponents of these views did much to clarify the precise meaning of efficacy or obedience in his theory. One interpretation is that a system exists if a certain ratio of cases of obedience to its laws to the total number of opportunities to obey them obtains. This is undoubtedly a crude interpretation, but it is better than none, and it can at least serve as a basis for comment and criticism. Some of the points made below can be met by refining and improving this interpretation of the principle of efficacy, but others show that the principle is inadequate and should be abandoned.

How should cases of disobedience be counted? Suppose that one drives a car for 50 miles exceeding the speed limit. How many times did one violate the law? How should the number of opportunities to obey the law be counted? How many opportunities not to murder does one have during a year? And how many opportunities not to steal? Suppose that an appropriate method of counting is established. Do the facts that a person did not murder 500 times and that he committed murder only once, that he paid income tax twice and did not pay it three times, do these facts add up to a (partial) ratio of efficacy of 4 to 506? It seems to me that no method of computation can make much sense.

---

[1] Cf. Ch. V, sect. 1 above.

Are all violations of all laws of equal importance to the existence of the legal system? Is the fact that a man breaks his contract or that he does not heed a road sign as detrimental to the existence of the legal system as the fact that he deserted from the army or conspired to rebel?

Furthermore, are all violations of the same law of equal importance to the existence of the legal system? Does not the murder of the head of state undermine the legal system more than other murders, regardless of whether or not it is a different type of offence? It seems also that the expressed intention with which a law is violated can make all the difference. Compare, for example, the effect of not paying taxes as an act of civil disobedience with the same offence committed by ordinary tax-evaders.

A general and very important question, which is left unanswered by most of the exponents of the principle of efficacy, is whether mere conformity to a law should be equated with obedience which entails at least some knowledge of the law, or even with obedience which entails that its existence affected the person's decision how to behave.

The principle of efficacy is concerned only with obedience and disobedience to D-laws. But is not the way in which people do or do not make use of powers conferred on them by P-laws of equal importance to the existence of the legal system? Suppose that in a certain country members of some racial or ethnic group are considered as second-class citizens and do not enjoy political rights. Suppose that the government appoint some of their members as a semi-autonomous legislative assembly, and that these persons, in protest against the regime, refuse to make use of their powers. Is not their action as detrimental to the existence of the legal system as any act of violating duties in civil disobedience? And is mass abstention from voting in parliamentary elections less relevant to this matter than an illegal public meeting? Similarly, if violation of certain contracts, or of certain duties of company directors, affects the existence of the legal system, so does the fact that the population refrains from making certain types of contract or that it refrains from creating certain types of commercial corporation.

Finally, it should be noticed that the existing legal system is not always the one to which a greater degree of obedience is rendered. There is, for example, a case for thinking that the post-U.D.I. legal system was the legal system existing in Rhodesia in 1968. This does not entail that it was the only efficacious legal system in Rhodesia. It may well be that the pre-U.D.I. legal system was also efficacious there; indeed, it may have been on balance the more efficacious system and yet it may not have been the existing system. The two systems are largely identical in content. It may be, for example, that a certain number of criminal laws enacted after U.D.I. were not fully obeyed. This could have given the pre-U.D.I. system the edge in the balance of efficacy, notwithstanding the fact that a new constitutional law of great importance replaced a previous constitutional law, and that the new law and not the old was obeyed. The efficacy of the one constitutional law may, however, determine that it was the post-U.D.I. system that existed in Rhodesia.

To sum up: Though obedience to all D-laws may be relevant to the existence of the legal system one must: (1) avoid over-simplified computation; (2) attribute different weight to different offences; (3) take into account legally irrelevant circumstances and intentions; (4) take into account knowledge of the law and its influence on people's behaviour;[1] (5) take into account the use of powers as well as the obedience to duties; (6) attach greater importance to important constitutional laws.[2]

IX.2: SOME FURTHER SUGGESTIONS

The complexity of the problem of existence defies a brief treatment, and it seems to me that most of the questions involved have, as yet, scarcely been touched by legal philosophers. The following pages contain only a few suggestions concerning the way in which the problem should be approached. They do not contain even the germ of a solution to it.

Two questions should be distinguished:

(1) Does a legal system exist in a certain society?

---

[1] The first three points and the first half of the fourth were explicitly recognized by Bentham; cf. his discussion of revolt, which is concerned with the change of legal systems: *Fragment*, pp. 45–6.

[2] The last two points are made by Hart: cf. *CL*, pp. 109–14.

(2) Assuming that a certain society is governed by a legal system, by which legal system is it governed? Which legal system exists in it?

The first question can be interpreted in two ways: It can be taken to mean (a) Given that S is a normative system existing in a certain society, is S a legal system? or (b) Does any complete description of a legal system describe a legal system which exists in a given society? It is only with the second interpretation that we shall be concerned here.

Corresponding to these two questions there are two distinct sets of tests: one is for determining whether in a given society there exists any legal system at all; the other is to determine, given a positive answer to the first question, which legal system exists there.

To the first set of tests, which can be called the 'preliminary test', all the laws of the system are relevant, though there is no reason to think that they are all equally relevant. Obedience to private law as well as to public law should be taken into account. The use of legal powers of all kinds by the population should also be considered. Particular attention should be paid to the degree to which the laws are known and to the influence they exercise on people's behaviour.

In considering the use made of legal powers not every unused opportunity to exercise a legal power is relevant, but only those in which its use might have been expected, for example, for the reason that it would have been to the obvious advantage of the person concerned. Needless to say, knowledge of the law is more important to the effectiveness of P-laws than it is to the conformity to D-laws.

The preliminary test is a test of the general efficacy of legal systems. (The term 'efficacy' is used here in a wider sense than hitherto.) More than one legal system may pass the preliminary test and be efficacious in a certain society. In such cases it may be necessary to use the second set of tests in order to find out which of the efficacious systems exists in that society. As was demonstrated in the previous section, the fact that one of two legal systems which pass the minimum preliminary test is more efficacious than the other is no proof that it is the existing system. This question is decided by a second set of tests, which will be called the 'test of exclusion'.

The preliminary test and the question it is designed to answer did not figure greatly in jurisprudential discussions. These are concerned either with the question of determining whether a certain normative system is a legal system, or with the question which of two legal systems is the one that exists. Examples are the question whether the rules of a primitive society are a legal system, and the question which legal system existed in Rhodesia in 1968.

To answer questions like the last one reference must be made to the test of exclusion. Before this test is applied, one must ascertain that the two legal systems under consideration are indeed mutually exclusive. A society may be governed by two legal systems, for example, one religious, the other a state legal system, which, even if sometimes conflicting, are compatible.

Whether or not two legal systems are compatible depends first of all on the social forms of organization of which they are part (e.g. the legal systems of a tribe, a state, a religion, etc.). In general, each social organization of a certain type is incompatible with other organizations of the same type, but can co-exist with social organizations of other types. (States are incompatible with one another, but are usually compatible with religions, etc.) Secondly, the compatibility of legal systems depends on the degree to which they conflict. (Certain religions may proscribe recognition of any non-religious authority, etc.)

Given two putative legal systems that are both efficacious in a certain society and are also incompatible, it is for the test of exclusion to determine which of them exists in that society. This test assigns special importance to people's attitude and actions towards the state, the regime, or the other form of social organization of which the legal system concerned is an integral part. Does the population defy or disregard part of one of the legal systems concerned because of its allegiance to one regime rather than another? It is here that people's intentions in violating certain duties, in exercising or abstaining from the exercise of legal powers, become relevant.

Other factors which are assigned special importance by the test of exclusion are the efficacy of major constitutional laws, i.e. the operations of the important law-applying and law-creating organs, and the efficacy of other laws that possess a political character. These vary from one legal system to another.

The test of exclusion is a comparative test. Of the competing legal systems, the one that comes out best is the existing one. In certain cases two competing systems may have roughly equal claim and the case must be judged unsettled.

Hitherto reference has constantly been made to the existence of legal systems in certain societies. The term 'society' should, in this context, be interpreted very loosely indeed. By saying of a legal system that it is the legal system of Britain or of the British people one means (a) that its laws apply (roughly speaking) only to acts performed in Britain or by British people; and (b) that when tested by the tests mentioned above in Britain or among the British people, i.e. in its sphere of application, it is proved to exist in them. Sometimes the sphere of a legal system's effective existence is narrower than its sphere of application. Thus, for all I know, the legal system in force in Formosa in 1968 may have applied also to mainland China. The criteria of existence make it possible to establish that this legal system in fact exists only in Formosa.

A legal system always exists at a certain moment or during a certain period. It must be remembered, however, that the tests of efficacy and exclusion yield results only if carried out during a certain minimum period of time. A legal system exists at any given moment if this moment is part of a period in which it exists.

These few remarks on the criteria of existence are only part of the preliminary clarification necessary before the problem of existence is fully tackled. Like most other suggestions made in this book they are merely pointers to the way to solve the problems involved. It is, however, my hope that the book has succeeded in formulating and demonstrating the importance of some major but neglected jurisprudential problems, and in throwing new light on the work of some great legal thinkers, as well as in making some contribution to the solution of these problems.

POSTSCRIPT

SOURCES, NORMATIVITY, AND INDIVIDUATION[1]

A THEORY of the nature of legal systems is one of the major elements of the analytical part of legal philosphy. Together with a theory of adjudication it provides the conceptual foundation of our understanding of the law as a social institution of great importance in society; they form the basis for the critical evaluation of the law which is the other part of legal philosophy.

Some authors maintain that laws do not necessarily belong to legal systems.[2] As a linguistic observation this is no doubt correct. The word 'law' is applied to rules of conduct which do not belong to legal systems. If philosophy of law was the study of the meaning of the word 'law' then it would not include the theory of legal systems as a major part. But legal philosophy is not and was never conceived to be by its main exponents an enquiry into the meaning of this or any other word.[3] It is the study of a distinctive form of social

---

[1] It would serve no useful purpose to list all the points on which I have developed or changed the views expressed in the first edition of *The Concept of a Legal System.* My purpose here is to concentrate on three main themes touched upon in the book: defending the views expressed on the dependence of law on sources and on the individuation of law and explaining how I was mistaken in the underlying assumptions concerning the normativity of law.

[2] See especially A. M. Honoré, 'What is a Group', *Archiv für Rechts und Sozialphilosophie* 61 (1975) 161; G. MacCormack, ' "Law" and "Legal System" ', (1979) 42 *M.L.R.* 285. Cf. also J. M. Eekelaar, 'Principles of Revolutionary Legality' in *Oxford Essays in Jurisprudence*, 2nd series, ed. by A. W. B. Simpson, Oxford, 1973, for an argument for the existence of system-transcending legal principles. R. M. Dworkin sometimes expresses himself as if he shares the view: *Taking Rights Seriously,* rev. edn., London, 1979, p. 344. But the views expressed there do not fit well with the main thrust of his essay 'Hard Cases' which identifies the law with the institutional morality of the courts and regards that as distinct both from what Dworkin calls 'background' morality as well as from the institutional moralities of other institutions.

[3] On the linguistic approach in legal philosophy see my 'The Problem about the Nature of Law', forthcoming, and *The Authority of Law*, Oxford, 1979, essay 3.

organization. This social organization provides one of the important contexts in which 'law' is used and is particularly closely associated with the use of 'legal' and 'legally'. But it is the study of the social organization and its normative structure which is the subject of this book, not the meaning of any word.

1. Sources

Of the four main questions belonging to a theory of legal systems the book concentrates on two, the identity of legal systems and their structure. The question whether there is any necessary content to law was not discussed at all.[4] The problem of existence was discussed mainly critically. It is commonly argued that a legal system is not in force unless it is efficacious to a certain degree. Kelsen points out that efficacy depends not only on conformity to law by the general population but also on the success of the courts and other law-enforcing agencies in applying sanctions to law-breakers. Hart has shown that to be efficacious conformity is not enough. Acceptance of the law at least on the part of officials is also necessary. In the last chapter of the book I discussed a number of confusions in our understanding of efficacy and pointed to several necessary differentiations of emphasis. And there the matter seems to rest at the moment. More refined tools borrowed from theoretical sociology would have to be employed to make any significant progress on this front.

This dependence on theoretical sociology is not accidental. Legal systems are not 'autarkic' social organizations. They are an aspect or a dimension of some political system. This fact bears on the temporal delimitation of continuous legal systems. In Chapter VIII I criticized legal theorists such as Austin, Kelsen, and Hart, who sought to provide autonomous legal criteria for the definition of the continuity of law.[5] Autonomous legal criteria are those derived from the

---

[4] I have tried to say something about it in *Practical Reason and Norms*, sect. 5.1, London, 1975.

[5] For similar criticism of Hart see J. M. Finnis, 'Revolution and Continuity in Law' in *Oxford Essays in Jurisprudence*, 2nd series, and see also *The Authority of Law*, essays 5, 7.

content of laws, their interrelations, and their efficacy. Reliance on them presupposes that not only the internal working but also the precise boundaries of the law can be fixed on the basis of specifically legal considerations alone. But the law is an aspect of a political system, be it a state, a church, a nomadic tribe, or any other. Both its existence and its identity are bound up with the existence and identity of the political system of which it is a part. If the book is at fault it is in not emphasizing this point enough. It argues that the identity of a legal system over time depends on the continuity of the political system of which the law is a part but it attempts an autonomous definition of the boundaries of a momentary legal system. Though it is true that autonomous criteria take one a long way towards the identification of the bounds of a momentary legal system they ultimately leave certain margins of doubt. A momentary legal system consists only of rules which a certain system of courts is bound to apply in accordance with their own customs and practices.[6] This leaves the notion of a system of courts unexplained.[7] Courts can be viewed as belonging to the same system if it is their practice to recognize rules on the basis of the same criteria of validity (i.e. if they practise the same rules of recognition). This test leaves wide-open borders.[8] It is possible to say that there is nothing wrong with that and that the notion of 'a legal system' is just vague and imprecise along this border. On the other hand it may make good sense to resort here again to the character of the political system of which that legal system is a part and to distinguish between those courts which are organs of that political system and those which are not. This will generate a more precise definition of momentary legal systems, but its main advantage is in highlighting the fact that law is an

[6] I am here following the definition of *Practical Reason and Norms*, sect. 4.3, rather than the one offered in Ch. VIII above, since the latter relies on the use of coercive sanctions and misinterprets the role of coercion in the law. Cf. H. Oberdiek, 'The Role of Sanctions and Coercion in Understanding Law and Legal Systems', *Am. J. of Juris.* 21 (1976) 71 and *Practical Reason and Norms*, sect. 5.2.

[7] The concept of a court can be explained by autonomous criteria: cf. *The Authority of Law*, essay 6; and 'The Problem about the Nature of Law'.

[8] Besides it has to be refined to allow for the different status of those rules applied because a legal system is an open system, see *The Authority of Law*, essays 5, 6. an

element in the political organization of a society. It can and should be treated as an autonomous system for many purposes but ultimately its boundaries are dependent upon the nature and boundaries of the larger political system of which it is a part.

Having emphasized the insufficiency of autonomous legal considerations in providing a doctrine of identity of legal systems, one should be wary of the reverse mistake. It is too easy to underestimate the importance of those autonomous considerations which do contribute to a doctrine of identity. They are part of the essence of law, part of those qualities which are present in all legal systems and in virtue of which they are legal systems. They are also among the features which explain the special role the law has in the political system.[9]

A legal system can be conceived of as a system of reasons for action. The question of its identity is the question which reasons are legal reasons or to put it more precisely: which reasons are legal reasons of one and the same legal system. I have mentioned above two features which are necessary to make a reason a legal one: (1) They are reasons applied and recognized by a system of courts. (2) Those courts are bound to apply them in accordance with their own practices and customs. These features account for the institutional character of law: law is a system of reasons recognized and enforced by authoritative law-applying institutions. These features provide the cornerstone of Hart's doctrine of the identity of law expressed in his doctrine of the rule of recognition.[10]

To these conditions another must be added. Legal reasons are such that their existence and content can be established on the basis of social facts alone, without recourse to moral argument. I have dubbed this condition 'the sources thesis'. It is tempting to regard the thesis as marking the difference between those notorious protagonists the legal positivists who accept it and the natural lawyers who reject it. But while the

---

[9] The necessary content of law, i.e. its being open, comprehensive, and supreme, is of course also crucial to the understanding of its role in the political system.

[10] *CL*, Ch. 6 and cf. my discussion aimed at justifying and somewhat modifying Hart's position in *The Authority of Law*, essays 4 to 6. Cf. also pp. 189ff. above.

thesis has no doubt a strong connection with that historical division, it cannot be claimed as the exclusive property of either school.[11]

The motivation for endorsing the sources thesis can best be explained in a somewhat metaphorical language: the other conditions briefly set out above explain that legal reasons lay claim to be authoritatively binding on members of a society. In the debate as to how members of a society should behave one may distinguish between the deliberative and executive stage. In the first the relative merit of alternative courses of action is assessed. In the second, executive, stage such assessment is excluded. The question what to do still arises but as an executive problem. Having decided in the deliberative stage what to do in certain circumstances the only questions remaining are one of memory (which action was decided upon in what circumstances) and of identification (is this an action of the specific kind and are the circumstances as specified) as well as a residual element of choice which is left as indifferent by the conclusion of the deliberative stage. (Such residual choice remains since deliberation ends always with a conclusion framed in general terms: to perform an action of a certain kind in circumstances of a certain character. There is invariably more than one way to comply with such instructions. Which way compliance is secured is indifferent from the point of view of that instruction.[12])

Naturally questions of identification may turn on moral issues, as when the question is which is the most just action. Clearly when this is the nature of the question it belongs, by definition, to the deliberative stage. Only when the identification of the required action does not depend on moral arguments does it belong to the executive stage. It is not

[11] It seems compatible with the writing of prominent natural lawyers such as L. Fuller in *The Morality of Law*, Cambridge, Mass., 1964, and J. M. Finnis in *Natural Law and Natural Rights*, Oxford, 1980. The extent that it is accepted by Hart has been recently queried by Soper in 'Legal Theory and the Obligation of a Judge: The Hart/Dworkin Dispute', *Mich. L. Rev.* 75 (1977) 473, and D. Lyons in 'Principles, Positivism and Legal Theory—Dworkin, *Taking Rights Seriously*', *Yale L. J.* 87 (1977) 415.

[12] Kelsen is the one prominent legal philosopher to emphasize this point. Cf. *PTL*, p. 349. For a similar point relating to intention generally see D. Davidson, 'Intending', Y. Yovel (ed.), *Philosophy of History and Action*, Dordrecht, 1978.

claimed that all societies necessarily separate between two stages. The only claim is that the distinction is coherent, that it is found in some societies and that its existence is a necessary condition for the existence of law. Law exists, according to the sources thesis, only in societies in which there are judicial institutions which recognize the distinction between the deliberative and executive stage, that is they hold themselves bound to recognize and enforce certain reasons not because they would have approved of them had they been entrusted with the question in the deliberative stage but because they regard their validity as authoritatively settled by custom, legislation, or previous judicial decisions so that the matter is held by the courts in the litigation in front of them as being in the executive stage. When this is the case the courts will not entertain moral arguments about the desirability of regarding a certain fact (e.g. a previous enactment) as a reason for a certain action but will once the existence of the relevant fact has been established through morally-neutral argument hold it to be a reason which they are bound to apply. Only reasons binding on the courts in such a way, i.e. only 'executive' reasons, reasons the existence of which can be established without invoking moral arguments, are legal reasons. The sources thesis assigns the law to the executive stage of social decision-making.

Several clarifications are called for to help to delineate the contours of the sources thesis. First, reference was made occasionally to valid or binding reasons. It should be clear, however, that the thesis itself does not involve any claim that any reasons are in fact good or binding reasons. It presupposes that binding considerations whatever they may be can be divided into those appropriate for the deliberative stage and those suitable to the executive stage and that the process leading to action passes sometimes through both stages. The thesis itself claims that legal reasons are 'executive'-type reasons held valid by the courts. It does not endorse the courts' point of view.

Second, it is not claimed that all the considerations which courts recognize and apply are facts identifiable without recourse to moral argument. The only claim is that of the considerations which courts legitimately recognize only those conforming to the above condition are legal considerations. Courts do and are entitled to act on extra-legal considerations as well.[13]

Third, the thesis identifies legal reasons through the eyes of the court, i.e. as 'executive' reasons which the courts hold themselves bound to recognize. But it is not part of the thesis that all legal reasons are addressed to the courts, that all legal reasons are reasons for action by the court. This was of course Kelsen's view but the better view is that legal reasons are addressed to all kinds of agents, though they all have it in common that courts are bound to recognize them and to draw appropriate conclusions from conformity or non-conformity with them.

Fourth, sometimes the courts are instructed by law to recognize the validity of a certain reason only if it is not unjust or morally undesirable to do so. On occasion such instructions result in a situation whereby a contract, for example, is legally valid only if it is morally unobjectionable. In such a case the validity of individual contracts is not based on 'social facts' only. To ascertain the validity of a particular contract one has to engage in moral argument. Only when the validity of a contract has been declared in court can it be established in accordance with the sources thesis, i.e. by reference to the court's decision. Therefore the sources thesis dictates that prior to such a decision by a court no contract can be said to be conclusively valid in law. Such contracts are of course *prima facie* valid in law provided they comform to the other tests of validity required by law.

Fifth, the point of the thesis is finality not certainty or predictability. The point is often missed by theorists who approve of the sources thesis. They dwell on the importance of certainty and predictability in law and legal decisions, assume that source-based laws are more certain than both moral considerations and judicial decisions based on moral considerations. Consequently, they claim, the law is source-based. Such arguments are flawed through and through. It is a matter of dispute whether moral considerations

---

[13] It is also possible that some courts are allowed a restricted power to revise legal considerations on the basis of some extra-legal considerations. Cf. *The Authority of Law,* essays 6, 10.

(of the kind likely to be relevant for legal decisions) are more or less certain than questions of social facts. Be that as it may, it is clear that questions of social fact can be complicated and subject to many uncertainties. The important point, however, is that the argument is at best an argument as to what *ought* to be the relative importance of legal and extra-legal considerations in judicial decisions. But the sources thesis is not a thesis about what ought to be the case. It is an element in the analysis of the concept of law.

Finality is a function of a division of labour between formal and informal stages of reflection and deliberation and formal and informal stages of implementation. Even in the life of a person deliberation is often followed by a decision which may anticipate action by a considerable period of time and which fixes the intention which thus becomes relatively immune from revision. Where social action is concerned, the need to fix the decision in advance of the action, the need to decide authoritatively what is to be done in a way which is binding on members of the community so that they are not allowed to differ from each other because of disagreement on what is best—such need for finality becomes overwhelming.

The above comments are designed to clarify and better to define the sources thesis. They contain no direct argument for accepting the thesis. The direct argument is brief and simple. The common conception of law prevalent in our society is consistent with the sources thesis. Furthermore, the sources thesis explains many fundamental beliefs about law current in our society such as the view that the law is sometimes settled, sometimes unsettled, that the courts sometimes apply pre-existing law and sometimes make new law, etc. Given that the distinction between the two kinds of reasons indicated by the sources thesis is important to the life and functioning of any society and that it is embedded in our common conception of law we have all the reason one can have for accepting it as an essential ingredient in our concept of law.

2. Individuation in General

There is little I would wish to add to the details of the

analysis of the doctrine of individuation as presented in this book. And yet it may be useful to say something more about the general nature of the doctrine elaborating and somewhat modifying the general approach adopted in the book and to defend in the next section one of its main theses, namely that power-conferring rules are a separate type of legal rules and that they are norms.

It is best to approach the question of individuation through an examination of legal statements. All (direct) legal statements can be expressed by sentences having the form 'legally p' or 'Lp', where 'p' is a sentential variable.[14] One special class of legal statements is normally expressed by sentences of the form 'There is a law that p' or 'The (legal) rule . . . determines that . . .'. The analysis of this class of legal statement is the concern of the doctrine of individuation. The point is made with admirable clarity by Honoré:

Lawyers talk freely about particular rules of law and sometimes name them: for example the 'rule against perpetuities' or the 'rule in *Rylands v. Fletcher*'. This suggests that there is a professional use of the term 'rule' or 'law' in which laws or rules are individuated. But this use of 'rule' or 'law' does not identify a law with a section of a statute or the statement of a judge in deciding a case. The legal adviser, advocate, or writer who sets out the 'rule in *Rylands v. Fletcher*' does not copy it exactly from the case of *Rylands v. Fletcher*. He takes account of subsequent decisions, of the traditional formulation in textbooks and in general or professional tradition to add and substract touches from the raw rule. Indeed, he may go further and extract from the raw material a law which is implicit in it but has not been enunciated, for example, that an interest in property of a certain type exists.[15]

The philospher's role is to provide a systematic account of

---

[14] See generally on legal statements pp. 48-50 above and 'The Problem about the Nature of Law'. 'Indirect' legal statements are best regarded as statements about the law. Only direct legal statements will be referred to as legal statements.

[15] 'Real Laws' in *Law, Morality and Society*, edited by P. M. S. Hacker and J. Raz, Oxford, 1977, pp. 100-1. Honoré accuses some writers, including me, of a wild goose chase. This seems to be based on a mistaken attribution of 'a strange form of analytical metaphysics' too mysterious for me to understand its nature. So far as I can see, all those whom he criticizes are engaged in essentially the same enterprises as he. The main difference between different writers on this problem has been in their solutions to it. This is not to deny that some philosophers' conception of the nature of the problem was confused.

the meaning of this class of legal statement. 'Legally you owe me £5' or 'According to law you ought to vacate the premises by the end of the month' may be true, while 'There is a law that you owe me £5', 'There is a law that you ought to vacate the premises', are false. The obligations concerned may simply arise out of contracts and not in virtue of any law alone.

True legal statements are either pure or applied or both. Pure legal statements are those true because the existence or non-existence of laws is sufficient to establish their truth, whereas applied legal statements have other facts among the conditions sufficient to establish their truth. 'Contracts are made by offer and acceptance', 'Illegal contracts are unenforceable', 'Contracts in restraint of trade are illegal', 'Contracts are frustrated by impossibility of performance', are all pure statements of English law. They are statements of the English law of contract. 'I owe two months' rent to my landlord', 'I should deliver the refrigerator to John by the end of the week', are, if true at all, applied legal statements. Their truth presumably depends on the existence of appropriate laws but also on other facts, e.g. that certain transactions took place or that certain non-law-creating events happened. A statement is both pure and applied if two sets of conditions obtain either of which is sufficient (independently of the other) to establish its truth, the one set consisting of the existence or non-existence of laws only, the other containing both the existence or non-existence of laws as well as some other facts.

Most legal statements are logically capable of being either pure or applied, i.e. there are logically possible states of affairs which if they obtain the legal statements concerned are both pure and applied. Some legal statements, however, are logically pure. These are those that if true are pure, those which cannot be made true by 'applicative facts'. (There are also logically applied statements but we are not concerned with them.)

'There is a law that p'-type statements are logically pure. If true they are pure. They cannot be applied statements. They cannot be made true by facts about legal transactions or by any other facts except those creating or repealing laws.

They are either true because of the existence or non-existence of laws or else they are not true.

It may be thought that 'There is a law that p' is the characteristic form of all logically pure legal statements just as 'legally p' is the characteristic form of all legal statements. But this is a mistake. Many logically pure legal statements cannot be expressed by the use of the 'There is a law . . .' operator. Consider the statement 'Women over 45 are liable to pay income tax'. It is a pure statement of English law. It is true and true because of the law alone. Revenue laws determine that liability to income tax is independent of sex or age; hence women over 45 are, like anyone else, liable to pay income tax. There is to be sure a logically pure statement stating that women over 45 are liable to pay income tax and that this is the result of the law itself and is not due to any applicative facts. But such a logically pure statement is commonly expressed by sentences such as (1) 'By law women over 45 are liable to tax'. The statement that (2) 'There is a law that women over 45 are liable to tax', far from being synonymous with (1), is actually false whereas (1) is true. That women over 45 are liable is the result of the general provisions of revenue laws. There just is no special law about their liability.

The lesson of this example is that 'There is a law that p'-type statements are a subclass of logically pure legal statements. They are statements each describing one complete law or (given that a complete description of a law with all its details is rare) the core idea of one complete law. We have now identified the basic characteristics of the 'There is a law that . . .' operator. Statements normally made by its use (1) are logically pure legal statements and (2) describe one complete law or the core idea of one complete law. I shall call the operator 'the individuating operator'. Statements it is normally used to make can be analysed as meaning 'Legally, there is a rule that p'. This shows that they are simply a subclass of ordinary legal statements. They too exhibit the form 'Lp'.

Some writers on legal philosophy, Holmes, Llewellyn, and Hohfeld among others, were interested in the general properties of legal statements and paid no special attention to the special properties of pure legal statements or of the individuating operator. Others, including Bentham, Austin, Kelsen, Hart, and Dworkin, paid special attention to features of legal statements which account for the properties of the individuating operator.

What is the importance of the individuating operator? What is missed by those who omit its examination? The answer consists of two parts corresponding to the two elements of the explanation of the individuating operator. First, then, what of value can be learned from the distinction between logically pure statements and the others? The distinction was introduced as one between statements which can only be true in virtue of the law alone and others the truth of which may depend on the existence or non-existence of applicative facts as well. Laws, it will be argued in the next section, exist in virtue of certain social facts only. Logically pure statements are, therefore, statements the truth conditions of which consist only of law-creating facts (these are taken to include facts which repeal or amend laws). Other legal statements include applicative facts among their truth conditions. The distinction between logically pure statements and other legal statements is important because it reflects the distinction between law-creating and law-applying facts[16] which is in itself the foundation of our understanding of the law.

Deeply embedded in our conception of the law is the picture of people's rights and duties, their status and their liabilities, etc., in short their legal situation being determined either directly by law or indirectly by the way the law determines the legal implications of various acts in the law (i.e. acts exercising legal powers such as the making of contracts or the effecting of a sale or a marriage) or of other events (such as the death of a person). Laymen often imagine that the difference lies in generality. Laws are general, and law-creating facts affect the fortunes of open classes of people, whereas other transactions and events having legal consequences affect only the fortunes of identifiable individuals. But, as every lawyer knows, this is very far from the truth. 'Individual norms', enacted by parliaments but

[16] Cf. pp. 60ff. above.

applying only to the action of a single person on a single occasion, though rather rare are possible. Sale and other transactions affecting rights *in rem* change the legal situation of open classes of persons without qualifying as 'law-creating'. Furthermore contracts and the rules and regulations of private associations are often legally enforceable without being themselves laws.

The distinction between law-creating and law-applying facts depends not on the generality of the former but on their being either custom or acts of the government in power or of its organs. This bold statement is oversimplified. Governments can make contracts, issue administrative or judicial orders, as well as perform physical actions not creating any norms. Law-creating acts are a subclass of governmental acts. They are the norm-creating acts of the supreme regular governmental authority and the acts creating general rules of other governmental organs.

The supreme regular legislator need not be the source of the superior laws of the legal system for one of two reasons: first, the superior law may be customary law. The supreme legislator's authority may be subordinate to that of customary law. Second, the supreme legislative authority may be a constitutional body acting with great infrequency. In such a country (e.g. the U.S.A.) the supreme regular legislator will not be supreme legislator, its powers being subject to the constitutional authority. (Some religious authorities may exercise similar infrequent supreme power.)

The conception of the law-creating facts I am advocating has three limbs. If an act is legally significant, if courts are bound to recognize it as valid, i.e. as having its intended effects, then law-creating facts are (1) all the legally significant acts of the supreme regular legislator; (2) all such acts of other governmental organs purporting to enact general rules; (3) those social customs which are legally significant. This is a political conception of law for it rests not on any technical or formal legal distinction but on the political role of the institutions and norms concerned. Its political character explains why some legal theories were indifferent to its existence. Many legal theorists are lawyers by training and outlook. Their theoretical interests are the clarification of concepts and techniques which play a role in the work of an attorney or a judge. From the point of view of the practising lawyer the distinction between law-applying and law-creating facts is of minor importance. There are in various legal systems legal regulations depending on this or similar distinctions such as differences in the way of establishing the existence of laws and of other facts. Different rules of construction may apply to statutory instrument or to private documents, etc. But these are relatively minor and local differences.

The legal philosophers who made a lot of the distinction between law-applying and law-creating facts are, not surprisingly, those who rose above the narrow horizon of the practising lawyer and his preoccupations. They were concerned in locating law and legal institutions in the wider context of the social and political life of a society. Here the distinction comes into its own. Law-creating acts are among the political events in the life of the society and they are enmeshed in the *political* life of the society in a way which differs significantly from other events.

It is time to recapitulate. A statement of the form 'There is a law that p' is true if and only if the corresponding statement that Lp

(1) is true;

(2) its truth is established by law-creating facts only (i.e. that Lp is a logically pure statement);

(3) represents the content of (the core of) a single complete law.

The preceding remarks explain the importance of such statements to our conception of the law by explaining the role of the distinction between law-creating and other legally significant facts. What is the role of the third element in the explanation? This is not a question of justifying its inclusion. The justification is through the linguistic argument provided above.[17] The question is about the role of this limb of the explanation in making such statements useful in legal discourse. Here the explanation is simple: an independent law is a unit of content. It contains some legal material

[17] p. 219.

sufficiently independent of the rest and of sufficient interest to deserve singling out as a separate unit—a rule or a law —and yet sufficiently simple to be regarded as one unit, one rule. The usefulness of having a standard way to refer to such units of content is self-evident.

The job of the legal philosopher is to articulate the conventions governing the use of such statements and present a systematic account of them. This is the job of the doctrine of individuation. The points I have just mentioned as guiding the use of the individuating operator are the source of the requirements determining the success of any doctrine of individuation as explained on pages 141-6 above.

The use of the individuating operator is often *ad hoc*. Every unit of content roughly meeting the conditions of relative independence, simplicity and interest can quite properly be picked out and designated a rule or a law for some transient purpose. Had the use of the operator been always *ad hoc* in this way there would have been nothing more to say on the doctrine of individuation. Its use, however, is not normally *ad hoc*. It is patterned in two ways. First, many legal units are crystallized in a stable form so that one and the same unit is normally referred to as a rule on many and diverse occasions. Secondly, even where the actual content of the unit referred to as a rule is not one which is crystallized into an accepted rule it is normally carved up in a recognizable pattern according to recognizable principles. In 'Real Laws', Honoré provides many such examples. Let me mention just two or three: statements of civil or criminal liability ('Anyone who . . . is liable to . . .'; 'Anyone who . . . is guilty of an offence'), statements of authorization ('. . . may . . .'), and statements of conditions for effecting a legal change (e.g. 'No overall will can be revived except by . . .') are often employed in individuating rules, i.e. in applying the individuating operator. It is the existence of those conventions (all of them meeting the basic requirements) which a doctrine of individuation articulates. They provide the foundation for the traditional philosophical discussion of types of laws. The typology of laws reflects the linguistic conventions governing the use of the individuating operator and illuminates our conception of the structure of law. The law is not thought of as a heap

of odds and ends but as a reasonably well-organized structure of different types of units interrelated in various fairly
standard ways. These are the products of those conventions
and their systematic study is what the doctrine of individuation is all about.[18]

3. Power-Conferring Rules

Five main theses constitute the main conclusions of the
doctrine of individuation in this book; they state some of the
general features governing the use of the individuating
operator:

I   In every legal system there are duty-imposing and
power-conferring rules.

II These are legal norms.[19]

III In every legal system there are several other types of laws
which are not norms.[20]

[18] Only the most naïve reader will think that the purpose of a doctrine of
individuation is to enable one to count how many rules there are. Questions of
individuation arise whenever one can employ count nouns 'a . . .' like 'a law', 'an
intention', 'an idea'. Those bring with them other forms of expression such as
quantification, identity, and difference: 'There is a law . . .', 'There is an idea', etc.;
'This is the same law', 'This is a different rule', 'I had the same idea', 'No, my
intention was different', 'I had another intention as well', etc. Doctrines of
individuation study the use of such expressions and the structures they give rise to.
In none of these cases does it make sense to count how many intentions did you
entertain yesterday?

[19] I have since abandoned the explanation provided in Ch. VI of the normative
character of these rules which is based on the sanctions or other consequences
attending behaviour designated by the rules. See for an alternative explanation
Practical Reason and Norms, Chs. 2 and 3, where it is also explained that legal
permissions are norms. Cf. also my 'Promises and Obligations' in *Law, Morality and
Society* for an account of obligations and duties, and P. M. S. Hacker, 'Sanction
Theories of Duty' in *Oxford Essays in Jurisprudence*, 2nd series, for a critical survey of
such theories.

[20] Honoré, on p. 112 of 'Real Laws' suggests that there are (at least) five types of
laws which are not norms:

1. *Existence* laws create, destroy, or provide for the existence or non-existence of
entities.
2. *Rules of inference* provide how facts may or must or should preferably be
proved and what inferences may or must or should preferably be drawn from
evidence.
3. *Categorizing rules* explain how to translate actions, events, and other facts into
the appropriate categories.
4. *Rules of scope* fix the scope of other rules.

IV All the laws which are not norms are internally related to legal norms.

V Legal rules may conflict.[21]

Some authors doubt the independent existence of power-conferring laws. Such doubts have a long and respectable tradition. They were recently aired again by J. W. Harris.[22] He claims that it is possible to describe the full content of a legal system as consisting of so many rules imposing duties and that it is desirable to do so. But it is doubtful whether such a project is indeed feasible. It has been convincingly argued by D. N. MacCormick[23] that rights can exist independently of duties. A statute or some private transaction

5. *Position-specifying rules* set out the legal position of persons or things in terms of rights, liabilities, status, and the like.

I do not necessarily agree with all the details of his analysis but I shall comment here on one point only. On p. 117, Honoré refers to 'a rule or assumption of law' that it is prohibited to commit offences. It is, however, part of the meaning of 'offence' that it should not be committed. Therefore there is no special normative law to that effect. Every law creating an offence is (*pace* Honoré) a norm.

---

[21] The opposite view is supported by J. W. Harris; see *Law and Legal Science,* pp. 81-3. Harris's mistake is to confuse conflict with contradiction and to deduce from the fact that a court faced with a conflict will do something to resolve it that the conflict did not exist in the first place. In *Taking Rights Seriously,* essay 2, Dworkin rightly emphasized the importance of conflicts in adjudication. He erroneously assumed, however, that only one type of legal standards (which he there called 'principles') can conflict (pp. 24f.). His stipulation that the other type (which he calls 'rules') cannot come into conflict with any legal standard is contradicted by his own admission that they may conflict with principles. In Ch. VII above I assumed that there are rules in every legal system for the resolution of all legal conflicts. This need not be the case. Cf. *The Authority of Law,* essay 4. The conflicts I have examined are those between duty-imposing rules and between them and permissions. For an attempt to apply the notion more widely see S. Munzer, 'Validity and Legal Conflicts', *Yale L.J.* 82 (1973) 1140.

[22] Their history dates back at least to Bentham's *Of Laws in General.* I have discussed his, Austin's, and Kelsen's treatment of the subject in Chs. I and V, and see Hart, 'Bentham on Legal Powers', *Yale L.J.* 81 (1972) 799. Cf. also D. N. MacCormick, 'Voluntary Obligations and Normative Powers', *Aristotelian Society,* Supp. Vol. 46 (1972) 59. J. W. Harris's argument is in Ch. 5 of *Law and Legal Science.*

[23] In 'Rights in Legislation', *Law, Morality and Society,* p. 189. A similar argument is advanced more obliquely by A. M. Honoré's 'Rights of Exclusion and Immunities against Divesting', *Tulane L. Rev.* 34 (1960) 453. See also the more general argument to the same effect in J. Feinberg, *Social Philosophy,* Englewood Cliffs, N.J., 1973, Ch. 4.

may vest a person with a right without there being a duty incumbent on anyone with respect to this right. Sometimes the absence of 'a corresponding' or 'a protecting' duty is due to the fact that the law makes its existence conditional and no one happens to satisfy the condition. The law, described schematically, provides that if someone has that right and if some other condition is satisfied then another person is subject to a duty. There are cases in which the right exists but the further condition is not satisfied. This would make it impossible to reduce rights to existing duties, although it is still possible to reduce them to conditional duties.[24] But rights have greater residual force than that of being part of the antecedent conditions of conditional duties. Rights are principles guiding the discretion of courts. Courts may rely on the existence of rights in justifying the creation of new duties (and new subsidiary rights). This role of rights is distinct from their being part of the antecedent of conditional duties. The relation between a right and a conditional duty exists in virtue of a valid rule of law, a constitutive rule in the terminology of Chapter XII above. But rights are also the 'source' of new rules. Duty-imposing rules which do not yet exist may be brought into existence in order to protect those rights, new powers may be conferred to facilitate their exercise, etc. It is crucial that the duties concerned cannot be deduced from the rights. The rights do not entail the existence of these duties. They simply authorize and direct the courts to act for their protection provided they judge such action best in light of all valid moral considerations. Legal rights in general have two dimensions. On the one hand rights are regulated by existing investitive, divestitive and constitutive rules. On the other hand they form a potential source of new laws, an authorization to the courts to generate new rules for their protection. This second dimension of legal rights defeats the reduction of them to duties. Notice that this does not mean that the concept of a right can be explained without reference to that of a duty. The explanation sketched above does represent rights as the 'source',

---

[24] It is still arguable that such a reduction distorts the nature of rights. See, for example, what amounts to an argument to this effect in MacCormick's 'The Obligations of Reparation', *Proc. of the Aristotelian Society* 78 (1977–8) 195.

among other things, of 'potential' duties. But it is a confusion
to think that the explanatory dependence of 'rights' on
'duties' warrants the conclusion that rules regulating rights
are merely parts of or are equivalent to duty rules.

Nor can they be reduced to more complicated conditional
obligations: 'If x has a right and if a court decides that
everyone ought to do A, then everyone ought to do A.' The
point is that a court's ruling may be a binding precedent (as
it is in English law) even if the court was not authorized by
the existence of a right to make it. Therefore, this rendering
of the dynamic aspect of rights fails. One ought to obey
courts' rulings anyway. The mention of the right in the
putative reduction is redundant.

Finally, and this is a crucial point, rights cannot be
reduced to *prima facie* reasons for courts to secure their
content. A's right to φ is a reason for the courts to allow him
to φ, to stop others from hindering him, etc., but quite apart
from the fact that there is no final and exhaustive list known
now which can replace the 'etc.', there is the further point
that the courts may have a reason for such action which is
based on different grounds. It may be based on considerations of general welfare or public safety, or public peace, etc.
Or it may be grounded on A's rights. Which it is is lost by
the reduction. But stating the legally recognized ground of
the court's reason to let A φ etc. is no mere rhetoric. It may
be crucial for determining the weight the court is allowed to
attribute to this reason when it conflicts with others.[25]

One may well wonder what the possibility or impossibility
of describing the content of a complete legal system as a set
of so many duties has to do with the individuation of laws.
It is beyond dispute that the individuating operator does
apply to other rules including power-conferring rules. Harris
thinks that such rules are 'duty excepting'. But this is
because of his failure to distinguish permissions from
authorizations. The latter confer powers as well as permissions to use them. He uses the following example: 'The judge

[25] Rights (or some kinds of rights) may be permissions but then one needs an
adequate theory of permissions to account for that. Harris offers no analysis of
permissions. On p. 93 he suggests in two successive sentences both that there are and
that there are no permission-granting rules.

may, (in certain circumstances) allocate the assets of a deceased person contrary to his will' (Harris, p. 94). This authorization clearly permits the judge to allocate assets but it also gives him power to do so. As a result of such a rule an allocation made by a judge is valid and confers valid title. The difference between me and a judge is not that I am not allowed to allocate assets contrary to the terms of a will but that I cannot do so. I do not have the required power.

It is clear that there are power-conferring rules. In legal discourse the individuating operator and other individuating devices are regularly used to refer to rules which are power-conferring.[26] But are such rules norms? Not if one equates 'a norm' with a requirement or a prohibition. Powers are normative abilities conferred on people because it is desirable to enable people to change normative situations when they choose to do so.[27] Where legal powers are concerned, for 'desirable' read 'accepted as desirable by the courts'. Such an ability means that the law itself attaches legal consequences to an action in order to determine the considerations for or against that action on the basis of which the power-holder will decide what to do. The law guides the action of the power-holder himself. It guides his decision whether or not to exercise the power. It does not merely guide the action of people subjected to duties or exempted from them in consequence of his exercise of his power. It is because of this fact that power-conferring rules are norms. They guide behaviour. But unlike duty-imposing rules they provide indeterminate guidance. Duties are requirements that defeat the agent's other reasons for action. The guidance provided by powers *depends* on the agent's other reasons. If he has reason for securing the result the power enables him to achieve then he has reason to exercise it. If he has reason to avoid that result then he has reason not to exercise the power.

[26] It is a separate question whether all power-conferring rules are also duty-imposing. I have discussed this question briefly on pp. 166-7 above and at greater length in 'Voluntary Obligations and Normative Powers', *Aristotelian Society*, Supp. Vol. 46 (1972) 79 at pp. 87-92.

[27] I am here deviating from the analysis I proposed on pp. 159ff. and follow the analysis in *Practical Reason and Norms*, sect. 3.2.

The core idea is simple: the law guides action if it intends to determine the reasons by which the agent is to be guided, on the basis of which he is to decide what to do. By imposing duties the law requires one decision. It holds the duty to be the only legitimate reason determining that decision. (I am here simplifying in disregarding the possibility of legal conflicts. But these can be easily accommodated within the boundaries of this account.) Here the law determines the reasons for action by constraining the agent's choice. It leaves him no options. Conferring powers too is a way of legally determining the agent's reasons for or against a certain action. The agent is endowed with the ability to change his or other people's legal position. This may affect his decision. But not every time an action attracts legal consequences which may affect the decision is it a case of normative guidance. Power-conferring is a case of normative guidance for there the law attaches those consequences to the action in order for the agents to base their decision for or against the action on the basis of these consequences alone. It is no coincidence that power-conferring acts have only trivial other consequences (power is typically exercised by word of mouth or a signature). Both duties and powers are intended to determine (in different ways) the reasons for or against the actions they affect. When a law guides behaviour, that is when it determines the reasons for an action of an agent in the way just described, then it is a norm. Therefore there are at least two kinds of legal norms, duty-imposing and power-conferring.[28]

It is through normatively guiding behaviour that the law strives to achieve whatever social purposes it has, first directly, by people actually being guided by the law, and secondly indirectly, by the causal consequences of knowledge of the law and of action guided by it. Since the law performs whatever social functions is has through its normative guidance the two are closely connected. But conceptually they are clearly distinct and neither social function nor social

[28] Some permission-granting rules are also norms (cf. *Practical Reason and Norms*, pp. 89-97, and the *Authority of Law*, pp. 64-7, 256) and the nature of right-instituting rules must await a more satisfactory analysis of rights. On the social functions of the law see *The Authority of Law*, essay 9.

purpose should be confused with mode of normative guidance.

4. Normativity

One major lacuna in the conception of the tasks of legal philosophy presented in the Introduction is the absence of any reference to the explanation of the normativity of law as an independent task. As a result of the omission the views about the normativity of law which are expressed in the book emerge obliquely from the discussion of other issues. Being usually out of focus they provide a misleading and distorted picture. Three questions have to be kept strictly separate: (1) How to determine the normative character of legal rules? (2) How does the existence of the law affect motivations for action? (3) Why do people use normative language in talking about the law?

The first question, concerning the determination of the normative character of legal rules, has already been discussed in the last section. It is not to be confused with the wider philosophical inquiry into the sense of the main normative terms. It adopts the conclusion of that inquiry and proceeds to investigate which legal rules should be described by which normative concepts. In other words, at this stage one assumes an understanding of 'duty', 'permission', 'power', and 'right', and considers on what grounds can a particular legal rule be regarded as a duty-imposing or a power-conferring rule, etc. As indicated above, this question is to be decided by the intention or purpose ascribed to the law by the courts. A rule is a norm if it is intended to guide action by determining the reasons for and against its performance. The intended character of the guidance decides what kind of a norm it is.

The question of the normative character of legal rules (i.e. are they norms and if so of what kind?) is closely related to the problem of the motivational impact of the law (i.e. does it affect people's attitudes and actions and if so how?). This connection though often perceived is frequently misconstrued. The normative character of a rule is often a crucial factor in determining its motivational influence. One version of the erroneous contrary suggestion that the motivational force of a rule decides its normative character has been convincingly refuted by Hart in criticizing Kelsen, one of the more forceful defendants of this fallacy.[29] He showed how one cannot identify legal duties as those actions omission of which attracts a legal sanction. Such a procedure assumes that there is a way of distinguishing sanctions from the other legal consequences which are normally undesirable from the agent's point of view (e.g. tax on earnings or import) other than by defining sanctions as those legal consequences attached to breach of duty. Hart's argument shows that the motivational influence of a rule is not sufficient to determine its normative character. The explanation which I professed above concerning the determination of the normative character of rules makes this character dependent on the law's intention to determine the reasons for the action. In the case of power this involves attaching legal consequences to the action but not all legal consequences are relevant to the determination of the normative character of rules. Consider the following situations:

(1) If I make a will then if I die without changing it, the beneficiaries designated in the will will have a right to my estate.

(2) If I apply for planning permission then the authority in question has a duty to consider my application following the proper procedure and to decide on the basis of lawful consideration.

(3) If I buy a TV receiver I ought to pay a TV licence.

(4) If I commit a tort in the course of my employment then my employer has a duty to pay damages to the injured party.

(5) If I dismiss an employee that employee has a right to unemployment benefits.

---

[29] In 'Kelsen Visited', 10 *U.C.L.A. Law Review* 709 (1963). Kelsen of course denies that he is dealing with the motivational influence that the law exercises. He is concerned merely with the potentially motivating consequences stipulated by law. His theory is a theory of law in the books, law as seen from a lawyer's point of view. The rest belongs to sociology. But one needs to add only that the law-enforcement machinery is by and large efficacious and that this is generally known, to derive (on the assumption of minimal rationality) at least weak generalizations about the law's motivational influences. Holmes's doctrine that the law should be regarded from the Bad Man's point of view is another version of the same mistake.

In all these situations performance gives rise to legal consequences. But only in the first two is it the law's intention that the decisions (to make a will or to apply for planning permission) should be determined by the legal consequences alone. In the others they are at best added to the agent's other considerations. Similarly, though breach of duty may attract a sanction it is the stipulation that the action is obligatory which is intended to determine the agent's judgment to the exclusion of all other non-legal consequences. The stipulation of a sanction provides a reinforcing consideration meant for those who fail to be moved by the existence of the duty itself. By itself deterrence through measures which are sanctions is no different from deterrence through taxation and similar other measures.

This approach emphasizes the law's intention as the decisive factor in determining the normative character of the law. This is in keeping with the basic intuition which informs the work of many legal scholars, namely that the character of the law depends on the activities and attitudes of the main legal institutions in charge of making law and enforcing it. What actually happens to it in 'the real world' is a separate question. It forms the subject of many of the sociological investigations about the law.

It is possible, however, to state several generalizations about the motivational influence of the law based on only the most general assumptions about the working of society. I shall make only one observation: the law motivates in two ways, by attaching consequences to various forms of behaviour and by setting standards for behaviour. Given that every legal system in force is by and large efficacious, there is some probability that legally stipulated consequences will be in fact implemented. Anyone with general knowledge of these bare facts, assuming he is rational to a minimal degree, will be motivationally affected. That is, he will be inclined, other things being equal, to adopt a course of action attracting favourable legal consequences and to avoid action to which unfavourable consequences are attached. This is just the truism it appears to be and it contains all the truth there is in theories which put down the law's motivational influence entirely to sanctions.

Theories which proclaim that the law motivates through sanctions only are committed to two mistakes and liable to fall into a third. They are liable to exaggerate the actual motivational force of sanctions. It is all too easy to put one's trust in them, as so many of the defenders of law and order do, and to forget that the actual success of sanctions to secure the desired results depends not on the general probability that they be applied given the general efficacy of the law but on that likelihood in particular classes of cases given the likelihood of detection and of successful prosecution, the likelihood that private citizens will choose to take legal action and will succeed in obtaining judgment in their favour, the ability of the man to pay (if the sanction is monetary) or submit to punishment (he may be too ill), the inclination of judges and juries to impose the sanctions the law allows or requires them to impose, the benefits to the culprit from breaking the law, his knowledge of the facts mentioned above, his willingness to run risks, etc.

Careful scholars have avoided the mistake of exaggerating the direct motivational influence of sanctions. If they committed themselves to the belief that the law motivates through sanctions only, however, they are guilty of two other mistakes, of overlooking the importance of other legally stipulated consequences and of disregarding the motivational impact of setting standards. It has already been remarked that legal powers exist where the law attaches legal consequences which are not sanctions to the exercise of legal powers. There are also many other legal consequences of action which are not sanctions, such as taxation, compulsory fees and other payments, planning requirements, evidential and procedural requirements, ordinary 'red tape', etc. Some of these are unconditional impositions, the majority, however, are conditional on one's desire to engage in various forms of action. Those perform a motivating role undistinguished from that of sanctions (except that some such consequences are attractive rather than disagreeable).

Compare a parking fine with an equivalent sum paid for permission to use a car park. Normally one would expect the fine to be more efficient in reducing parking than the parking charge. The difference in motivational power cannot be explained in terms of a difference in legally stipulated consequences which are by definition the same. It is to be accounted for by the fact that the law does in the one case set a standard prohibiting parking, whereas no such legal standard exists in the second. This motivating influence of the law is sometimes considered irrelevant to our understanding of the nature of law on the ground that it is not a universal feature of law but rather depends on independent motivation which may or may not be present. In this it does indeed differ from sanctions which rely on motives which are universal (though not always decisive) such as one's interest in one's life, health, liberty, or property. On the other hand other legally stipulated consequences need not rely on universal motives. They are important to our understanding the law because even if their detailed operation varies they are as a group systematically used and invariably relied upon both by legal institutions and by the law's subjects.

The same is true of the law's motivating by setting standards for behaviour. This is done simply by declaring which actions are prohibited and which are permitted, what a person has a duty to do and what he has a right to. In most societies various groups, even apart from the officials, accept conventions requiring compliance with the law generally or with certain groups of laws (e.g. excluding traffic laws or including only the laws relating to serious crime and to honest dealings, etc.). Their acceptance may be due to superstition, to moral or religious convictions, to considerations of self-interest, or simply to the fact that that is what everyone believes. In any case the existence of such conventions enables the law to motivate by setting standards which trigger them off and apply their motivating power to new forms of behaviour. Their importance must be acknowledged in any general account of the nature of law for they account in large degree for the efficacy of the law, such as it is, and because law-making is quite consciously designed to rely on them, to invoke their existence and bring them into operation.

5. *Normative Statements*

Neither the explanation of the normative character of legal

rules nor an understanding of the motivating force of the law is sufficient to explain why people use normative language in describing the law. Why do people describe legal situations in terms of duties and rights, entitlements, permissions, etc.? The first thing to note is that one has an alternative vocabulary for describing the law which is not infrequently used. One can talk of that which one is required by law to do, of what one had better do to avoid prison, of what the ruling class, the power élite, the tyrant, etc., dictate or demand. These and many other expressions provide a rich non-normative vocabulary for describing legal situations which is more often used than some legal scholars would like to admit.

Resort to normative language normally implies acceptance of the validity, the bindingness of the legal rules concerned. Avoidance of normative language often suggests dissent from belief in the validity of law. Acceptance here does not impart moral approbation of the rule nor even belief that there are adequate moral reasons for obeying it. Acceptance could be for moral, prudential, or any other reasons, or for no reason at all. All it means is belief that the agent should follow the rule according to its terms. Accepting rules is sometimes contrasted with acting for fear of sanction. This is mistaken. Fear of sanction is a self-interested reason, and if other reasons of self-interest can lead to acceptance, why not fear of sanction? 'Honesty is the best policy' is the sort of consideration that leads to accepting rules of conduct whether the rewards are profits or the avoidance of penalties. Acceptance of rules can be based on fear of punishment provided it leads to a general policy rather than to a one-off decision. One accepts a rule of conduct if one behaves according to it as a rule, if it is one's regular policy to do so. One does not accept a rule if one reconsiders the merits of conforming to it on every occasion to which it applies.

A person describing legal situations by the use of normative terms normally implies his acceptance of the bindingness of the rules on which his statement rests. This can be called the committed use of normative language. Not all statements made by the use of normative language are of this kind. It has been often remarked that normative language can be used to describe other people's normative views as in 'During the last decade it has become common among professional people to believe that a woman has a right to abortion on demand'. Many authors assume that all non-committed use of normative language is of this kind. But consider a solicitor advising a client or a writer discussing a point of law. Typically they will not be asserting what other people believe the law to be, rather they will be stating what it is. Since the law is normally a matter of public knowledge it may well be that others believe it to be as the solicitor or writer states. But this is incidental to their purpose and in typical cases is not what they state. It may well be that the point of law clarified by them, though correct, never occurred to anyone before. The solicitor may, for practical reasons, be worried by this. The author on the other hand is likely to regard such novelty as a feather in his cap. In any case neither the content nor the truth of their statement is affected by whether or not it is a novel point of law. To deny this is to deny the possibility of non-committed statements of novel points of law.

It may be objected that all this argument establishes is that non-committed normative statements do not always state what people believe *explicitly*. Sometimes they state what others believe implicitly. The objection has force only if one accepts the erroneous principle that every person necessarily believes in all the logical consequences of his beliefs, i.e. in all the propositions which are entailed by whatever propositions he believes in. This is not the place to explain why this principle is erroneous. Abandoning it does not lead to a denial of implicit knowledge, merely to a more restricted use of this notion. Once restricted, however, it becomes insufficient to explain the kind of non-committed statements we are discussing and which I shall call detached statements or statements from the legal point of view.[30]

[30] The alternative of analysing detached statements as a kind of internal statements (in an extended sense of that term) – is equally unsuccessful. In attempting such an analysis one's best bet is to regard such statements as a conditional reason-statement. Such an interpretation may proceed somewhat along the following lines: 'Legally one ought to φ' when used to make a detached statement (i.e. one which is compatible with 'but one has no reason whatsoever to φ') means: 'If law-creating facts were reasons then it would be true that one ought

Imagine a person who believes in the binding force of the English rules of recognition (and that of the other ultimate rules of English law if there are such). Imagine further that he believes that no duty is binding, no right is valid, no normative consequence has any claim on those subject to it unless it can be traced back to the ultimate rules of English law. Assume further that that person has complete knowledge of all factual information, is completely and unwaveringly rational, and has worked out all the consequences of the ultimate rules of English law including all those which follow from them when applied to the facts as they are. Such a person, clearly too diabolical to contemplate in any way except as an abstract logical model, represents exclusive acceptance of the legal point of view. Detached statements are true only in cases where our imaginary person believes in their committed counterpart (i.e. in the committed normative statement normally expressed by the use of the same normative sentence, when it is used to make a committed statement). A detached statement is true if and only if the legal point of view is valid and exhaustive. In other words a detached statement normally made by the use of a certain sentence is true if and only if the committed statement normally made by the use of the same sentence is true—given the non-normative facts of this world—if all the

---

to φ.' One should be wary of interpreting apparently categorical statements as elliptical conditionals. One requires a very strong reason for doing so, especially in a case in which, as in the present case, the complete conditional is very rarely stated in its complete, explicit form. Quite apart from these general doubts there are additional reasons for rejecting this interpretation. It may be the case that law-creating facts are reasons for action and yet that it is false that one ought to φ. There may be other non-legal reasons for x not to φ which override the legal reasons for φ-ing. It is not possible to avoid this problem by saying that the 'ought' in the conditional is a *prima facie* 'ought' equivalent merely to the assertion of the existence of a reason for action. Detached statements may be statements of *prima facie* 'ought', but they may also be statements of conclusive 'ought' and any interpretation of them must allow for this. The proposed interpretation does not allow for this.

A more complicated interpretation may now be proposed. 'Legally one ought to φ' may be thought to be equivalent to 'If law-creating facts are reasons then, in so far as such reasons affect the issue, one ought to φ.' This is true but rather empty and uninformative. It is tantamount to saying: 'If because according to law one ought to φ one ought to φ then one ought to φ.' True enough but hardly an explanation of 'Legally one ought to φ. The conditional statement is tautological whereas the legal statement it purports to explain is not.

ultimate rules of the legal system referred to are binding and if there are no other binding normative considerations.

On page 49 above I distinguished between direct and indirect normative legal statements. The comments on the use of normative language advanced here mean that indirect legal statements are mostly statements about people's attitudes, beliefs, and practices. Direct normative statements are either committed or detached depending on the intentions of the speakers as revealed by their utterances or by the contexts in which they are made.

BIBLIOGRAPHY

(including only works cited or referred to)

AUSTIN, JOHN. *Lectures on Jurisprudence.* John Murray, London, 5th edn., 1885.

—— *The Province of Jurisprudence Determined.* The Noonday Press, New York, 1954.

—— 'The Uses of the Study of Jurisprudence', published in the same volume with *The Province.*

BENTHAM, J. *A Fragment on Government.* Blackwell, Oxford, 1960.

—— 'A General View of a Complete Code of Laws' in *The Works of J. Bentham.*

—— *The Limits of Jurisprudence Defined.* Columbia University Press, 1945.

—— *Of Laws in General,* The Athlone Press, 1970.

—— *The Works of J. Bentham,* ed. J. Bowrigg. William Tait, Edinburgh, 1863.

BROWN, J. *The Austinian Theory of Law.* John Murray, London, 1920.

BRYCE, J. 'The Nature of Sovereignty' in *Studies in History and Jurisprudence,* Vol. ii. Clarendon Press, Oxford, 1901.

BUCKLAND, W. W. *Some Reflections on Jurisprudence.* Cambridge University Press, 1949.

D'ARCY, E. *Human Acts.* Clarendon Press, Oxford, 1963.

DAVIDSON, D. 'Intending', Y. Yovel (ed.), *Philosophy of History and Action,* Dordrecht, 1978.

DICEY, A. V. *Introduction to the Study of the Law of the Constitution.* Macmillan & Co., London, 10th edn., 1964.

DWORKIN, R. M. *Taking Rights Seriously,* rev. edn., London, 1979.

EEKELAAR, J. M. 'Principles of Revolutionary Legality' in A. W. Simpson (ed.), *Oxford Essays in Jurisprudence.*

FEINBERG, J. *Social Philosophy,* Englewood Cliffs, N.J., 1973.

FINNIS, J. M. *Natural Law and Natural Rights,* Oxford, 1980.

—— 'Revolution and Continuity in Law' in A. W. B. Simpson (ed.), *Oxford Essays in Jurisprudence.*

FULLER, L. *The Morality of Law,* Cambridge, Mass., 1964.

GRAY, J. C. *The Nature and Sources of the Law.* Beacon Press, Boston, 2nd edn., 1963.

HACKER, P. M. S. 'Sanction Theories of Duty' in A. W. B. Simpson (ed.), *Oxford Essays in Jurisprudence.*

HACKER, P. M. S. and RAZ., J. (eds.) *Law, Morality and Society*, Oxford, 1977.

HARE, R. M. *The Language of Morals.* Oxford University Press, 1964.

HARRIS, J. W. *Law and Legal Science,* Oxford, 1979.

HART, H. L. A. 'Bentham on Legal Powers', *Yale L.J.* 81 (1972).

—— *Definition and Theory in Jurisprudence,* Clarendon Press, Oxford, 1959.

—— 'Kelsen Visited', 10 *U.C.L.A. Law Review* 709.

—— 'Legal and Moral Obligation' in A. I. Melden (ed.), *Essays in Moral Philosophy.* University of Washington Press, 1958.

—— 'Positivism and the Separation of Law and Morals', (1958) 71 *Harvard Law Review* 593.

—— 'Self-Referring Laws' in *In Honour of Karl Olivecrona.*

—— *The Concept of Law.* Clarendon Press, Oxford, 1961.

HOBBES, T. *Leviathan.* Blackwell, Oxford, 1960.

HOHFELD, W. N. *Fundamental Legal Conceptions.* Yale University Press, New Haven & London, 1964.

HONORÉ, A. M. 'Real Laws' in *Law, Morality and Society,* edited by P. M. S. Hacker and J. Raz, Oxford, 1977.

—— 'Rights of Exclusion and Immunities against Divesting', (1960) 34 *Tulane Law Review* 453.

—— 'What is a Group' *Archiv für Rechts und Sozialphilosophie* 61 (1975) 161.

HOLLAND, T. E. *The Elements of Jurisprudence.* Clarendon Press, Oxford, 10th edn., 1906.

KELSEN, H. *General Theory of Law and State.* Russell & Russell, New York, 1961.

—— 'On the Pure Theory of Law', (1966) 1 *Israel Law Review* 1.

—— 'Prof. Stone and the Pure Theory of Law', (1965) 17 *Stanford Law Review,* vol. 2, p. 1128.

—— *Théorie pure du droit.* Dalloz, Paris, 1962.

—— *The Pure Theory of Law.* University of California Press, Berkeley & Los Angeles, 1967.[1]

—— 'The Pure Theory of Law', (1934) 50 *Law Quarterly Review* 477, and (1935) 51 *Law Quarterly Review* 517.

—— 'The Pure Theory of Law and Analytic Jurisprudence' published in *What is Justice?*

—— *What is Justice?* University of California Press, 1960.

KENNY, A. 'Intention and Purpose', (1966) 63 *The Journal of Philosophy* 642.

---

[1] Usually I used this translation of *Reine Rechtslehre* (2nd edn.), but occasionally, when I found that the translation deviated from the original in a way significant to my purpose, I used the French translation listed above.

LYONS, D. 'Principles, Positivism and Legal Theory—Dworkin, *Taking Rights Seriously*', *Yale L.J.* 87 (1977) 415.

MacCORMACK, G. ' "Law" and "Legal System" ', (1979) 42 *M.L.R.* 285.

MacCORMICK, D. N. 'Rights in Legislation', *Law, Morality and Society*, p. 189.

—— 'The Obligations of Reparation', *Proc. of the Aristotelian Society*, 78 (1977-8) 195.

—— 'Voluntary Obligations and Normative Powers', *Aristotelian Society*, Supp. Vol. 46 (1972) 59.

MARKBY, W. *Elements of Law*. Clarendon Press, Oxford, 5th edn., 1896.

MUNZER, S. 'Validity and Legal Conflicts', *Yale L.J.* 82 (1973) 1140.

OBERDIEK, H. 'The Role of Sanctions and Coercion in Understanding Law and Legal Systems', *Am. J. of Juris.* 21 (1976) 71.

PRIOR, A. *Formal Logic*. Clarendon Press, Oxford, 2nd edn., 1962.

RAZ, J. 'Voluntary Obligations and Normative Powers', *Aristotelian Society*, Supp. Vol. 46 (1972) 79.

—— *Practical Reason and Norms*, London, 1975.

—— 'Promises and Obligations' in *Law, Morality and Society*.

—— *The Authority of Law*, Oxford, 1979.

—— 'The Problem about the Nature of Law', forthcoming.

ROSS, A. 'A Review of Kelsen's *What is Justice?*', 45 *California Law Review* 564.

—— *On Law and Justice*. Stevens, London, 1958.

—— 'Tû Tû', 70 *Harvard Law Review*, vol. 1, p. 812.

SALMOND, J. W. *The First Principles of Jurisprudence*. Stevens & Haynes, 1893.

—— *Salmond on Jurisprudence: Eleventh Edition*, ed. G. Williams, Sweet & Maxwell, London, 1957.

SIMPSON, A. W. B. (ed.) *Oxford Essays in Jurisprudence*, 2nd series, Oxford, 1973.

—— 'The Analysis of Legal Concepts', (1964) 80 *L.Q.R.* 535.

SOPER, E. P. 'Legal Theory and the Obligation of a Judge: The Hart/Dworkin Dispute', *Mich. L. Rev.* 75 (1977) 473.

STENIUS, E. *Wittgenstein's 'Tractatus'*. Blackwell, Oxford, 1960.

STRAWSON, P. 'Intention and Convention in Speech Acts', (1964) 73 *Philosophical Review* 439.

VON WRIGHT, G. H. *Norm and Action*. Routledge & Kegan Paul, New York, 1963.

WILLOUGHBY, W. W. *The Fundamental Concepts of Public Law*, Macmillan, London, 1924.

INDEX

Normativity of law, the, 3, 157–9, 168–70, 201–2, 230–5
  Kelsen's view, 130–7
Nullity, as sanction, 22

Obedience, 5–7, 11, 14–16, 33–5, 94
  Obedience laws, 21–3, 166–7
Oberdiek, H., 211
O-norms, 159–65
Operative structure, 185
Origin, principle of, 18–19, 27, 93, 95, 108–9
Original law, 60–1, 188

Paper rules, 201–2
Permissions, 46, 56–8, 77–8, 84–6, 109, 114, 170–5, 227, 229–30
Power-conferring laws, 156–67, 181–3, 185–6, 196, 199, 204, 206, 224-30
  PL-laws, 161–4, 166–7, 181–2
  PR-laws, 161–4, 181–2
Powers, 19–23, 29–32, 105–9, 112, 116–7, 138, 159–66, 171, 177
  Regulative and legislative powers, 162–6
Prescriptive norms, 128–9, 156, 159, 161
Prior, A. N., 56
Punitive relations, 24, 114, 140, 156, 185

Regulative relations, 162–5, 181–3, 185
Repealing laws, 58, 62–4, 117, 184

Rights, 19–21, 28–32, 175–83
Ross, A., 127, 129
Rule of recognition, the, 197–200

Salmond, J. W., 28, 42–3, 190–1, 197
Sanctions, 76, 150–6, 185–6, 193–5
  Austin's view, 12–14, 22–3, 25
  Kelsen's view, 78–81, 84, 90, 118–9, 125–6
Sanction-stipulating laws, 114, 154–6, 174, 185–6
Simpson, A. W. B., 179, 209
Social functions of the law, the, 158, 229–30, 231–4
Soper, E. P., 213
Sources thesis, 210–6
Sovereignty, 5–11, 13–4, 27–33, 34–43, 93, 95, 99–100, 105–8
Stenius, E., 46
Strawson, P., 62
Structure of a legal system, 1–2, 24, 45, 50, 70, 73, 114, 140–1, 155–6, 169–70, 175, 181–7, 193, 196
  Austin's view, 6, 22–6
  Kelsen's view, 109–120
  Operative and genetic structure, 183–5

Willoughby, W. W., 30
von Wright, G. H., 46, 51, 59

Yovel, Y., 213